PATHOPHYSIOLOGY AND TREATMENT OF ATHEROSCLEROTIC DISEASE IN PERIPHERAL ARTERIES

PATHOPHYSIOLOGY AND TREATMENT OF ATHEROSCLEROTIC DISEASE IN PERIPHERAL ARTERIES

Edited by

ALOKE VIRMANI FINN

CVPath Institute, Gaithersburg, MD, United States
University of Maryland, School of Medicine, Baltimore, MD, United States

ELSEVIER

Elsevier
Radarweg 29, PO Box 211, 1000 AE Amsterdam, Netherlands
125 London Wall, London EC2Y 5AS, United Kingdom
50 Hampshire Street, 5th Floor, Cambridge, MA 02139, United States

Notices
Knowledge and best practice in this field are constantly changing. As new research and experience broaden our understanding, changes in research methods, professional practices, or medical treatment may become necessary.

Practitioners and researchers must always rely on their own experience and knowledge in evaluating and using any information, methods, compounds, or experiments described herein. In using such information or methods they should be mindful of their own safety and the safety of others, including parties for whom they have a professional responsibility.

To the fullest extent of the law, neither the Publisher nor the authors, contributors, or editors, assume any liability for any injury and/or damage to persons or property as a matter of products liability, negligence or otherwise, or from any use or operation of any methods, products, instructions, or ideas contained in the material herein.

ISBN: 978-0-443-13593-4

For information on all Elsevier publications visit our website at
https://www.elsevier.com/books-and-journals

Publisher: Stacy Masucci
Acquisitions Editor: Patricia Osborn
Editorial Project Manager: Susan Ikeda
Production Project Manager: Neena S. Maheen
Cover Designer: Christian Bilbow

Working together
to grow libraries in
developing countries

www.elsevier.com • www.bookaid.org

Typeset by TNQ Technologies

Contents

Chapter 10 Atherectomy in endovascular procedures 175

Craig Walker, McCall Walker and Matthew T. Finn

Chapter 11 Interventional treatment of PAD: Drug-coated balloons and stents 197

Gary M. Ansel

List of contributors

Shaunak Adkar
Division of Vascular Surgery, Department of Surgery, Stanford University, Palo Alto, CA, United States

Gary M. Ansel
Department of Medicine, University of Toledo, Toledo, OH, United States

Joshua Beckman
University of Texas Southwestern Medical Center, Dallas, TX, United States

Arielle Bellissard
Department of Vascular Surgery and Kidney Transplantation, Strasbourg University Hospitals, Strasbourg, France; CVPath Institute, Gaithersburg, MD, United States

Nabil Chakfe
Department of Vascular Surgery and Kidney Transplantation, Strasbourg University Hospitals, Strasbourg, France

Aloke V. Finn
Division of Cardiovascular Medicine, Department of Medicine, University of Maryland Medical Center, Baltimore, MD, United States; CVPath Institute, Gaithersburg, MD, United States; University of Maryland, School of Medicine, Baltimore, MD, United States

Matthew T. Finn
Cardiovascular Institute of the South, Gray, LA, United States

Sareena George
Division of Cardiology, Department of Medicine, Columbia University Irving Medical Center, New York, NY, United States

Kenji Kawai
CVPath Institute, Gaithersburg, MD, United States

Nicholas Leeper
Stanford University, Palo Alto, CA, United States

Kunihiro Matsushita
Division of Cardiology, Johns Hopkins University School of Medicine, Baltimore, MD, United States; Department of Epidemiology, Johns Hopkins Bloomberg School of Public Health, Baltimore, MD, United States

Ramya Mosarla
NYU Langone Health, New York, NY, United States

Sahil Parikh
Division of Cardiology, Department of Medicine, Columbia University Irving Medical Center, New York, NY, United States

Ji-Eun Park
Division of Cardiovascular Medicine, Department of Medicine, University of Maryland Medical Center, Baltimore, MD, United States

Sonal Pruthi
Division of Cardiology, Department of Medicine, Columbia University Irving Medical Center, New York, NY, United States

Maya Salameh
Division of Cardiology, Johns Hopkins University School of Medicine, Baltimore, MD, United States

Eric Secemsky
Beth Israel Medical Center, Harvard University, Boston, MA, United States

Renu Virmani
CVPath Institute, Gaithersburg, MD, United States

Craig Walker
Cardiovascular Institute of the South, Gray, LA, United States

McCall Walker
University of Texas Southwestern, Dallas, TX, United States; Cardiovascular Institute of the South, Gray, LA, United States

Preface

Although the epidemiology, pathogenesis, and treatment of atherosclerotic coronary artery disease has been the subject of intense research for many decades, relatively less focus has been devoted to peripheral vascular disease (PAD) despite the fact that is estimated to affect over 200 million people worldwide. Even today, our treatments for PAD have been primarily based upon our learning from CAD despite emerging knowledge that these diseases have overlapping but also distinctive pathogenesis. It is my hope that by putting together a collection of experts from diverse disciplines in the field of PAD that clinicians and researchers can benefit from this knowledge to enhance the care of these patients and perhaps be an impetus to enhance research in the field of PAD.

This book is dedicated to the many patients throughout the world who suffer from this disease. They should be aware that this remains an important area of research for cardiovascular researchers throughout the world. I would also like to acknowledge my former mentor Herman (Chip) Gold, MD, at Massachusetts General Hospital whose enthusiasm for learning and research still inspires me to this day. This book is dedicated to his memory.

Sincerely,
Aloke Virmani Finn, MD
Gaithersburg, MD

Introduction

Ji-Eun Park[1] and Aloke V. Finn[2,3]

[1]*Division of Cardiovascular Medicine, Department of Medicine, University of Maryland Medical Center, Baltimore, MD, United States;* [2]*CVPath Institute, Gaithersburg, MD, United States;* [3]*University of Maryland, School of Medicine, Baltimore, MD, United States*

Peripheral arterial disease (PAD) is a common cardiovascular disease affecting 200 million people worldwide. It is characterized by stenosis or occlusion in the region extending from the aortoiliac bifurcation to the pedal arteries. Although the vast majority of PAD is caused by atherosclerosis, compared to coronary artery disease (CAD), the pathophysiology of PAD remains poorly understood and distinctive in its epidemiology, pathogenesis, disease morphologies, and clinical treatments. It is often assumed that PAD develops and should be treated similarly to CAD, but differing genetic risk factors and pathophysiological patterns should guide distinct but overlapping treatment paradigms. Here, we discuss the most up-to-date data and areas of continued research regarding PAD. We have brought together a multidisciplinary group of experts to update the reader on the most important new developments in the field of PAD. We will review the current understanding of pathology, pathophysiology, and diagnosis of lower extremity atherosclerosis and discuss current and future medical, interventional, and surgical treatments. Our hope is that in bringing this group of world-renowned experts, we have created an invaluable text and resource for interventional radiologists, general and interventional cardiologists, vascular medicine physicians, vascular surgeons, trainees, and students alike.

Pathophysiology and Treatment of Atherosclerotic Disease in Peripheral Arteries. https://doi.org/10.1016/B978-0-443-13593-4.00001-9

Epidemiology of peripheral artery disease

Maya Salameh[1] and Kunihiro Matsushita[1,2]

[1]Division of Cardiology, Johns Hopkins University School of Medicine, Baltimore, MD, United States; [2]Department of Epidemiology, Johns Hopkins Bloomberg School of Public Health, Baltimore, MD, United States

Pathophysiology and Treatment of Atherosclerotic Disease in Peripheral Arteries. https://doi.org/10.1016/B978-0-443-13593-4.00002-0

Introduction

Peripheral artery disease (PAD) is a vascular syndrome caused by obstruction of the aorta and arteries to the lower extremities, leading to stenosis or occlusion. The majority of cases are due to atherosclerosis, a systemic process characterized by inflammation and changes in endothelial cells lining the vessel walls. The arterial lumen eventually becomes obstructed by plaque leading to reduced blood flow to the lower extremities. Nonatherosclerotic causes of PAD are uncommon and include vasculitis, fibromuscular dysplasia, thromboangiitis obliterans, and cystic adventitial disease. PAD can also technically refer to disease in other vascular beds, exclusive of the coronary vessels. In this chapter, the term PAD will be used to denote atherosclerotic occlusive disease of the aorta and lower extremity arteries.

Prevalence

Given that up to 50% of patients with PAD are asymptomatic (Hirsch et al., 2005), the ankle-brachial index (ABI) is currently used as a first-line test for PAD detection (Ouriel et al., 1982; Yao et al., 1969). The ABI is measured using a standard sphygmomanometer and a Doppler instrument to detect pulses and is calculated by dividing the ankle systolic pressure by the higher brachial systolic pressure. An ABI ≤ 0.9 is considered up to 97% specific for angiographically confirmed lower extremity arterial disease (Fowkes, 1988). The sensitivity is lower, approximately 80%, likely due to limitations of the ABI, which include noncompressible arteries and false-negative ABIs in patients with more proximal disease (Criqui & Aboyans, 2015).

Based on low ABI, PAD is estimated to affect more than 230 million adults worldwide, with a reported global prevalence of approximately 5.6% (Song et al., 2019). Fowkes et al. reported that the PAD prevalence increased by 23.5% from 2000 to 2010, with the increase being higher in low-to middle-income countries (28.7%) compared with high-income countries (13.1%) (Fowkes et al., 2013). This is likely due to increased life expectancy, with more people reaching the age of 55 and over in low-to middle-income countries and the age of 80 years and over in high-income countries. Like with other atherosclerotic diseases, the risk of developing PAD is accelerated with increasing age. For example, a study using data from the National Health and Nutrition Examination Survey (NHANES) reported a prevalence of PAD of 14.5% in US adults aged 70 or older, compared with a prevalence of 0.9% in US adults aged 40–49 (Selvin & Erlinger, 2004).

Another study by Allison et al. combined data from community-based studies to estimate the race/ethnic-specific prevalence of PAD in the United States (Allison et al., 2007). Overall, the prevalence of PAD for African Americans (AA) was twice that of Non-Hispanic Whites (NHW), at any given age (Allison et al., 2007) (Figs. 2.1 and 2.2). The Atherosclerosis Risk in Communities (ARIC) study also reported a higher prevalence of PAD in Black males compared with White males (3.3% versus 2.3%) as well as in Black females compared with White females (4.0% versus 3.3%) (Zheng et al., 1997). NHANES reported that a prevalence of PAD in non-Hispanic Blacks was as high as 7.8%, compared with 4.4% in Whites (Selvin & Erlinger, 2004). The

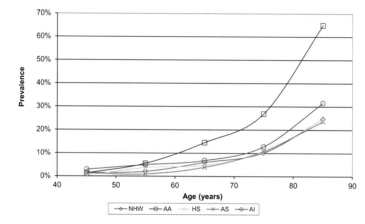

Figure 2.1 Ethnic-specific prevalence of peripheral arterial disease in men in the United States (Allison et al., 2007).

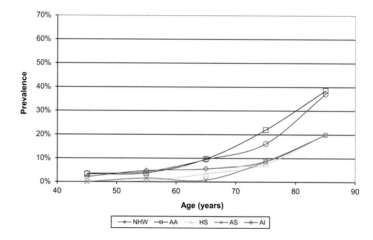

Figure 2.2 Ethnic-specific prevalence of peripheral arterial disease in women in the United States (Allison et al., 2007).

Multi-Ethic Study of Atherosclerosis (MESA) also reported a higher prevalence of PAD in Blacks compared with Whites and Hispanics, with an odds ratio of 1.67 for Blacks compared with Non-Hispanic Whites (McDermott et al., 2005). Using data from six US community-based cohorts, Matsushita et al. studied the lifetime risk for PAD and estimated that approximately 30% of Black men and women would develop PAD during their lifetime, compared with approximately 20% of Whites and Hispanics (Matsushita et al., 2019). Of note, while multiple community-based studies have shown a similar or lower prevalence of PAD in Hispanics compared with non-Hispanic whites (McDermott et al., 2005; Selvin & Erlinger, 2004), Morrissey et al. reported that Hispanics present with more advanced stages of disease, demonstrating higher rates of limb-threatening ischemia, failed lower extremity revascularization, and amputations than non-Hispanic Whites (Morrissey et al., 2007).

Allison et al. reported that, unlike other atherosclerotic diseases, the prevalence of PAD between men and women appears to be similar (Allison et al., 2007). Other epidemiologic studies have also shown comparable results. For example, the Multi-Ethnic Study of Atherosclerosis (MESA) reported that the prevalence of PAD was 3.7% in both men and women (McDermott et al., 2005). Matsushita et al. reported a similar lifetime risk of PAD between men and women, and in fact, reported a somewhat higher prevalence of PAD in women compared with men, particularly in younger age groups (Matsushita et al., 2019).

Risk factors

Several cardiovascular risk factors have been associated with increased risk for PAD (Fig. 2.3). Of those, smoking and diabetes are particularly strongly associated with PAD.

Cigarette smoking

Cigarette smoking is one of the most important modifiable risk factors for PAD, with up to 80% of PAD patients being current or former smokers (Meijer et al., 1998). Smoking increases the risk of PAD by two- to sixfold (Hirsch et al., 2005) and is twice as likely to cause PAD than coronary artery disease (CAD) (Price et al., 1999). Similarly, a recent report from the ARIC study observed that participants who smoked for ≥40 pack years had a fourfold increased risk of PAD, compared with a hazard ratio (HR) of 2.1 for CAD and 1.8 for stroke (Ding et al., 2019). This study also

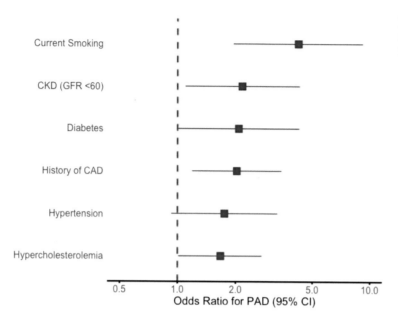

Figure 2.3 Risk factors and odds ratios for PAD (Selvin & Erlinger, 2004).

revealed that, compared with never smokers, the elevated risk of PAD persisted for up to 30 years after smoking cessation (Ding et al., 2019). In addition, current smokers with PAD demonstrate lower survival rates, reduced bypass graft patency rates, and increased likelihood of progression to critical limb ischemia (CLI) and amputation (Olin & Sealove, 2010). Conversely, PAD patients who quit smoking have improved survival rates and are less likely to develop CLI (Jonason & Bergström, 1987).

Diabetes mellitus

Diabetes mellitus is strongly associated with an elevated risk of PAD. Studies have shown that diabetes increases the risk of developing both symptomatic and asymptomatic PAD by up to fourfold. The Edinburgh Artery Study demonstrated a PAD prevalence of up to 20.6% in participants with diabetes or impaired glucose tolerance, compared with 12.5% in those with normal glucose tolerance. The NHANES study reported that the prevalence of PAD was 10.8% in US adults aged 40 or older with diabetes versus 3.6% in those without diabetes. PAD patients with diabetes are also at increased risk of complications, including major limb amputations and higher mortality. One study reported that diabetic patients with PAD were five times more likely to undergo limb amputation and had three times the odds for mortality compared with PAD patients without diabetes. In addition, a recent study examining data from Nationwide Inpatient Sample and the National Health Interview Survey revealed a troubling increase in amputation rates among patients with diabetes after 2009 (Geiss et al., 2019).

Dyslipidemia

Several studies have reported a significant association between total cholesterol and PAD. The Framingham Study demonstrated that an elevated total cholesterol level was associated with a twofold increased risk of intermittent claudication (McGee, 1985). The NHANES study reported that the prevalence of PAD was 5.8% in US adults (age $\geq$40 years) with hyperlipidemia versus 3.2% in those without (Selvin & Hirsch, 2008). One study demonstrated that the likelihood of developing PAD increased by 10% for every 10 mg/dL increase in total cholesterol (Hiatt et al., 1995). In addition, a recent study using data from the ARIC study showed that triglyceride-related and HDL-related lipids were particularly robustly associated with the future risk of PAD (Kou et al., 2021).

Hypertension

Several population-based studies have demonstrated a strong association between hypertension and PAD. Data from the ARIC study demonstrated an independent association between systolic blood pressure and the risk of PAD, with a relative risk of about 2.6 for systolic blood pressure $\geq$140 mmHg compared with a reference of systolic blood pressure <120 mmHg (Lu et al., 2017). Furthermore, given its high prevalence in the elderly population, hypertension is considered a significant contributor to the burden of PAD in the global population. For example, the Heart Professionals Follow-up Study revealed that hypertension had a population-attributable risk of more than 40% (Joosten et al., 2012) for incident PAD, while the Framingham Study reported that 30% of the PAD risk in the population was attributable to blood pressure above 160/100 mmHg (Murabito et al., 1997).

Homocysteine

Elevated levels of homocysteine have been associated with a two- to threefold increased risk of developing atherosclerosis (Hirsch et al., 2005). It is estimated that approximately 30%–40% of patients with PAD have high levels of homocysteine

(Taylor et al., 1991). The European Concerted Action Project reported that plasma homocysteine concentrations greater than the 80th percentile for control subjects were associated with a twofold increased risk of vascular disease, including PAD, CAD, and stroke, independent of major traditional risk factors (Robinson et al., 1998). A metaanalysis of 14 epidemiological studies revealed that patients with PAD had consistently higher levels of homocysteine as compared with controls, suggesting that elevated homocysteine levels may either serve as a marker of PAD or contribute to the development of PAD (Khandanpour et al., 2009).

Inflammatory markers

C-reactive protein (CRP) and fibrinogen are serologic markers of systemic inflammation, which is considered an important pathophysiological condition in the development of systemic atherosclerosis. Numerous studies have reported that elevated levels of these markers are associated with incident PAD. An analysis of previously healthy people from the Physicians Health Study (PHS) reported that both CRP and fibrinogen were significantly associated with PAD in multivariable models, with the relative risk of incident PAD for those with baseline levels in the highest versus the lower quartiles being 2.8 for CRP and 2.2 for fibrinogen (Ridker et al., 2001). The study also noted that baseline CRP levels were higher in individuals who required lower extremity revascularization. A recent study from the ARIC study showed that galectin-3, a marker of fibrosis and inflammation, is also independently associated with incident PAD (Ding et al., 2020).

Chronic kidney disease

Mild-to-moderate chronic kidney disease (CKD) is an established risk factor for cardiovascular disease (Garg et al., 2002; Manjunath et al., 2003). Several studies have also shown an association between CKD and PAD, including a high prevalence of PAD among dialysis patients (O'Hare & Johansen, 2001). A recent individual participant data metaanalysis including more than 0.8 million adults demonstrated that both lower glomerular filtration rate and elevated albuminuria are associated with PAD risk independently of each other and other confounders such as age, diabetes, and hypertension (Matsushita, Ballew, Coresh, et al., 2017). This study found an especially strong association of albuminuria with leg amputation. Other studies have also reported that patients with PAD and concomitant CKD are at increased risk for poorer outcomes, such as higher mortality and increased risk of limb loss (O'Hare et al., 2004; Pasqualini et al., 2007). In fact, one Veterans Administration study of PAD patients undergoing lower extremity revascularization found that those patients receiving dialysis had a very high risk of amputation within the first year after lower extremity revascularization (29% versus 10% in patients with normal or mildly reduced renal function) (O'Hare et al., 2004).

Natural history of PAD

PAD as a marker for disease in other vascular beds

Due to the systemic nature of atherosclerosis, PAD patients are at risk for polyvascular disease. Multiple studies have shown that PAD overlaps with disease in other vascular beds. For example, the Reduction of Atherothrombosis for Continued Health (REACH) international registry reported that 63% of patients with PAD have concomitant symptomatic cerebrovascular or coronary disease (Bhatt et al., 2006). The Swiss Atherothrombosis Survey revealed that 52% of symptomatic PAD patients reported a concurrent history of stroke/transient ischemic attack (TIA) and/or CAD and that 23% of patients with a history of stroke/TIA or CAD were found to have previously undiagnosed, asymptomatic PAD (Hayoz et al., 2005). An analysis from the Clopidogrel versus Aspirin in Patients at Risk of Ischemic Events (CAPRIE) trial showed that 26% of participants had symptomatic disease in at least two vascular beds (A randomised, blinded, trial of clopidogrel versus aspirin in patients at risk of ischaemic events (CAPRIE), 1996). In addition, the REACH registry reported that patients with PAD only at baseline had the highest risk of progressing to polyvascular disease at 3 years, with approximately 10% progressing to polyvascular disease (specifically, 6.1% CAD and 3.8% stroke), compared with approximately 4% of patients with either CAD or stroke (Alberts et al., 2009).

Cardiovascular morbidity and mortality in PAD

The Framingham Heart Study initially described the association between intermittent claudication and both CAD and stroke and reported a twofold age-adjusted increased risk of death in both men and women with claudication (Kannel et al., 1970). In fact, the overall 5-year mortality for PAD patients has been reported to be as high as 15%—30%, with over 75% attributable to cardiovascular causes (Hirsch et al., 2005). The presence of PAD as defined by an ABI <0.9 has been associated with a sixfold increased risk of cardiovascular death at 10 years (Criqui et al., 1992) and a two- to threefold increased risk of ischemic stroke (Abbott et al., 2001) when compared with the general population. Furthermore, while an ABI between 0.9 and 1.3 has been traditionally considered normal (Hirsch et al., 2001), the Multi-Ethnic Study of Atherosclerosis (MESA) has reported excess coronary and carotid atherosclerosis in patients with borderline low ABIs (0.9—1.1) (McDermott et al., 2005). In addition, the Strong Heart Study reported an increased risk of all-cause and cardiovascular mortality for participants with a low ABI (<0.9) and borderline ABI (0.9—1.0) (Resnick et al., 2004). These studies also demonstrated elevated cardiovascular risk related to high ABIs (>1.3 or 1.4), indicative of incompressible arteries due to medial calcification.

Multiple recent studies have demonstrated that patients with PAD are at higher risk of major adverse cardiovascular events compared with patients with CAD or stroke. For example, the REACH registry reported that patients with PAD had the highest 3-year event rate of MI/stroke/death/rehospitalization, at 40.4%, compared with 29.7% in patients with CAD and 28.1% in patients with history of stroke (Alberts et al., 2009). In addition, patients with PAD were most likely to have vascular death (2.9 events per 100 patient-years), followed by patients with cerebrovascular disease (2.1 events per 100 patient-years) and those with CAD (1.9 events per 100 patient-years) (Alberts et al., 2009). A post hoc analysis of 3096 patients with PAD from the CHARISMA trial observed that the risk of cardiovascular death, myocardial infarction (MI), or stroke (primary endpoint) was higher in patients with PAD than in those without: 8.2% versus 6.8%, with HR of 1.25. Patients with PAD had also higher risk of death from any cause (HR, 1.8), death from cardiovascular causes (HR, 1.7), MI (HR, 1.3), and hospitalization for ischemic events (HR, 2.0) (Cacoub et al., 2009). More recently, the Further Cardiovascular Outcomes Research with PCSK9 Inhibition in Subjects with Elevated Risk (FOURIER) trial, which included 3642 with symptomatic PAD, reported that patients with PAD only at baseline (no prior MI or stroke), had higher risk of CV death, MI, or stroke than patients with prior MI or stroke but no symptomatic PAD (10.3% versus 7.6%; adjusted HR, 2.1) (Bonaca et al., 2018). In addition, patients with PAD with concomitant history of prior MI or stroke (polyvascular disease) exhibited higher risk of CV death, MI, or stroke than those without (14.9% versus 10.3%) (Bonaca et al., 2018). A recent study using data from NHANES in US adults aged 40 years or older revealed that those with both PAD and CHD/stroke had the worst prognosis, with a 12-year survival of 25.5%, compared with 87.2% in patients with neither CHD/stroke or PAD (Matsushita et al., 2022). In addition, patients with PAD without CHD/stroke had a worse prognosis than those with CHD/stroke without PAD, with a survival of 47.7% versus 53.2% (Fig. 2.4).

Limb outcomes in PAD

Patients with PAD are at risk for multiple limb complications, including functional impairment/claudication, ischemic rest pain, ischemic ulceration, hospitalization for revascularization, and limb loss. These complications are associated with poor quality of life and a high rate of depression (McDermott et al., 2003; Regensteiner et al., 2008). Studies have shown that over 50% of patients with PAD have some degree of walking impairment (Selvin & Hirsch, 2008). Therefore, based on current estimates of PAD prevalence worldwide, it is likely that over 100 million people could experience diminished mobility leading to a reduced quality of life. Further, patients with more severe manifestations of PAD may require revascularization to improve mobility and prevent tissue loss. Data have shown that PAD patients who undergo peripheral revascularization are at high risk for subsequent vascular complications, including acute limb ischemia, major amputation, or death from cardiovascular causes (Bonaca et al., 2020).

Functional impairment

Several studies have shown that patients with PAD experience significant functional impairment and loss of mobility, including those who report no leg symptoms (Matsushita, Ballew, Sang, et al., 2017; McDermott et al., 2013; McDermott et al., 2000). The Women's Health and Aging Study examined the lower extremity functioning of 933 women, 328 of whom had PAD as defined by ABI <0.9 (McDermott et al., 2002). In the cohort of patients with PAD, 63% reported no leg symptoms with exertion and were therefore classified as asymptomatic; however, after objective testing, these individuals were found to have worse lower extremity functioning than an age-matched cohort (McDermott et al.,

(a)

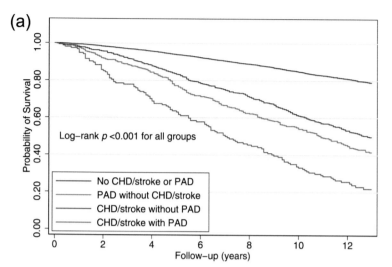

(b)

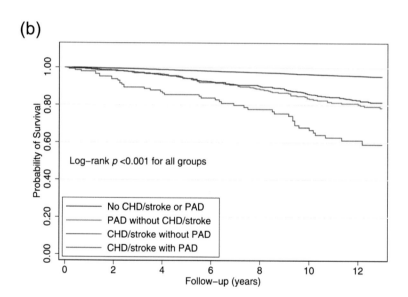

Figure 2.4 Survival estimates by the status of PAD and CHD/stroke (Matsushita et al., 2022). (a) All-cause mortality and (b) Cardiovascular mortality.

2002). Specifically, women who were classified as having asymptomatic PAD were actually found to have slower walking velocities and poorer standing balance scores and walked fewer blocks per week than women without PAD, even after adjustment for other comorbidities (McDermott et al., 2002). Another study revealed that asymptomatic patients with PAD based on abnormal ABI have poorer functional performance, poorer quality of life, and smaller calf muscle area than an age-matched group of patients without PAD (McDermott et al., 2000). The ARIC study reported that community-dwelling older adults with abnormal ABI (ABI $\leq$0.9) and borderline low ABI (0.9—1.0) exhibited significantly reduced physical function as measured by the Short Physical Performance Battery instrument compared with those with normal ABI (Matsushita, Ballew, Sang, et al., 2017). The association was significant even after adjusting for traditional risk factors and history of other cardiovascular diseases, CAD, stroke, and heart failure (Matsushita, Ballew, Sang, et al., 2017).

Critical limb ischemia and amputations

CLI is defined by pain in the lower extremities that occurs with rest or evidence of tissue loss in the setting of severely compromised arterial flow. In individuals with CLI, occlusive disease progresses to the point where blood flow at rest becomes insufficient for tissue viability, and ischemic rest pain, nonhealing ulcerations, and/or gangrene can develop. CLI is considered a severe manifestation of PAD and is associated with significant limb morbidity and cardiovascular mortality. It is estimated that CLI is present in up to 10% of all patients with PAD (Shishehbor et al., 2016), with up to 2% of those patients presenting with CLI at initial diagnosis. Patients with diabetes are particularly prone to developing this syndrome, which is associated with a substantial risk of limb loss (Hiatt, 2001). One in four patients may require amputation or die from cardiovascular causes 1 year after the initial diagnosis of CLI (Hirsch et al., 2005). An analysis of 186,338 Medicare recipients, who underwent major lower extremity amputation from 2000 to 2008, showed a mortality of 13.5% at 30 days and up to 70.9% at 3 years (Jones et al., 2013). A more recent analysis of the Medicare claims data reported a poor long-term prognosis after the diagnosis of CLI, with 54% mortality at 4 years (Mustapha et al., 2018). In addition, 71% of patients underwent at least one revascularization or amputation procedure within the 4-year period, with 3% experiencing major amputation (Mustapha et al., 2018). The ARIC study examined the prospective association between ABI and severe ischemic leg outcomes in a middle-aged community-based cohort of 13,375 participants, with a median follow-up of 28 years (Paskiewicz et al., 2021). Low ABI ($\leq$0.90) had a nearly threefold increased risk for CLI (adjusted HR 2.4) and ischemic leg amputation (adjusted HR 2.7). Borderline low ABI (0.91—1.00), and even ABI 1.01—1.10, showed a significant association, with adjusted HR of about 1.7—2.0 for both outcomes (Paskiewicz et al., 2021). The FOURIER trial revealed that patients with symptomatic PAD had a higher risk of limb outcomes relative to those without PAD including major adverse limb events (2.4% versus 0.2%; adjusted HR, ~12) and the composite of acute limb ischemia (ALI) and major amputation (1.5% versus 0.1%; adjusted HR, ~8) (Bonaca et al., 2018).

Acute limb ischemia

ALI occurs due to a sudden deterioration in limb perfusion and may be a form of CLI but is more commonly related to an acute event such as embolism or local thrombosis. In patients with PAD, atherosclerotic plaques may undergo rupture or erosion causing thrombosis and abrupt cessation of blood flow in the affected vascular bed. ALI is a particularly serious complication of PAD and is associated with long hospitalizations and high incidences of limb loss, disability, and death (Bonaca et al., 2016, 2020). The Examining Use of Ticagrelor in Peripheral Artery Disease (EUCLID) trial reported 293 ALI events out of 13,885 participants with symptomatic PAD (Hess et al., 2019). In a multivariable analysis, ALI was significantly associated with an increased risk of major amputation (HR ~14), as well as increased risk of all-cause mortality (HR ~3) (Hess et al., 2019). In the VOYAGER trial, which included PAD patients who had recently undergone lower-extremity revascularization, nearly 20% of patients in the placebo group had the primary composite outcome of ALI, major amputation for vascular causes, MI, ischemic stroke, or death from cardiovascular causes at 3 years (Bonaca et al., 2020).

Other outcomes in PAD

While several studies have documented an association between PAD and lower extremity infections, particularly after revascularization (Bodewes et al., 2017), the presence of PAD has also recently been studied as a risk factor for overall infections (Mok et al., 2022). An analysis from the ARIC study revealed that patients with PAD had a 1.5–2.1-fold increased risk of four subtypes of infection, including cellulitis, bloodstream infection, pneumonia, and urinary tract infection. After multivariable adjustment, patients with PAD had a 1.6-fold increased risk for overall infection, while patients with both PAD and CHD/stroke had a close to twofold increased risk (Mok et al., 2022).

PAD awareness

Despite the rising prevalence, awareness of PAD is poor, particularly in general practice. The PARTNERS program was a cross-sectional study aimed at studying the prevalence of PAD in primary care practices in the United States. Using an ABI <0.9 to define PAD, PARTNERS found that the diagnosis of PAD was new in 55% of patients with PAD only (exclusive of CAD). In addition, while 83% of patients with prior PAD were aware of their diagnosis, only 49% of their physicians were aware of this diagnosis (Hirsch et al., 2001). A study conducted in vascular surgery specialty clinics for PAD revealed that awareness and understanding of the disease among patients enrolled in the clinics were poor, with only 65% of participants aware of their PAD diagnosis (Byskosh et al., 2022). Further, among patients who had undergone major leg amputation, 35% were unaware of a diagnosis of PAD.

Screening for PAD

Current PAD management guidelines recommend the routine use of ABIs in general medical practices, specifically in patients who exhibit risk factors for PAD: age $\geq$65; age 50−64 years with risk factors such as smoking or diabetes; exertional leg symptoms suggestive of claudication; ischemic rest pain; abnormal lower extremity pulse examination; and known atherosclerotic disease (Gerhard-Herman et al., 2016, p. 135). The Population Screening for Intervention in Vascular Disease in Danish men (VIVA) trial randomized 50,156 men aged 65−74 years to screening for abdominal aortic aneurysm (AAA), PAD, and hypertension, or to no screening (Lindholt & Søgaard, 2017). After a median follow-up of 4.4 years, the screening and subsequent intervention significantly reduced overall mortality, with HR of 0.93, and a number needed to invite for screening to avert one death of 169. In addition, fewer inpatient hospitalization days due to PAD were observed in the screening group compared with the nonscreening group. After removal of the effect of hypertension treatment and surgical repair of AAA, the observed major benefit persisted, suggesting that in this screening trial, the mortality benefit observed may be in large part related to the initiation of medical therapy based on the detection of AAA and PAD, specifically statins and antiplatelet therapy. Despite this data, the US Preventive Services Task Force still currently recommends against routine screening for PAD by ABI testing ("United States Preventive Services Task Force. Recommendation Statement: Screening for Peripheral Arterial Disease," 2005).

Several barriers to the routine use of ABIs in primary care practice have been reported, including time constraints, lack of reimbursement, and staff availability (Mohler et al., 2004). Given limitations of routine ABI use in the primary care setting, physicians may consider screening for possible PAD by simply querying their patients for the presence of exertional leg symptoms. This is especially important because a significant number of patients may not even report their symptoms to their physician, as they attribute them to aging, arthritis, or other musculoskeletal pain (McDermott et al., 2001). In fact, the Northern Manhattan Study (NOMAS) found that self-reported PAD, defined as a positive answer to one of two questions related to exertional leg symptoms or a known history of prior PAD, was independently associated with an increased risk of future vascular events in a population-based cohort (Salameh et al., 2008). Despite the potential value of screening for PAD based on leg symptoms, this is not routinely performed in the primary care setting. One study aimed at assessing the factors affecting the diagnosis of PAD revealed that only 37% of internists reported taking a history of claudication from their patients; in contrast, 92% reported taking a cardiac history most of the time (McLafferty et al., 2000).

Undertreatment of PAD

PARTNERS and other studies have reported that patients with PAD are less frequently treated with evidence-based therapy for atherosclerotic disease than those with CAD (Hirsch et al., 2001; McDermott et al., 1997). Specifically, patients with PAD were less likely to be treated with aspirin and statins than their CAD counterparts (Hirsch et al., 2001). An analysis of NHANES 1999–2004 revealed that statin use was reported in only 30.5% of patients with PAD, aspirin use in 35.8%, and use of angiotensin-converting enzyme inhibitor (ACE-I)/angiotensin receptor blocker (ARB) in 24.9% (Pande et al., 2011). A separate analysis of patients with PAD enrolled in ambulatory care in the United States from 2005 to 2013, antiplatelet therapy was used in 36.3% of patients, a statin was used in 30.5%, and an ACE-I or ARB in 32.9% (Berger & Ladapo, 2017). The same analysis revealed that PAD patients who also had a known diagnosis of CAD were much more likely to receive treatment with antiplatelets, statins, and ACE-Is/ARBs at a given outpatient visit compared with patients with PAD alone. These findings highlight the need for increased awareness of PAD in general practice settings, with the goal of training primary care physicians to routinely screen for leg symptoms and/or functional impairment in patients considered high-risk for PAD, so that they may benefit from early diagnosis. This would in turn lead to institution of appropriate early treatment for cardiovascular risk reduction and the use of specific strategies (e.g., supervised exercise treatment) to improve health-related quality of life in patients with PAD.

Conclusion

PAD is a global problem that is increasing in prevalence worldwide in both high-income and low-/middle-income countries. With the aging of the population and the expected increase in associated risk factors such as diabetes, the burden of PAD is expected to rise in the near future, especially in low- and middle-income countries. While PAD shares common risk factors with CAD and cerebrovascular disease, it has also emerged as a distinct syndrome associated with a significantly increased risk of cardiovascular morbidity and mortality and considerable disability and poor quality of life due to functional impairment and major adverse limb events. Despite its increasing prevalence, PAD continues to be underdiagnosed and undertreated due to a general lack of awareness on the part of both patients and practitioners. As a result, PAD patients are less frequently treated with evidence-based therapy for atherosclerotic disease compared to those with CAD. The detection of PAD early in its course through ABI screening and evaluation of leg symptoms would be beneficial in instituting appropriate therapies aimed at prevention and treatment of vascular risk factors on a global level, with the ultimate goal of reducing major cardiovascular and limb events in this high-risk population.

References

A randomised, blinded, trial of clopidogrel versus aspirin in patients at risk of ischaemic events (CAPRIE). *The Lancet, 348*(9038), (1996), 1329–1339. https://doi.org/10.1016/s0140-6736(96)09457-3

2005 United States preventive Services Task Force. Recommendation Statement: Screening for peripheral arterial disease. *Agency for Healthcare Research and Quality*, , (2005)1–8.

Abbott, R. D., Rodriguez, B. L., Petrovitch, H., Yano, K., Schatz, I. J., Popper, J. S., Masaki, K. H., Webster Ross, G., & David Curb, J. (2001). Ankle-brachial blood pressure in elderly men and the risk of stroke: The Honolulu Heart Program. *Journal of Clinical Epidemiology, 54*(10), 973–978. https://doi.org/10.1016/S0895-4356(01)00373-0

Alberts, M. J., Bhatt, D. L., Mas, J. L., Ohman, E. M., Hirsch, A. T., Röther, J., Salette, G., Goto, S., Smith, S. C., Liau, C. S., Wilson, P. W. F., & Steg, P. G. (2009). Three-year follow-up and event rates in the international REduction of atherothrombosis for continued health registry. *European Heart Journal, 30*(19), 2318–2326. https://doi.org/10.1093/eurheartj/ehp355

Allison, M. A., Ho, E., Denenberg, J. O., Langer, R. D., Newman, A. B., Fabsitz, R. R., & Criqui, M. H. (2007). Ethnic-specific prevalence of peripheral arterial disease in the United States. *American Journal of Preventive Medicine, 32*(4), 328–333. https://doi.org/10.1016/j.amepre.2006.12.010

Berger, J. S., & Ladapo, J. A. (2017). Underuse of prevention and lifestyle counseling in patients with peripheral artery disease. *Journal of the American College of Cardiology, 69*(18), 2293–2300. https://doi.org/10.1016/j.jacc.2017.02.064

Bhatt, D. L., Gabriel Steg, P., Magnus Ohman, E., Hirsch, A. T., Ikeda, Y., Mas, J. L., Goto, S., Liau, C. S., Richard, A. J., Röther, J., & Wilson, P. W. F. (2006). International prevalence, recognition, and treatment of cardiovascular risk factors in outpatients with atherothrombosis. *Journal of the American Medical Association, 295*(2), 180–189. https://doi.org/10.1001/jama.295.2.180

Bodewes, T. C. F., Soden, P. A., Ultee, K. H. J., Zettervall, S. L., Pothof, A. B., Deery, S. E., Moll, F. L., & Schermerhorn, M. L. (2017). Risk factors for 30-day unplanned readmission following infrainguinal endovascular interventions. *Journal of Vascular Surgery, 65*(2), 484–494.e3. https://doi.org/10.1016/j.jvs.2016.08.093

Bonaca, M. P., Bauersachs, R. M., Anand, S. S., Debus, E. S., Nehler, M. R., Patel, M. R., Fanelli, F., Capell, W. H., Diao, L., Jaeger, N., Hess, C. N., Pap, A. F., Kittelson, J. M., Gudz, I., Mátyás, L., Krievins, D. K., Diaz, R., Brodmann, M., Muehlhofer, E., … Hiatt, W. R. (2020). Rivaroxaban in peripheral artery disease after revascularization. *New England Journal of Medicine, 382*(21), 1994–2004. https://doi.org/10.1056/NEJMoa2000052

Bonaca, M. P., Gutierrez, J. A., Creager, M. A., Scirica, B. M., Olin, J., Murphy, S. A., Braunwald, E., & Morrow, D. A. (2016). Acute limb ischemia and outcomes with vorapaxar in patients with peripheral artery disease. *Circulation, 133*(10), 997–1005. https://doi.org/10.1161/CIRCULATIONAHA.115.019355

Bonaca, M. P., Nault, P., Giugliano, R. P., Keech, A. C., Pineda, A. L., Kanevsky, E., Kuder, J., Murphy, S. A., Jukema, J. W., Lewis, B. S., Tokgozoglu, L., Somaratne, R., Sever, P. S., Pedersen, T. R., & Sabatine, M. S. (2018). Low-density lipoprotein cholesterol lowering with evolocumab and outcomes in patients with peripheral artery disease: Insights from the FOURIER trial (further cardiovascular outcomes Research with PCSK9 inhibition in subjects with elevated risk). *Circulation, 137*(4), 338–350. https://doi.org/10.1161/CIRCULATIONAHA.117.032235

Byskosh, N., Pamulapati, V., Xu, S., Vavra, A. K., Hoel, A. W., Tian, L., McDermott, M. M., Butt, Z., & Ho, K. J. (2022). Identifying gaps in disease knowledge among patients with peripheral artery disease. *Journal of Vascular Surgery, 75*(4), 1358–1368.e5. https://doi.org/10.1016/j.jvs.2021.11.036

Cacoub, P. P., Bhatt, D. L., Steg, P. G., Topol, E. J., & Creager, M. A. (2009). Patients with peripheral arterial disease in the CHARISMA trial. *European Heart Journal, 30*(2), 192–201. https://doi.org/10.1093/eurheartj/ehn534

Criqui, M. H., & Aboyans, V. (2015). Epidemiology of peripheral artery disease. *Circulation Research, 116*(9), 1509–1526. https://doi.org/10.1161/CIRCRESAHA.116.303849

Criqui, M. H., Langer, R. D., Feigelson, H. S., Klauber, M. R., Mccann, T. J., Browner, D., Criqui, M. H., & Fronek, A. (1992). Mortality over a period of 10 years in patients with peripheral arterial disease. *New England Journal of Medicine, 326*(6), 381–386. https://doi.org/10.1056/NEJM199202063260605

Ding, N., Sang, Y., Chen, J., Ballew, S. H., Kalbaugh, C. A., Salameh, M. J., Blaha, M. J., Allison, M., Heiss, G., Selvin, E., Coresh, J., & Matsushita, K.

(2019). Cigarette smoking, smoking cessation, and long-term risk of 3 major atherosclerotic diseases. *Journal of the American College of Cardiology, 74*(4), 498–507. https://doi.org/10.1016/j.jacc.2019.05.049

Ding, N., Yang, C., Ballew, S. H., Kalbaugh, C. A., McEvoy, J. W., Salameh, M., Aguilar, D., Hoogeveen, R. C., Nambi, V., Selvin, E., Folsom, A. R., Heiss, G., Coresh, J., Ballantyne, C. M., & Matsushita, K. (2020). Fibrosis and inflammatory markers and long-term risk of peripheral artery disease: The ARIC study. *Arteriosclerosis, Thrombosis, and Vascular Biology*, 2322–2331. https://doi.org/10.1161/ATVBAHA.120.314824

Fowkes, F. G. R. (1988). The measurement of atherosclerotic peripheral arterial disease in epidemiological surveys. *International Journal of Epidemiology, 17*(2), 248–254. https://doi.org/10.1093/ije/17.2.248

Fowkes, F. G. R., Rudan, D., Rudan, I., Aboyans, V., Denenberg, J. O., McDermott, M. M., Norman, P. E., Sampson, U. K. A., Williams, L. J., Mensah, G. A., & Criqui, M. H. (2013). Comparison of global estimates of prevalence and risk factors for peripheral artery disease in 2000 and 2010: A systematic review and analysis. *The Lancet, 382*(9901), 1329–1340. https://doi.org/10.1016/S0140-6736(13)61249-0

Garg, A. X., Clark, W. F., Haynes, R. B., & House, A. A. (2002). Moderate renal insufficiency and the risk of cardiovascular mortality: Results from the NHANES I. *Kidney International, 61*(4), 1486–1494. https://doi.org/10.1046/j.1523-1755.2002.00270.x

Geiss, L. S., Li, Y., Hora, I., Albright, A., Rolka, D., & Gregg, E. W. (2019). Resurgence of diabetes-related nontraumatic lower-extremity amputation in the young and middle-aged adult U.S. population. *Diabetes Care, 42*(1), 50–54. https://doi.org/10.2337/dc18-1380

Gerhard-Herman, Gornik, Barrett, Barshes, Corriere, Drachman, Fleisher, Fowkes, F. G., Hamburg, Kinlay, S., Lookstein, Misra, S., Mureebe, Olin, J. W., Patel, Regensteiner, J. G., Schanzer, Shishehbor, M. H., Stewart, K. J., Treat-Jacobson, D., & Walsh, M. E. (2016). *AHA/ACC guideline on the management of patients with lower extremity peripheral artery disease: A report of the American College of Cardiology/American Heart Association Task Force on clinical practice guidelines* (p. 135), 2016.

Hayoz, D., Bounameaux, H., & Canova, C. R. (2005). Swiss atherothrombosis Survey: A field report on the occurrence of symptomatic and asymptomatic peripheral arterial disease. *Journal of Internal Medicine, 258*(3), 238–243. https://doi.org/10.1111/j.1365-2796.2005.01536.x

Hess, C. N., Huang, Z., Patel, M. R., Baumgartner, I., Berger, J. S., Blomster, J. I., Fowkes, F. G. R., Held, P., Jones, W. S., Katona, B., Mahaffey, K. W., Norgren, L., Rockhold, F. W., & Hiatt, W. R. (2019). Acute limb ischemia in peripheral artery disease. *Circulation, 140*(7), 556–565. https://doi.org/10.1161/circulationaha.119.039773

Hiatt, W. R., Hoag, S., & Hamman, R. F. (1995). Effect of diagnostic criteria on the prevalence of peripheral arterial disease: The San Luis Valley Diabetes Study. *Circulation, 91*(5), 1472–1479. https://doi.org/10.1161/01.CIR.91.5.1472

Hiatt, W. R. (2001). Medical treatment of peripheral arterial disease and claudication. *New England Journal of Medicine, 344*(21), 1608–1621. https://doi.org/10.1056/NEJM200105243442108

Hirsch, A. T., Criqui, M. H., Treat-Jacobson, D., Regensteiner, J. G., Creager, M. A., Olin, J. W., Krook, S. H., Hunninghake, D. B., Comerota, A. J., Walsh, M. E., McDermott, M. M., & Hiatt, W. R. (2001). Peripheral arterial disease detection, awareness, and treatment in primary care. *Journal of the American Medical Association, 286*(11), 1317–1324. https://doi.org/10.1001/jama.286.11.1317

Hirsch, Haskal, Z. J., & Hertzer, N. R. (2005). 2005 guidelines for the management of patients with peripheral arterial disease (lower extremity, renal, mesenteric, and abdominal aortic): Executive summary a collaborative report from the American association for vascular surgery/society for vascular surgery, society for cardiovascular angiography and interventions, society for vascular medicine and biology, society of interventional radiology, and the ACC/AHA Task Force on practice guidelines (writing committee to develop guidelines for the management of patients with peripheral arterial disease) endorsed by the American association of cardiovascular and pulmonary rehabilitation; national heart, lung, and blood institute; society for vascular nursing; TransAtlantic inter-society consensus; and vascular disease foundation. *Journal of the American College of Cardiology, 47*, 2–192.

Jonason, T., & Bergström, R. (1987). Cessation of smoking in patients with intermittent claudication: Effects on the risk of peripheral vascular complications, myocardial infarction and mortality. *Acta Medica Scandinavica, 221*(3), 253–260. https://doi.org/10.1111/j.0954-6820.1987.tb00891.x

Jones, W. S., Patel, M. R., Dai, D., Vemulapalli, S., Subherwal, S., Stafford, J., & Peterson, E. D. (2013). High mortality risks after major lower extremity amputation in Medicare patients with peripheral artery disease. *American Heart Journal, 165*(5), 809–815.e1. https://doi.org/10.1016/j.ahj.2012.12.002

Joosten, M. M., Pai, J. K., Bertoia, M. L., Rimm, E. B., Spiegelman, D., Mittleman, M. A., & Mukamal, K. J. (2012). Associations between conventional cardiovascular risk factors and risk of peripheral artery disease in men. *JAMA, 308*(16), 1660–1667. https://doi.org/10.1001/jama.2012.13415

Kannel, W. B., Skinner, J. J., Schwartz, M. J., & Shurtleff, D. (1970). Intermittent claudication. Incidence in the Framingham study. *Circulation, 41*(5), 875–883. https://doi.org/10.1161/01.CIR.41.5.875. undefined.

Khandanpour, N., Loke, Y. K., Meyer, F. J., Jennings, B., & Armon, M. P. (2009). Homocysteine and peripheral arterial disease: Systematic review and meta-analysis. *European Journal of Vascular and Endovascular Surgery, 38*(3), 316–322. https://doi.org/10.1016/j.ejvs.2009.05.007

Kou, M., Ding, N., Ballew, S. H., Salameh, M. J., Martin, S. S., Selvin, E., Heiss, G., Ballantyne, C. M., Matsushita, K., & Hoogeveen, R. C. (2021). Conventional and novel lipid measures and risk of peripheral artery disease. *Arteriosclerosis, Thrombosis, and Vascular Biology, 41*(3), 1229–1238. https://doi.org/10.1161/ATVBAHA.120.315828

Lindholt, J. S., & Søgaard, R. (2017). Population screening and intervention for vascular disease in Danish men (VIVA): A randomised controlled trial. *The Lancet, 390*(10109), 2256–2265. https://doi.org/10.1016/S0140-6736(17)32250-X

Lu, Y., Ballew, S. H., Tanaka, H., Szklo, M., Heiss, G., Coresh, J., & Matsushita, K. (2017). 2017 ACC/AHA blood pressure classification and incident peripheral artery disease: The atherosclerosis risk in Communities (ARIC) study. *Eur J Prev Cardiol, 27*, 51–59.

Manjunath, G., Tighiouart, H., Ibrahim, H., MacLeod, B., Salem, D. N., Griffith, J. L., Coresh, J., Levey, A. S., & Sarnak, M. J. (2003). Level of kidney function as a risk factor for atherosclerotic cardiovascular outcomes in the community. *Journal of the American College of Cardiology, 41*(1), 47–55. https://doi.org/10.1016/S0735-1097(02)02663-3

Matsushita, K., Ballew, S. H., Coresh, J., Arima, H., Ärnlöv, J., Cirillo, M., Ebert, N., Hiramoto, J. S., Kimm, H., Shlipak, M. G., Visseren, F. L. J., Gansevoort, R. T., Kovesdy, C. P., Shalev, V., Woodward, M., Kronenberg, F., Chalmers, J., Perkovic, V., Grams, M. E., … Kwak, L. (2017). Measures of chronic kidney disease and risk of incident peripheral artery disease: A collaborative meta-analysis of individual participant data. *Lancet Diabetes & Endocrinology, 5*(9), 718–728. https://doi.org/10.1016/S2213-8587(17)30183-3

Matsushita, K., Ballew, S. H., Sang, Y., Kalbaugh, C., Loehr, L. R., Hirsch, A. T., Tanaka, H., Heiss, G., Windham, B. G., Selvin, E., & Coresh, J. (2017). Ankle-brachial index and physical function in older individuals: The Atherosclerosis Risk in Communities (ARIC) study. *Atherosclerosis, 257*, 208–215. https://doi.org/10.1016/j.atherosclerosis.2016.11.023

Matsushita, K., Gao, Y., Sang, Y., Ballew, S. H., Salameh, M., Allison, M., Selvin, E., & Coresh, J. (2022). Comparative mortality according to peripheral artery disease and coronary heart disease/stroke in the United States. *Atherosclerosis, 354*, 57–62. https://doi.org/10.1016/j.atherosclerosis.2022.04.029

Matsushita, K., Sang, Y., Ning, H., Ballew, S. H., Chow, E. K., Grams, M. E., Selvin, E., Allison, M., Criqui, M., Coresh, J., Lloyd-Jones, D. M., & Wilkins, J. T. (2019). Lifetime risk of lower-extremity peripheral artery disease defined by ankle-brachial index in the United States. *Journal of the American Heart Association, 8*(18). https://doi.org/10.1161/JAHA.119.012177

McDermott, M. M. G., Mehta, S., Ahn, H., & Greenland, P. (1997). Atherosclerotic risk factors are less intensively treated in patients with peripheral arterial disease than in patients with coronary artery disease. *Journal of General Internal Medicine, 12*(4), 209–215. https://doi.org/10.1007/s11606-006-5042-4

McDermott, M. M., Applegate, W. B., Bonds, D. E., Buford, T. W., Church, T., Espeland, M. A., Gill, T. M., Guralnik, J. M., Haskell, W., Lovato, L. C., Pahor, M., Pepine, C. J., Reid, K. F., & Newman, A. (2013). Ankle brachial index values, leg symptoms, and functional performance among community-dwelling older men and women in the lifestyle interventions and independence for elders study. *Journal of the American Heart Association, 2*(6). https://doi.org/10.1161/JAHA.113.000257

McDermott, M. M. G., Ferrucci, L., Simonsick, E. M., Balfour, J., Fried, L., Ling, S., Gibson, D., & Guralnik, J. M. (2002). The ankle brachial index and change in lower extremity functioning over time: The women's health and aging study. *Journal of the American Geriatrics Society, 50*(2), 238–246. https://doi.org/10.1046/j.1532-5415.2002.50054.x

McDermott, M. M. G., Fried, L., Simonsick, E., Ling, S., & Guralnik, J. M. (2000). Asymptomatic peripheral arterial disease is independently associated with impaired lower extremity functioning: The women's health and aging study. *Circulation, 101*(9), 1007–1012. https://doi.org/10.1161/01.CIR.101.9.1007

McDermott, M. M. G., Greenland, P., Guralnik, J. M., Liu, K., Criqui, M. H., Pearce, W. H., Chan, C., Schneider, J., Sharma, L., Taylor, L. M., Arseven, A., Quann, M., & Celic, L. (2003). Depressive symptoms and lower extremity functioning in men and women with peripheral arterial disease. *Journal of General Internal Medicine, 18*(6), 461–467. https://doi.org/10.1046/j.1525-1497.2003.20527.x

McDermott, M. M. G., Greenland, P., Liu, K., Guralnik, J. M., Criqui, M. H., Dolan, N. C., Chan, C., Celic, L., Pearce, W. H., Schneider, J. R., Sharma, L., Clark, E., Gibson, D., & Martin, G. J. (2001). Leg symptoms in peripheral arterial disease associated clinical characteristics and functional impairment. *JAMA, 286*(13), 1599–1606. https://doi.org/10.1001/jama.286.13.1599

McDermott, M. M. G., Liu, K., Criqui, M. H., Ruth, K., Goff, D., Saad, M. F., Wu, C., Homma, S., & Sharrett, A. R. (2005). Ankle-brachial index and subclinical cardiac and carotid disease: The Multi-Ethnic Study of Atherosclerosis. *American Journal of Epidemiology, 162*(1), 33–41. https://doi.org/10.1093/aje/kwi167

McGee, D. L. (1985). Update on some epidemiologic features of intermittent claudication: The Framingham study. *Journal of the American Geriatrics Society, 33*(1), 13–18. https://doi.org/10.1111/j.1532-5415.1985.tb02853.x

McLafferty, R. B., Dunnington, G. L., Mattos, M. A., Markwell, S. J., Ramsey, D. E., Henretta, J. P., Karch, L. A., Hodgson, K. J., & Sumner, D. S. (2000). Factors affecting the diagnosis of peripheral vascular disease before vascular surgery referral. *Journal of Vascular Surgery, 31*(5), 870–879. https://doi.org/10.1067/mva.2000.106422

Meijer, W. T., Hoes, A. W., Rutgers, D., Bots, M. L., Hofman, A., & Grobbee, D. E. (1998). Peripheral arterial disease in the elderly: The Rotterdam study. *Arteriosclerosis, Thrombosis, and Vascular Biology, 18*(2), 185–192. https://doi.org/10.1161/01.ATV.18.2.185

Mohler, E. R., Treat-Jacobson, D., Reilly, M. P., Cunningham, K. E., Miani, M., Criqui, M. H., Hiatt, W. R., & Hirsch, A. T. (2004). Utility and barriers to performance of the ankle-brachial index in primary care practice. *Vascular Medicine, 9*(4), 253–260. https://doi.org/10.1191/1358863x04vm559oa

Mok, Y., Ishigami, J., Lutsey, P. L., Tanaka, H., Meyer, M. L., Heiss, G., & Matsushita, K. (2022). Peripheral artery disease and subsequent risk of infectious disease in older individuals: The ARIC study. *Mayo Clinic Proceedings, 97*(11), 2065–2075. https://doi.org/10.1016/j.mayocp.2022.03.038

Morrissey, N. J., Giacovelli, J., Egorova, N., Gelijns, A., Moskowitz, A., McKinsey, J., Kent, K. C., & Greco, G. (2007). Disparities in the treatment and outcomes of vascular disease in Hispanic patients. *Journal of Vascular Surgery, 46*(5), 971–978. https://doi.org/10.1016/j.jvs.2007.07.021

Murabito, J. M., D'Agostino, R. B., Silbershatz, H., & Wilson, P. W. F. (1997). Intermittent claudication: A risk profile from the Framingham heart study. *Circulation, 96*(1), 44–49. https://doi.org/10.1161/01.CIR.96.1.44

Mustapha, J. A., Katzen, B. T., Neville, R. F., Lookstein, R. A., Zeller, T., Miller, L. E., & Jaff, M. R. (2018). Disease burden and clinical outcomes following initial diagnosis of critical limb ischemia in the Medicare population. *JACC: Cardiovascular Interventions, 11*(10), 1011–1012. https://doi.org/10.1016/j.jcin.2017.12.012

O'Hare, A., & Johansen, K. (2001). Lower-extremity peripheral arterial disease among patients with end-stage renal disease. *Journal of the American Society of Nephrology, 12*(12), 2838–2847.

O'Hare, A. M., Sidawy, A. N., Feinglass, J., Merine, K. M., Daley, J., Khuri, S., Henderson, W. G., & Johansen, K. L. (2004). Influence of renal insufficiency on limb loss and mortality after initial lower extremity surgical revascularization. *Journal of Vascular Surgery, 39*(4), 709–716. https://doi.org/10.1016/j.jvs.2003.11.038

Olin, J. W., & Sealove, B. A. (2010). Peripheral artery disease: Current insight into the disease and its diagnosis and management. *Mayo Clinic Proceedings, 85*(7), 678–692. https://doi.org/10.4065/mcp.2010.0133

Ouriel, K., McDonnell, A. E., Metz, C. E., & Zarins, C. K. (1982). A critical evaluation of stress testing in the diagnosis of peripheral vascular disease. *Surgery, 91*(6), 686–693.

Pande, R. L., Perlstein, T. S., Beckman, J. A., & Creager, M. A. (2011). Secondary prevention and mortality in peripheral artery disease: National health and nutrition examination study, 1999 to 2004. *Circulation, 124*(1), 17–23. https://doi.org/10.1161/CIRCULATIONAHA.110.003954

Paskiewicz, A., Wang, F. M., Yang, C., Ballew, S. H., Kalbaugh, C. A., Selvin, E., Salameh, M., Heiss, G., Coresh, J., & Matsushita, K. (2021). Ankle-brachial index and subsequent risk of severe ischemic leg outcomes: The aric study. *Journal of the American Heart Association, 10*(22). https://doi.org/10.1161/JAHA.121.021801

Pasqualini, L., Schillaci, G., Pirro, M., Vaudo, G., Siepi, D., Innocente, S., Ciuffetti, G., & Mannarino, E. (2007). Renal dysfunction predicts long-term mortality in patients with lower extremity arterial disease. *Journal of Internal Medicine, 262*(6), 668–677. https://doi.org/10.1111/j.1365-2796.2007.01863.x

Price, J. F., Mowbray, P. I., Lee, A. J., Rumley, A., Lowe, G. D. O., & Fowkes, F. G. R. (1999). Relationship between smoking and cardiovascular risk factors in the development of peripheral arterial disease and coronary artery disease. Edinburgh Artery Study. *European Heart Journal, 20*(5), 344–353. https://doi.org/10.1053/euhj.1998.1194

Regensteiner, J. G., Hiatt, W. R., Coll, J. R., Criqui, M. H., Treat-Jacobson, D., McDermott, M. M., Hirsch, A. T., & Rooke, T. (2008). The impact of peripheral arterial disease on health-related quality of life in the peripheral arterial disease awareness, risk, and treatment: New resources for survival (PARTNERS) program. *Vascular Medicine, 13*(1), 15–24. https://doi.org/10.1177/1358863X07084911

Resnick, H. E., Lindsay, R. S., McDermott, M. M. G., Devereux, R. B., Jones, K. L., Fabsitz, R. R., & Howard, B. V. (2004). Relationship of high and low ankle brachial index to all-cause and cardiovascular disease mortality. *Circulation, 109*(6), 733–739. https://doi.org/10.1161/01.cir.0000112642.63927.54

Ridker, P. M., Stampfer, M. J., & Rifai, N. (2001). Novel risk factors for systemic atherosclerosis: A comparison of C-reactive protein, fibrinogen, homocysteine, lipoprotein(a), and standard cholesterol screening as predictors of peripheral arterial disease. *JAMA, 285*(19), 2481–2485. https://doi.org/10.1001/jama.285.19.2481

Robinson, K., Arheart, K., Refsum, H., Brattström, L., Boers, G., Ueland, P., Rubba, P., Palma-Reis, R., Meleady, R., Daly, L., Witteman, J., & Graham, I. (1998). Low circulating folate and vitamin B6 concentrations risk factors for stroke, peripheral vascular disease, and coronary artery disease. *Circulation, 97*(5), 437–443. https://doi.org/10.1161/01.CIR.97.5.437

Salameh, M. J., Rundek, T., Boden-Albala, B., Jin, Z., Ratchford, E. V., Di Tullio, M. R., Homma, S., & Sacco, R. L. (2008). Self-reported peripheral arterial disease predicts future vascular events in a community-based cohort. *Journal of General Internal Medicine, 23*(9), 1423–1428. https://doi.org/10.1007/s11606-008-0694-x

Selvin, E., & Erlinger, T. P. (2004). Prevalence of and risk factors for peripheral arterial disease in the United States: Results from the national health and nutrition examination Survey, 1999–2000. *Circulation, 110*(6), 738–743. https://doi.org/10.1161/01.CIR.0000137913.26087.F0

Selvin, E., & Hirsch, A. T. (2008). Contemporary risk factor control and walking dysfunction in individuals with peripheral arterial disease: Nhanes 1999–2004. *Atherosclerosis, 201*(2), 425–433. https://doi.org/10.1016/j.atherosclerosis.2008.02.002

Shishehbor, M. H., White, C. J., Gray, B. H., Menard, M. T., Lookstein, R., Rosenfield, K., & Jaff, M. R. (2016). Critical limb ischemia: An expert statement. *Journal of the American College of Cardiology, 68*(18), 2002–2015. https://doi.org/10.1016/j.jacc.2016.04.071

Song, P., Rudan, D., Zhu, Y., Fowkes, F. J. I., Rahimi, K., Fowkes, F. G. R., & Rudan, I. (2019). Global, regional, and national prevalence and risk factors for peripheral artery disease in 2015: An updated systematic review and analysis. *Lancet Global Health, 7*(8), e1020−e1030. https://doi.org/10.1016/S2214-109X(19)30255-4

Taylor, L. M., DeFrang, R. D., Harris, E. J., & Porter, J. M. (1991). The association of elevated plasma homocyst(e)ine with progression of symptomatic peripheral arterial disease. *Journal of Vascular Surgery, 13*(1), 128−136. https://doi.org/10.1016/0741-5214(91)90020-U

Yao, S. T., Hobbs, J. T., & Irivne, W. T. (1969). Ankle systolic pressure measurements in arterial disease affecting the lower extremities. *British Journal of Surgery, 56*(9), 676−679. https://doi.org/10.1002/bjs.1800560910

Zheng, Z. J., Sharrett, A. R., Chambless, L. E., Rosamond, W. D., Nieto, F. J., Sheps, D. S., Dobs, A., Evans, G. W., & Heiss, G. (1997). Associations of ankle-brachial index with clinical coronary heart disease, stroke and preclinical carotid and popliteal atherosclerosis: The Atherosclerosis Risk in Communities (ARIC) study. *Atherosclerosis, 131*(1), 115−125. https://doi.org/10.1016/S0021-9150(97)06089-9

3

Atherosclerosis—Pathology of lower extremity atherosclerosis

Kenji Kawai[1], Renu Virmani[1] and Aloke V. Finn[1,2]
[1]CVPath Institute, Gaithersburg, MD, United States; [2]University of Maryland, School of Medicine, Baltimore, MD, United States

Introduction

Peripheral arterial disease (PAD) risk factors include diabetes, hypertension, and chronic kidney disease (CKD), as well as other comorbidities such as smoking, obesity, and hyperlipidemia (Virani et al., 2020), with a worldwide prevalence reported to be 10%–20% of individuals over 60 years of age (Aday & Matsushita, 2021; Fowkes et al., 2017; Roth et al., 2017; Song et al., 2020). While PAD affects a large proportion of those with established cardiovascular disease, it is difficult to determine the exact prevalence of PAD because early lesions are asymptomatic in the pathogenesis of the disease and symptoms are often delayed due to the development of collateral channels with chronic progression. PAD is an important phenotype of vascular disease, causing an increased risk of all-cause mortality, cardiovascular mortality, coronary artery disease (CAD), and cerebrovascular disease. Lower extremity arterial disease (LEAD) is one of the types of PAD in which the lesions are localized in the legs. Approximately, 1%–3% of patients with LEAD develop critical limb ischemia (CLI) associated with high mortality and frequent amputations. CLI is a treatment-resistant condition, with only 25% of patients achieving symptom-free recovery (Anand et al., 2018; Sampson et al., 1990). Therefore, despite improvement of therapeutic devices, LEAD is associated with high morbidity, frequency of procedural intervention, hospitalization, readmission rates, and low quality of life indicators; further research is needed to improve invasive treatment with pharmacological agents, therapy exercise approaches, and device-based interventions.

The lower extremity consists of multiple arteries that vary greatly in size, as they anatomically branch from the aorta to the iliac artery, the femoral artery above the knee, the below-knee artery, and the plantar artery. On the other hand, these arteries are subjected to bending and twisting motions at the joint site, which causes unique stresses on the arteries that are specific and different from other arteries in the body. Therefore, understanding the unique morphology of atherosclerosis in the arteries of the lower extremities is very important in terms of treatment strategies for LEAD. While the pathogenesis of atherosclerosis in the arteries of the lower extremities is similar to that of the coronary arteries and carotid arteries (Burke et al., 1997; Davies & Thomas, 1985; O'Neill et al., 2015; Soor et al., 2008; Van Oostrom et al., 2005), the unique atherosclerotic characteristics of LEAD are becoming better understood. This section provides a comprehensive overview highlighting the pathology of atherosclerotic lesions in the arteries of the lower extremities and contrasts to that of CAD.

General understanding of progression of atherosclerosis

At the basic anatomic level, an artery is composed of an intima containing an endothelial layer, tunica media, and adventitia. The intima is located in the innermost layer of the artery and consists of the endothelium and a subendothelial layer composed of a few smooth muscle cells and internal elastic lamina (IEL) in a proteoglycan—collagen matrix. The media is located between the inner and outer membranes and consists of a muscular layer composed of smooth muscle cells and an external elastic lamina (EEL) with the outer layer. The progression of atherosclerosis is caused by successive injury to these vascular structures starting with the endothelial layer.

Preatherosclerotic lesions develop at the arterial bifurcations and at regions with low shear stress and progress slowly to early atherosclerotic lesion called pathological intimal thickening (PIT) (Yahagi et al., 2016). PIT is characterized by scattered extracellular matrix (ECM) consisting of proteoglycans and collagen type III (i.e., lipid pools) in areas of abundant smooth muscle cells (SMC). The ECM is mainly composed of hyaluronic acid, the proteoglycans biglycan, decorin, and versican, with mixed triglycerides and free cholesterol. Lipid pools are formed by infiltration and deposition of lipids derived from plasma and show intracellular droplets of lipids in the region of macrophages. Macrophage infiltration causes the lipid pool of the PIT lesion to transform into a necrotic core, resulting in matrix disruption and the formation of early fibroatheroma. Dead and calcified macrophages are seen in and at the borders of the necrotic core (Otsuka et al., 2016). Infiltration of macrophages into lipid pool causes a transition from early to advanced atherosclerotic lesions, which is early and late fibroatheroma with a small to large necrotic core (Otsuka et al., 2016). Therefore, the number of macrophages is greater in late-stage fibroatheroma compared to early-stage fibroatheroma.

In PIT, the chemical composition of lipids in the lipid pool is mainly composed of cholesterol esters (77%) and phospholipids (10%), with less than 10% of free cholesterol. On the other hand, in the intermediate stage of atherosclerosis, there are more phospholipids (20%) and free cholesterol (20%) and less cholesterol esters (55%) (Katz et al., 1976). On the other hand, fibroatheroma with necrotic cores have significantly more free cholesterol and less cholesterol esters and phospholipids (Felton et al., 1997; Katz et al., 1976).

Some histological characteristics have been identified as contributing to atherosclerotic vulnerability. Intraplaque hemorrhage is one of the pathological conditions that contributes to plaque vulnerability by causing an increase in the size of the necrotic core. Intraplaque hemorrhage caused by rupture from intimal microvessels leads to further expansion of the necrotic core due to free cholesterol derived from the erythrocyte membrane of the leaking red blood cells and secondary macrophage infiltration (Kolodgie et al., 2003). Microvessels are another factor contributing to plaque vulnerability, the density of which correlates with the progression of atherosclerosis. The wall of microvessels is incompetent, leading to extensive hemorrhage and subsequent macrophage infiltration (Sluimer et al., 2009).

These progressive stages of atherosclerosis can be histologically categorized into four major stages: (1) nonatherosclerotic intimal lesions (intimal thickening, intimal xanthomas) (Fig. 3.1). (2) progressive atherosclerotic lesions (pathological

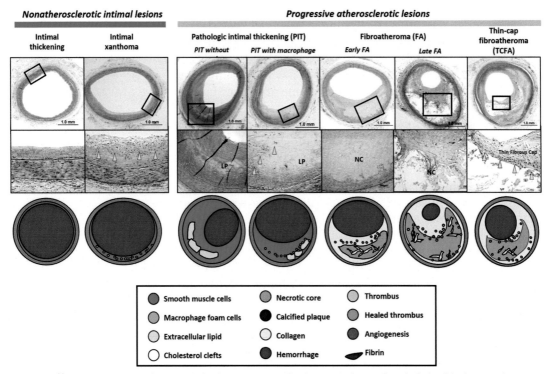

Figure 3.1 Human coronary lesion morphologies are categorized as nonatherosclerotic intimal lesions and progressive atherosclerotic lesions. Nonatherosclerotic lesions, including intimal thickening and intimal xanthoma, progress into atherosclerotic lesions beginning with pathological intimal thickening, leading to fibroatheroma and thin-cap fibroatheroma. *LP*, lipid pool; *NC*, necrotic core. Images were reproduced with permission from Yahagi, K., Kolodgie, F. D., Otsuka, F., Finn, A. V., Davis, H. R., Joner, M., & Virmani, R. (2016). Pathophysiology of native coronary, vein graft, and in-stent atherosclerosis. *Nature Reviews Cardiology, 13*(2), 79–98. https://doi.org/10.1038/nrcardio.2015.164.

intimal thickening, fibroatheroma, thin-cap fibroatheroma) (Fig. 3.1), (3) acute thrombotic lesions (Fig. 3.2), and (4) other lesions including healed plaque (Fig. 3.3) (Yahagi et al., 2016).

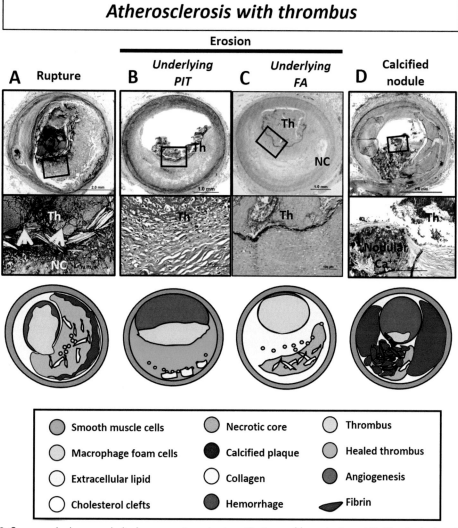

Figure 3.2 Coronary lesion morphologies are categorized as "lesions with acute thrombi". Histological and schematic images are shown for (A) plaque rupture, (B) plaque erosion with underlying pathological intimal thickening, (C) plaque erosion with underlying fibroatheroma, and (D) calcified nodule. *Arrowheads* indicate fibrous cap. *NC*, necrotic core; *Th*, thrombus. (A, B, and D) were reproduced with permission from Falk, E., Nakano, M., Bentzon, J. F., Finn, A. V., & Virmani, R. (2013). Update on acute coronary syndromes: The pathologists' view. *European Heart Journal*, *34*(10), 719—728. doi:10.1093/eurheartj/ehs411. Other images were reproduced with permission from Yahagi, K., Kolodgie, F. D., Otsuka, F., Finn, A. V., Davis, H. R., Joner, M., & Virmani, R. (2016). Pathophysiology of native coronary, vein graft, and in-stent atherosclerosis. *Nature Reviews Cardiology*, *13*(2), 79—98. https://doi.org/10.1038/nrcardio.2015.164.

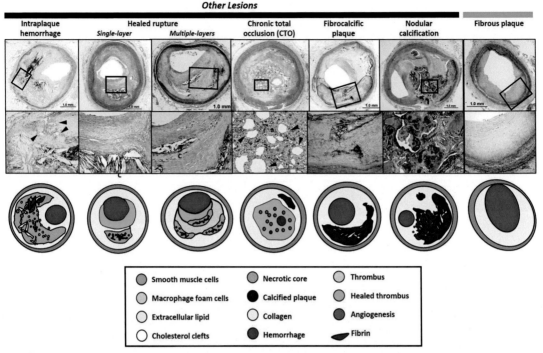

Figure 3.3 Human coronary lesion morphologies are categorized as complications of hemorrhage and/or thrombus with healing and stabilization. Other lesions include intraplaque hemorrhage and stable lesion, which is categorized as healed rupture, chronic total occlusion, fibrocalcific plaque, and nodular calcification. Fibrous plaque is also included as stable plaque. Images were reproduced with permission from Yahagi, K., Kolodgie, F. D., Otsuka, F., Finn, A. V., Davis, H. R., Joner, M., & Virmani, R. (2016). Pathophysiology of native coronary, vein graft, and in-stent atherosclerosis. *Nature Reviews Cardiology*, *13*(2), 79—98. https://doi.org/10.1038/nrcardio.2015.164.

In general, LEAD is mostly caused by atherosclerotic plaques, and the risk factors for LEAD are similar to those for CAD, with diabetes and smoking having a greater impact (Criqui et al., 2021). The following paragraphs address the morphological characteristics of nonatherosclerotic and atherosclerotic lesions seen in coronary and lower extremity arteries (Fig. 3.4).

Nonatherosclerotic intimal lesions

Adaptive or diffuse intimal thickening/intimal xanthoma

Intimal thickening is the earliest change in the arterial wall detectable with current imaging modalities such as intravascular imaging. Adaptive and diffuse intimal thickening is a

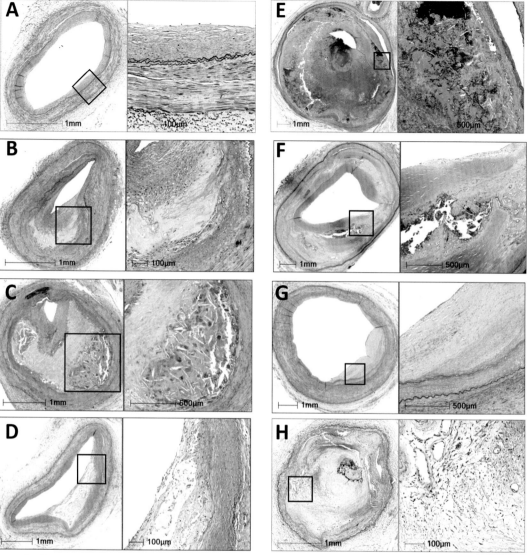

Figure 3.4 Representative histological sections showing plaque progression in human lower extremity arteries. (A) Adaptive intimal thickening characterized by natural accumulation of smooth muscle cells (SMCs) within a proteoglycan—collagen matrix with absence of lipid and macrophage foam cells infiltration. (B) Pathological intimal thickening, characterized by a lipid pool that lacks SMCs but is rich in proteoglycan and lipid. (C) Fibroatheroma characterized by a dense fibrous cap with macrophages located at the periphery of the necrotic core. (D) thin-cap fibroatheroma showing a necrotic core covered by a thin fibrous cap. (E) Rupture characterized by disrupted fibrous cap; the thrombus is in continuity with the underlying hemorrhagic necrotic core. Note the presence of punctate areas of calcification in the periphery of the necrotic core. (F) Healed plaque characterized by the underlying thin collagen-rich fibrous cap over the necrotic core and a luminal healed thrombus consisting of SMCs surrounded by proteoglycan-rich matrix. (G) Fibrous plaque characterized by collagen-rich neointimal tissue with few SMCs but no lipid pool or necrotic core. (H) Chronic total occlusion characterized by an occluded lumen showing an organized thrombus rich in neoangiogenesis surrounded by a loose proteoglycan-rich neointimal tissue and few SMC-rich area. Images were reproduced with permission from Torii, S., Mustapha, J. A., Narula, J., Mori, H., Saab, F., Jinnouchi, H., Yahagi, K., Sakamoto, A., Romero, M. E., Narula, N., Kolodgie, F. D., Virmani, R., & Finn, A.V. 2019. Histopathologic characterization of peripheral arteries in subjects with abundant risk factors: Correlating imaging with pathology. *Journal of the American College of Cardiology: Cardiovascular Imaging, 12*(8), 1501—1513. https://doi.org/10.1016/j.jcmg.2018.08.039.

physiological response to blood flow and can be detected as early as in the postnatal state (Ikari et al., 1999). This stage has less pathological significance and is mainly composed of a proteoglycan-rich matrix and smooth muscle cells. When formed near bifurcations, it precedes the lesions of atherosclerosis, increases with age, and may progress to PIT, one of the earliest lesions characterizing the atherosclerotic condition. Intimal xanthomas are fatty streaks composed mainly of macrophage foam cells infiltrating into the intima and SMCs containing a small fraction of lipids (Aikawa et al., 1998; Fan & Watanabe, 2003). Intimal xanthomas are classified as nonatherosclerotic lesions and do not always exhibit the essential features of more advanced atherosclerotic plaques. It has been reported that arterial morphology at this stage can regress, especially in coronary arteries of young individuals (McGill et al., 2000; Velican, 1969, 1981). The progression from AIT to PIT, i.e., from a nonatherosclerotic lesion to an early stage of atherosclerosis, involves lipid extravasation and apoptosis of SMC.

Progressive atherosclerotic lesions

Pathological intimal thickening (PIT)

PIT is defined as the initial stage of progressive atherosclerosis leading more advanced lesions (Kolodgie et al., 2007), which is considered a crucial stage in the development of atherosclerosis in terms of the histomorphology that bridge nonatherosclerotic and atherosclerotic lesions (Kolodgie et al., 2007). The classic histology of PIT consists of SMC remnants and lipid pools in an ECM composed of several proteoglycans and type III collagen, without evidence of a necrotic core. The ECM is composed of hyaluronic acid, biglycan, decorin, versican, triglycerides, and free cholesterol. The precise origin of the free cholesterol in PIT is still unclear. A classic PIT is observed near the bifurcation point, where extracellular lipids are present underneath the layer of foamy cells derived from macrophages (Nakashima et al., 2007).

PIT is also the earliest stage that presents with calcification and can exhibit microcalcifications ($>0.5\,\mu m$, usually $<15\,\mu m$) that are detectable using specific stains with alizarin red or Von Kossa (Otsuka, Sakakura, et al., 2014). Apoptotic SMCs in the PIT contribute to the progression of lipid pools, and this process eventually leads to the enlargement of the plaque itself (Sakamoto et al., 2018). While the presence of macrophages is rare in the early stages of PIT, these are seen during the advanced stages of PIT and are usually localized to the luminal side of the lipid pool. The presence of macrophages in PIT compared to the absence of macrophages is at a more advanced stage of atherosclerosis than in the absence of macrophages (Otsuka et al., 2015). The precise mechanism of which macrophages initiate accumulation in PIT lesions is not fully elucidated but is thought to involve the expression of potent chemoattractant proteins, especially proteoglycans, and changes in lipid composition (Nakashima et al., 2007).

Fibroatheroma

Fibroatheroma is an advanced stage of atherosclerosis, which histologically consists of a necrotic core covering with a fibrous cap (Virmani et al., 2000). Necrotic cores, described as "graveyards of macrophages," are noncellular structures that are histologically caused by macrophage infiltration into the lipid pool accompanied by necrosis or apoptosis of macrophages (Tabas, 2010). When apoptosis of macrophages is accompanied by loss of phagocytic clearance of apoptotic cells, plaque necrosis is enhanced by further necrosis of macrophage (Tabas, 2000; Tabas et al., 1996). Therefore, the expression of ECM components decreases in the necrotic core as well as in the lipid pool. The fibrous capsule covering the necrotic core is composed of type I and type III collagen, proteoglycans, and SMCs (Sakakura et al., 2013). The size of the necrotic core and the thickness of the fibrous component are strictly related to plaque vulnerability.

Fibroatheroma is classified into "early" and "late" stages, based on the relative degree of necrosis and ECMs (Yahagi et al., 2016). Early fibroatheroma shows necrosis or apoptosis of macrophages infiltrating within the necrotic core in the early stages transitioned from the lipid pool, and the expression of ECM in the lipid pool is markedly decreased (Yahagi et al., 2016). As the plaque progresses, the lipid core undergoes sclerotic change and consists of necrotic debris and cholesterol crystals. The necrotic core of late fibroatheroma shows various tissue components such as lacerations of free cholesterol, free cholesterol from apoptotic macrophages, calcification, intraplaque hemorrhage, and surrounding angiogenesis (FitzGibbon et al., 1996; Sluimer et al., 2009; Virmani et al., 2014). ECM is markedly absent in late stage compared to early stage, and the density of apoptotic cells in the necrotic core is higher in late-stage fibromas compared to early stage (Otsuka et al., 2015).

Thin-cap fibroatheroma

Thin-cap fibroatheroma (TCFA), classically known as vulnerable plaque, is a high-risk atherosclerosis-causing intraluminal thrombus formation after plaque rupture. Since thrombus occlusion in coronary arteries leads to myocardial ischemia, the majority of sudden cardiac deaths are associated with plaque rupture and subsequent thrombus formation (Burke et al., 2003). Mechanical stress is also involved in the process of plaque rupture in vulnerable plaques (Arroyo & Lee, 1999). The thickness of the fibrous cap is one of the indexes of plaque vulnerability and is defined as less than 65 μm in the thinnest region of the plaque. This evidence is from a study reporting 113 cadaver subjects of sudden death, in which 95% of the ruptured cap were measured less than 65 μm (Burke et al., 1997). The thin fibrous cap is mostly constructed of type I collagen, while SMCs are not present or rarely observed. The necrotic core is also smaller in size compared to ruptured plaques. Matrix metalloproteinases (MMPs) released from abundant macrophages contribute to the destruction of collagen/proteoglycans constituting the fibrous capsule and extensive apoptosis of the smooth muscle layer, causing the thin capsule to rupture (Johnson et al., 2014; Lee et al., 2011).

Lesion with thrombus formation

Plaque rupture

A ruptured plaque consists of a necrotic core and an overlying ruptured thin fibrous cap. The ruptured fibrous cap is often seen with infiltration of macrophages and T-lymphocytes. When the fibrous capsule is ruptured, the contents of the necrotic core are exposed to the lumen of the vessel, and a coagulation cascade is activated in response to exposure to lipids and tissue factors. Eventually, it forms a platelet-rich occlusive or nonocclusive luminal thrombus, which is called a white thrombus. Rupture of the fibrous cap is prone to occur in the shoulder of plaque where it is common of the weak region in the structure of plaque, especially at rest. However, it can also rupture at the center of the fibrous cap during exertion (Burke et al., 1999); rupture is often additionally seen destroying the media, especially the inner elastic lamina. As mentioned above, selective proteases secreted by macrophages are involved in the thinning of the fibrous capsule, as well as high shear and tensile stress with hemodynamic factors also contributing to plaque rupture (Gijsen et al., 2008; Lenglet et al., 2013; Sukhova et al., 1999). Microcalcification and iron accumulation are other potential triggers of plaque rupture and can cause stress-induced rupture of fibrous cap (Kolodgie et al., 2000; Vengrenyuk et al., 2006). Intraplaque hemorrhage and spotty calcification are the most common plaque components seen in plaque rupture compared to plaque erosion and stable CAD, and spotty calcification is found around the necrotic core, usually near the tunica media (Otsuka, Sakakura, et al., 2014).

Plaque erosion

Plaque erosion develops in nonruptured conditions and is defined as an acute thrombus having direct contact with a denuded, endothelium-free intimal surface enriched in SMC and type III collagen, hyaluronic acid, or proteoglycan substrates (Burke et al., 2002; Falk et al., 2013). The underlying plaque in the region of erosion consists of a PIT or fibroatheroma with a thick fibrous cap, without communication between the thrombus and the necrotic core, and is a thrombotic pathogenesis that can occur at a relatively early stage of atherosclerosis (Yahagi et al., 2014; Sakakura et al., 2013). In contrast with plaque rupture, macrophages and lymphocytes are rarely observed and the medial layer is intact (van der Wal et al., 1994; Virmani et al., 2000). These findings in plaque erosions suggest that vasospasm is involved in their pathogenesis in CAD (Bentzon et al., 2014; Sakakura et al., 2013). A morphological hallmark of plaque erosion manifests mild to moderate luminal narrowing at the site of the erosion, with evidence of repeated development and healing of the overlying platelet-rich erosion, often showing negative remodeling (Burke et al., 2002). Eroded lesions are prone to eccentricity, and calcified sheets are rarely seen in eroded lesions, while microcalcifications and fragmented calcium are seen in about 30% (Yahagi et al., 2014; Mori et al., 2018). Thrombus on eroded plaques often is formed at a later stage than thrombus on ruptured plaques. In a previous pathological study, the prevalence of late thrombus in eroded plaques was 88%, compared to 54% in ruptured plaques (Kramer et al., 2010).

Calcified nodule

The incidence of calcified nodules (CN) is highest in the lower extremities (62.5%), followed by the carotid arteries (4%−14%) and lowest in the coronary arteries (2%−7%) (Mauriello et al., 2010; Torii et al., 2019; Yahagi et al., 2015, 2016). In coronary arteries, CN is most frequently seen in the proximal to middle portion of the right coronary artery, where torsional stress is greatest, and in the bifurcation of the left coronary artery. The presence of necrotic core calcification is a key factor in thrombus formation, which is often sandwiched between proximal and distal hard collagen-rich calcifications (Torii et al., 2021). Necrotic core calcification is fragmented and erupts from the inside of plaque to the luminal side in coronary arteries that are vulnerable to mechanical stress, ultimately leading to thrombus formation (Torii et al., 2021). Therefore, the presence of thrombus adhesion on the erupted calcification is essential to identify CN. Intraplaque hemorrhage is found in 40% of CN lesions, suggesting that it is the result of destruction of surrounding capillaries during calcium fragmentation (Torii et al., 2021).

Other lesions including healed plaque and fibrocalcific plaque

In CAD, individuals who died from unstable angina or acute myocardial infarction experienced an average of 2.4 episodes of minor nonobstructive coronary thrombi (Mann & Davies, 1999). Nonobstructive thrombi can result from asymptomatic plaque rupture or erosion, and healed plaque rupture (HPR) is found in 61% of coronary arteries in patients with sudden coronary death (Burke, Kolodgie et al., 2001). When looking at plaque types, the incidence is highest in patients with stable plaques (80%), followed by acute plaque rupture (75%) and plaque erosion (9%) (Burke, Kolodgie et al., 2001). Healed lesions include HPRs, healed plaque erosions, and healed calcified nodules. Therefore, ruptured fibrous caps, necrotic cores, or nodular calcifications are seen within the plaque (Fig. 3.4) (Yahagi et al., 2016). The thrombus in early lesions of healed plaques is composed primarily of granulation tissue and subsequent proteoglycan and type III collagen over time are replaced with type I collagen (Otsuka, Joner, et al., 2014; Mann & Davies, 1999; Sakakura et al., 2014). HPR is characterized by the presence of a ruptured collagen-rich thin fibrous cap overlying a necrotic core that can be observed by microscopy (Torii et al., 2019).

Similarly, in LEAD, an incidence of lesions with HPR was noted to increase along with an increase in percent stenosis, and this trend was specifically more apparent in above-knee lesions than below-knee (Fig. 3.5) (Torii et al., 2019).

These data indicate that HPR is a form of plaque wound healing in both CAD and LEAD, and that repeated asymptomatic plaque rupture contributes to plaque progression (Mann & Davies, 1999). Fibrocalcific plaques (FCPs) are defined as lesions with a thick fibrous cap and extensive calcification deposits typically found in the deep intima (Kragel et al., 1989; Virmani et al., 2000). Different from healed plaques, FCPs are not considered true FAs because they have minimal or no necrotic cores. In CAD, FCP is commonly observed in patients with a history of stable angina (Sakamoto et al., 2019).

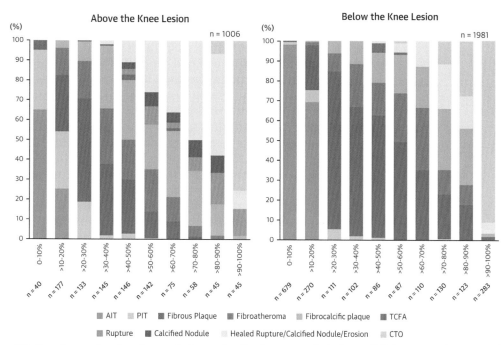

Figure 3.5 Prevalence of various types of atherosclerotic plaque morphologies at 10% incremental cross-sectional area narrowing in sections above and below the knee. Acute thrombotic lesions (plaque rupture and calcified nodule) were exclusively observed in above-the-knee (AK) lesions. AK lesions demonstrated a higher incidence of lipid-rich plaque (pathological intimal thickening [PIT], fibroatheroma, thin-cap fibroatheroma [TCFA], rupture, and healed rupture), whereas the majority of the narrowing in below-the-knee lesions is from fibrous plaque and chronic total occlusion (CTO). Images were reproduced with permission from Torii, S., Mustapha, J. A., Narula, J., Mori, H., Saab, F., Jinnouchi, H., Yahagi, K., Sakamoto, A., Romero, M. E., Narula, N., Kolodgie, F. D., Virmani, R., & Finn, A.V. 2019. Histopathologic characterization of peripheral arteries in subjects with abundant risk factors: Correlating imaging with pathology. *Journal of the American College of Cardiology: Cardiovascular Imaging, 12*(8), 1501–1513. https://doi.org/10.1016/j.jcmg.2018.08.

Differences of cause of acute thrombotic event between CAD and LEAD

In CAD, the underlying plaque morphology leading to acute luminal thrombosis is most frequent in plaque rupture (60%), followed by plaque erosion (35%) and calcified nodules (5%) (Torii et al., 2021; Yahagi et al., 2016). On the other hand, more than half of the thrombogenic mechanisms in LEAD originated from calcified nodules (62.5%) and less than half from plaque rupture (27.5%) (Torii et al., 2021). Since mechanical stress is a major contributing factor of thrombus formation in calcified nodules, active and mechanical stress in the superficial femoral artery (SFA) presents high incidence of calcified nodules, resulting from rupture of sheet calcium (MacTaggart et al., 2014).

In CAD, acute luminal thrombosis leads to acute coronary syndromes and sudden cardiac death, while acute arterial occlusion of the lower extremities, called acute limb ischemia (ALI), is essentially a sudden loss of blood supply to the extremities, with a 14.2-fold higher risk of limb amputation (Low Wang et al., 2018). Therefore, ALI is a disease requiring early revascularization because extensive ischemia leads to tissue loss. The pathogenesis of ALI presents not only in situ (atherogenic) thrombosis but also embolization from the heart or proximal vessels, and graft occlusion in a variety of embolic and occlusive patterns, differing in pathogenetic variation from acute CAD in which atherothrombosis is the primary causative pathogenesis (Bonaca et al., 2013; Creager et al., 2012). For the distribution of thrombus lesion, LEAD is characterized by localized acute thrombotic lesions only in above-knee lesions and not in below-knee lesions (Torii et al., 2019).

Differences of manifestation of calcifications between PAD and CAD

The severity of calcified lesions in atherosclerosis is a predictor of clinical outcome in CAD (Fumiyuki Otsuka, Sakakura, et al., 2014). In atherosclerotic plaques of LEAD, calcification is more frequent and more severe than in patients with CAD (Burke, Weber, et al., 2001; Demer & Tintut, 2008; Otsuka et al., 2013; Torii et al., 2019). Calcification is formed by the crystallization of calcium/phosphate with the formation of hydroxyapatite in the ECM. Calcification formation in atherosclerosis is considered to develop by overlapped multiple processes including inflammation, apoptosis, disruption of calcium–phosphate homeostasis, matrix vesicle release, altered bone formation, degeneration of the ECM, and genetic disorders (Lanzer et al., 2021). Spotty calcification in early-stage atherosclerosis can progress to around the necrotic core, and when calcified sheets are fractured, this can cause the formation of nodular calcification (Fig. 3.4). Nodular calcification is defined as the nodular calcium seen within the plaque that does not protrude the lumen, and it is characterized by breaks in calcified plates with fragments of calcium separated by fibrin (Jinnouchi et al., 2019, pp. 1–25; Mori et al., 2018).

Intimal and medial calcification

In general, vascular calcification can be classified into two types based on the site of localization: intimal calcification and medial calcification (Demer & Tintut, 2008; Torii et al., 2019).

Risk factors such as age, diabetes, and chronic kidney disease (CKD) contribute to the development pattern of calcification, and both intimal and medial calcification may occur in the same vessel wall depending on the combination of these risk factors (Vos et al., 2018). Since currently available imaging modalities including CT and intravascular imaging such as OCT and IVUS are unreliable for precise differentiation of these two types of calcifications, histological diagnosis is the only way to determine these two types of calcifications (Jinnouchi et al., 2021; Lanzer et al., 2014). Intimal calcification is associated with luminal narrowing of vessels, while medial calcification increases vascular stiffness, and reduced flexibility and compliance of arterial wall leads to reduction of peripheral tissue perfusion, resulting in diffuse thrombus formation (Ho & Shanahan, 2016; Lanzer et al., 2014; Mustapha et al., 2017). Medial calcification is rarely seen in coronary arteries, is more frequent in patients with LEAD, and is associated with adverse cardiovascular motility and increased mortality (Lehto et al., 1996; Nakamura et al., 2009). In the cadaver study with elderly subjects from Torii et al., the presence of atherosclerotic plaque in the lower extremities decreased from the proximal popliteal artery to the more distal posterior tibial artery, with atherosclerotic lesions below the knee determined as smaller lipid pool lesions compared to lesions above the knee, which had larger lipid pool lesions (Torii et al., 2019). The presence of severe intimal calcification was greater in above-the-knee than below-the-knee lesions, while the medial calcification was not as frequent in above- as well as below-the-knee lesions (Torii et al., 2019). Thus, the understanding that these two types of calcified lesions each have different contributions to ischemic pathophysiology requires different treatment approaches to the characteristics of each tissue.

Bone formation

Another hallmark of calcification seen in lower extremity arteries is bone formation, which is the most advanced stage of calcification. Bone formation consisting of trabeculae with a marrow space is rarely observed in CAD (Otsuka, Sakakura, et al., 2014; Mori et al., 2018), while the incidence of bone formation in LEAD has been reported to be 19%–83% (Lanzer et al., 2014; Otsuka, Sakakura, et al., 2014; Soor et al., 2008; Torii et al., 2019), suggesting bone formation is more histologically apparent in LEAD compared to CAD. Bone formation is a severely calcified formation and is considered a locally stable plaque. The presence of bone formation indirectly suggests a high-risk clinical events because cardiovascular risk factors are also often comorbid (Otsuka, Sakakura, et al., 2014). The detection of bone formation in LEAD may help to better understand risk stratification and local plaque stability.

Perspective of histology of LEAD

Here, we comprehensively summarized our understanding of the histology of LEAD and its characteristic histopathology in comparison with the pathogenesis in CAD. Pathological characteristics, origin of thrombosis, and manifestation of calcification are different between CAD and LEAD (Fig. 3.6) (Narula et al., 2020).

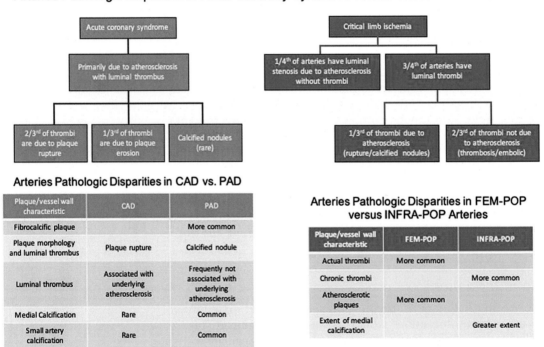

Figure 3.6 Arterial pathological disparities in coronary artery disease versus peripheral artery disease. Images were reproduced with permission from Narula, N., Olin, J. W., & Narula, N. (2020). Pathologic disparities between peripheral artery disease and coronary artery disease. *Arteriosclerosis, Thrombosis, and Vascular Biology, 40*(9), 1982—1989. https://doi.org/10. 1161/ATVBAHA.119.312864.

The underlying disease of acute occlusion in the lower extremity arteries does not only feature lesions of atherosclerotic origin but also displays a higher frequency of conditions such as embolism from proximal vessels and graft vessels compared to coronary arteries, which results in a greater number of target pathologies; the diversity in the distribution of these conditions and target lesions will require various treatment modalities. Furthermore, calcified lesions in the lower extremity atherosclerosis are characterized by the presence of medial calcification and bone formation, which are not commonly seen in coronary arteries. The pathological diversity of LEAD, as well as mechanical stress specific to lower extremity arteries, could explain the high rate of revascularization of vessels compared to coronary arteries. To overcome the recurrence of disease and treatment resistance of LEAD, which is a critical issue in the LEAD, a further understanding of the pathophysiology of the lower extremity atherosclerosis is warranted. Improvements in our understanding of the disease will lead to the development of improved therapeutic devices and new pharmacological treatment strategies.

References

Aday, A. W., & Matsushita, K. (2021). Epidemiology of peripheral artery disease and polyvascular disease. *Circulation Research, 128*(12), 1818–1832. https://doi.org/10.1161/CIRCRESAHA.121.318535

Aikawa, M., Rabkin, E., Okada, Y., Voglic, S. J., Clinton, S. K., Brinckerhoff, C. E., Sukhova, G. K., & Libby, P. (1998). Lipid lowering by diet reduces matrix metalloproteinase activity and increases collagen content of rabbit atheroma: A potential mechanism of lesion stabilization. *Circulation, 97*(24), 2433–2444. https://doi.org/10.1161/01.CIR.97.24.2433

Anand, S. S., Caron, F., Eikelboom, J. W., Bosch, J., Dyal, L., Aboyans, V., Abola, M. T., Branch, K. R. H., Keltai, K., Bhatt, D. L., Verhamme, P., Fox, K. A. A., Cook-Bruns, N., Lanius, V., Connolly, S. J., & Yusuf, S. (2018). Major adverse limb events and mortality in patients with peripheral artery disease: The COMPASS trial. *Journal of the American College of Cardiology, 71*(20), 2306–2315. https://doi.org/10.1016/j.jacc.2018.03.008

Arroyo, L. H., & Lee, R. T. (1999). Mechanisms of plaque rupture: Mechanical and biologic interactions. *Cardiovascular Research, 41*(2), 369–375. https://doi.org/10.1016/S0008-6363(98)00308-3

Bentzon, J. F., Otsuka, F., Virmani, R., & Falk, E. (2014). Mechanisms of plaque formation and rupture. *Circulation Research, 114*(12), 1852–1866. https://doi.org/10.1161/CIRCRESAHA.114.302721

Bonaca, M. P., Scirica, B. M., Creager, M. A., Olin, J., Bounameaux, H., Dellborg, M., Lamp, J. M., Murphy, S. A., Braunwald, E., & Morrow, D. A. (2013). Vorapaxar in patients with peripheral artery disease results from TRA2°P-TIMI 50. *Circulation, 127*(14), 1522–1529. https://doi.org/10.1161/CIRCULATIONAHA.112.000679

Burke, A. P., Farb, A., Malcom, G. T., Liang, Y. H., Smialek, J. E., & Virmani, R. (1999). Plaque rupture and sudden death related to exertion in men with coronary artery disease. *JAMA, 281*(10), 921–926. https://doi.org/10.1001/jama.281.10.921

Burke, A. P., Farb, A., Malcom, G. T., Liang, Y. H., Smialek, J., & Virmani, R. (1997). Coronary risk factors and plaque morphology in men with coronary disease who died suddenly. *New England Journal of Medicine, 336*(18), 1276–1282. https://doi.org/10.1056/NEJM199705013361802

Burke, A. P., Kolodgie, F. D., Farb, A., Weber, D. K., Malcom, G. T., Smialek, J., & Virmani, R. (2001). Healed plaque ruptures and sudden coronary death: Evidence that subclinical rupture has a role in plaque progression. *Circulation, 103*(7), 934–940. https://doi.org/10.1161/01.CIR.103.7.934

Burke, A. P., Kolodgie, F. D., Farb, A., Weber, D., & Virmani, R. (2002). Morphological predictors of arterial remodeling in coronary atherosclerosis. *Circulation, 105*(3), 297–303. https://doi.org/10.1161/hc0302.102610

Burke, A. P., Virmani, R., Galis, Z., Haudenschild, C. C., & Muller, J. E. (2003). 34th Bethesda Conference: Task force #2–What is the pathologic basis for new atherosclerosis imaging techniques? *Journal of the American College of Cardiology, 41*(11), 1874–1886. https://doi.org/10.1016/s0735-1097(03)00359-0

Burke, A. P., Weber, D. K., Kolodgie, F. D., Farb, A., Taylor, A. J., & Virmani, R. (2001). Pathophysiology of calcium deposition in coronary arteries. *Herz, 26*(4), 239–244. https://doi.org/10.1007/PL00002026

Creager, M. A., Kaufman, J. A., & Conte, M. S. (2012). Acute limb ischemia. *New England Journal of Medicine, 366*(23), 2198–2206. https://doi.org/10.1056/NEJMcp1006054

Criqui, M. H., Matsushita, K., Aboyans, V., Hess, C. N., Hicks, C. W., Kwan, T. W., McDermott, M. M., Misra, S., & Ujueta, F. (2021). Lower extremity peripheral artery disease: Contemporary epidemiology, management gaps, and future directions: A scientific statement from the American heart association. *Circulation, 144*(9), E171–E191. https://doi.org/10.1161/CIR.0000000000001005

Davies, M. J., & Thomas, A. C. (1985). Plaque fissuring–the cause of acute myocardial infarction, sudden ischaemic death, and crescendo angina. *Heart, 53*(4), 363–373. https://doi.org/10.1136/hrt.53.4.363

Demer, L. L., & Tintut, Y. (2008). Vascular calcification: Pathobiology of a multifaceted disease. *Circulation, 117*(22), 2938–2948. https://doi.org/10.1161/CIRCULATIONAHA.107.743161

Falk, E., Nakano, M., Bentzon, J. F., Finn, A. V., & Virmani, R. (2013). Update on acute coronary syndromes: The pathologists' view. *European Heart Journal, 34*(10), 719–728. https://doi.org/10.1093/eurheartj/ehs411

Fan, J., & Watanabe, T. (2003). Inflammatory reactions in the pathogenesis of atherosclerosis. *Journal of Atherosclerosis and Thrombosis, 10*(2), 63–71. https://doi.org/10.5551/jat.10.63

Felton, C. V., Crook, D., Davies, M. J., & Oliver, M. F. (1997). Relation of plaque lipid composition and morphology to the stability of human aortic plaques. *Arteriosclerosis, Thrombosis, and Vascular Biology, 17*(7), 1337–1345. https://doi.org/10.1161/01.ATV.17.7.1337

FitzGibbon, G. M., Kafka, H. P., Leach, A. J., Keon, W. J., Hooper, G. D., & Burton, J. R. (1996). Coronary bypass graft fate and patient outcome: Angiographic follow-up of 5,065 grafts related to survival and reoperation in 1,388 patients during 25 years. *Journal of the American College of Cardiology, 28*(3), 616–626. https://doi.org/10.1016/S0735-1097(96)00206-9

Fowkes, F. G. R., Aboyans, V., Fowkes, F. J. I., McDermott, M. M., Sampson, U. K. A., & Criqui, M. H. (2017). Peripheral artery disease:

Epidemiology and global perspectives. *Nature Reviews Cardiology, 14*(3), 156–170. https://doi.org/10.1038/nrcardio.2016.179

Gijsen, F. J. H., Wentzel, J. J., Thury, A., Mastik, F., Schaar, J. A., Schuurbiers, J. C. H., Slager, C. J., Van Der Giessen, W. J., De Feyter, P. J., Van Der Steen, A. F. W., & Serruys, P. W. (2008). Strain distribution over plaques in human coronary arteries relates to shear stress. *American Journal of Physiology - Heart and Circulatory Physiology, 295*(4), H1608–H1614. https://doi.org/10.1152/ajpheart.01081.2007

Ho, C. Y., & Shanahan, C. M. (2016). Medial arterial calcification: An overlooked player in peripheral arterial disease. *Arteriosclerosis, Thrombosis, and Vascular Biology, 36*(8), 1475–1482. https://doi.org/10.1161/ATVBAHA.116.306717

Ikari, Y., McManus, B. M., Kenyon, J., & Schwartz, S. M. (1999). Neonatal intima formation in the human coronary artery. *Arteriosclerosis, Thrombosis, and Vascular Biology, 19*(9), 2036–2040. https://doi.org/10.1161/01.ATV.19.9.2036

Jinnouchi, H., Sakamoto, A., Torii, S., Virmani, R., & Finn, A. (2019). *Chapter 1 - types and pathology of vascular calcification.* Academic Press.

Jinnouchi, H., Sato, Y., Bhoite, R. R., Kuntz, S. H., Sakamoto, A., Kutyna, M., Torii, S., Mori, M., Kawakami, R., Amoa, F. C., Kolodgie, F. D., Virmani, R., & Finn, A. V. (2021). Intravascular imaging and histological correlates of medial and intimal calcification in peripheral artery disease. *EuroIntervention, 17*(8), E688–E698. https://doi.org/10.4244/EIJ-D-20-01336

Johnson, J. L., Jenkins, N. P., Huang, W. C., Di Gregoli, K., Sala-Newby, G. B., Scholtes, V. P. W., Moll, F. L., Pasterkamp, G., & Newby, A. C. (2014). Relationship of MMP-14 and TIMP-3 expression with macrophage activation and human atherosclerotic plaque vulnerability. *Mediators of Inflammation, 2014*. https://doi.org/10.1155/2014/276457

Katz, S. S., Shipley, G. G., & Small, D. M. (1976). Physical chemistry of the lipids of human atherosclerotic lesions. Demonstration of a lesion intermediate between fatty streaks and advanced plaques. *Journal of Clinical Investigation, 58*(1), 200–211. https://doi.org/10.1172/JCI108450

Kolodgie, F. D., Burke, A. P., Nakazawa, G., & Virmani, R. (2007). Is pathologic intimal thickening the key to understanding early plaque progression in human atherosclerotic disease? *Arteriosclerosis, Thrombosis, and Vascular Biology, 27*(5), 986–989. https://doi.org/10.1161/ATVBAHA.0000258865.44774.41

Kolodgie, F. D., Gold, H. K., Burke, A. P., Fowler, D. R., Kruth, H. S., Weber, D. K., Farb, A., Guerrero, L. J., Hayase, M., Kutys, R., Narula, J., Finn, A. V., & Virmani, R. (2003). Intraplaque hemorrhage and progression of coronary atheroma. *New England Journal of Medicine, 349*(24), 2316–2325. https://doi.org/10.1056/NEJMoa035655

Kolodgie, F. D., Narula, J., Burke, A. P., Haider, N., Farb, A., Hui-Liang, Y., Smialek, J., & Virmani, R. (2000). Localization of apoptotic macrophages at the site of plaque rupture in sudden coronary death. *American Journal Of Pathology, 157*(4), 1259–1268. https://doi.org/10.1016/S0002-9440(10)64641-X

Kragel, A. H., Reddy, S. G., Wittes, J. T., & Roberts, W. C. (1989). Morphometric analysis of the composition of atherosclerotic plaques in the four major epicardial coronary arteries in acute myocardial infarction and in sudden coronary death. *Circulation, 80*(6), 1747–1756. https://doi.org/10.1161/01.cir.80.6.1747

Kramer, M. C. A., Rittersma, S. Z. H., de Winter, R. J., Ladich, E. R., Fowler, D. R., Liang, Y. H., Kutys, R., Carter-Monroe, N., Kolodgie, F. D., van der Wal, A. C., & Virmani, R. (2010). Relationship of thrombus healing to underlying plaque morphology in sudden coronary death. *Journal of the American College of Cardiology, 55*(2), 122−132. https://doi.org/10.1016/j.jacc.2009.09.007

Lanzer, P., Boehm, M., Sorribas, V., Thiriet, M., Janzen, J., Zeller, T., St Hilaire, C., & Shanahan, C. (2014). Medial vascular calcification revisited: Review and perspectives. *European Heart Journal, 35*(23), 1515−1525. https://doi.org/10.1093/eurheartj/ehu163

Lanzer, P., Hannan, F. M., Lanzer, J. D., Janzen, J., Raggi, P., Furniss, D., Schuchardt, M., Thakker, R., Fok, P. W., Saez-Rodriguez, J., Millan, A., Sato, Y., Ferraresi, R., Virmani, R., & St Hilaire, C. (2021). Medial arterial calcification: JACC state-of-the-art review. *Journal of the American College of Cardiology, 78*(11), 1145−1165. https://doi.org/10.1016/j.jacc.2021.06.049

Lee, C. W., Hwang, I., Park, C. S., Lee, H., Park, D. W., Kang, S. J., Lee, S. H., Kim, Y. H., Park, S. W., & Park, S. J. (2011). Comparison of ADAMTS-1, -4 and -5 expression in culprit plaques between acute myocardial infarction and stable angina. *Journal of Clinical Pathology, 64*(5), 399−404. https://doi.org/10.1136/jcp.2010.088484

Lehto, S., Niskanen, L., Suhonen, M., Rönnemaa, T., & Laakso, M. (1996). Medial artery calcification: A neglected harbinger of cardiovascular complications in non-insulin-dependent diabetes mellitus. *Arteriosclerosis, Thrombosis, and Vascular Biology, 16*(8), 978−983. https://doi.org/10.1161/01.ATV.16.8.978

Lenglet, S., Mach, F., & Montecucco, F. (2013). Role of matrix metalloproteinase-8 in atherosclerosis. *Mediators of Inflammation, 2013*, 1−6. https://doi.org/10.1155/2013/659282

Low Wang, C. C., Blomster, J. I., Heizer, G., Berger, J. S., Baumgartner, I., Fowkes, F. G. R., Held, P., Katona, B. G., Norgren, L., Jones, W. S., Lopes, R. D., Olin, J. W., Rockhold, F. W., Mahaffey, K. W., Patel, M. R., & Hiatt, W. R. (2018). Cardiovascular and limb outcomes in patients with diabetes and peripheral artery disease: The EUCLID trial. *Journal of the American College of Cardiology, 72*(25), 3274−3284. https://doi.org/10.1016/j.jacc.2018.09.078

MacTaggart, J. N., Phillips, N. Y., Lomneth, C. S., Pipinos, I. I., Bowen, R., Timothy Baxter, B., Johanning, J., Matthew Longo, G., Desyatova, A. S., Moulton, M. J., Dzenis, Y. A., & Kamenskiy, A. V. (2014). Three-dimensional bending, torsion and axial compression of the femoropopliteal artery during limb flexion. *Journal of Biomechanics, 47*(10), 2249−2256. https://doi.org/10.1016/j.jbiomech.2014.04.053

Mann, J., & Davies, M. J. (1999). Mechanisms of progression in native coronary artery disease: Role of healed plaque disruption. *Heart, 82*(3), 265−268. https://doi.org/10.1136/hrt.82.3.265

Mauriello, A., Sangiorgi, G. M., Virmani, R., Trimarchi, S., Holmes, D. R., Kolodgie, F. D., Piepgras, D. G., Piperno, G., Liotti, D., Narula, J., Righini, P., Ippoliti, A., & Spagnoli, L. G. (2010). A pathobiologic link between risk factors profile and morphological markers of carotid instability. *Atherosclerosis, 208*(2), 572−580. https://doi.org/10.1016/j.atherosclerosis.2009.07.048

McGill, H. C., McMahan, C. A., Herderick, E. E., Tracy, R. E., Malcom, G. T., Zieske, A. W., & Strong, J. P. (2000). Effects of coronary heart disease risk factors on atherosclerosis of selected regions of the aorta and right coronary artery. *Arteriosclerosis, Thrombosis, and Vascular Biology, 20*(3), 836−845. https://doi.org/10.1161/01.atv.20.3.836

Mori, II., Torii, S., Kutyna, M., Sakamoto, A., Finn, A. V., & Virmani, R. (2018). Coronary artery calcification and its progression: What does it really mean? *Journal of the American College of Cardiology: Cardiovascular Imaging, 11*(1), 127−142. https://doi.org/10.1016/j.jcmg.2017.10.012

Mustapha, J. A., Diaz-Sandoval, L. J., & Saab, F. (2017). Infrapopliteal calcification patterns in critical limb ischemia: Diagnostic, pathologic and therapeutic implications in the search for the endovascular holy grail. *The Journal of Cardiovascular Surgery, 58*(3), 383–401. https://doi.org/10.23736/S0021-9509.17.09878-0

Nakamura, S., Ishibashi-Ueda, H., Niizuma, S., Yoshihara, F., Horio, T., & Kawano, Y. (2009). Coronary calcification in patients with chronic kidney disease and coronary artery disease. *Clinical Journal of the American Society of Nephrology, 4*(12), 1892–1900. https://doi.org/10.2215/cjn.04320709

Nakashima, Y., Fujii, H., Sumiyoshi, S., Wight, T. N., & Sueishi, K. (2007). Early human atherosclerosis: Accumulation of lipid and proteoglycans in intimal thickenings followed by macrophage infiltration. *Arteriosclerosis, Thrombosis, and Vascular Biology, 27*(5), 1159–1165. https://doi.org/10.1161/ATVBAHA.106.134080

Narula, N., Olin, J. W., & Narula, N. (2020). Pathologic disparities between peripheral artery disease and coronary artery disease. *Arteriosclerosis, Thrombosis, and Vascular Biology, 40*(9), 1982–1989. https://doi.org/10.1161/ATVBAHA.119.312864

O'Neill, W. C., Han, K. H., Schneider, T. M., & Hennigar, R. A. (2015). Prevalence of nonatheromatous lesions in peripheral arterial disease. *Arteriosclerosis, Thrombosis, and Vascular Biology, 35*(2), 439–447. https://doi.org/10.1161/ATVBAHA.114.304764

Otsuka, F., Nakano, M., Sakakura, K., Ladich, E., Kolodgie, F. D., & Virmani, R. (2013). Unique demands of the femoral anatomy and pathology and the need for unique interventions. *The Journal of Cardiovascular Surgery, 54*(2), 191–210.

Otsuka, F., Joner, M., Prati, F., Virmani, R., & Narula, J. (2014). Clinical classification of plaque morphology in coronary disease. *Nature Reviews Cardiology, 11*(7), 379–389. https://doi.org/10.1038/nrcardio.2014.62

Otsuka, F., Kramer, M. C. A., Woudstra, P., Yahagi, K., Ladich, E., Finn, A. V., de Winter, R. J., Kolodgie, F. D., Wight, T. N., Davis, H. R., Joner, M., & Virmani, R. (2015). Natural progression of atherosclerosis from pathologic intimal thickening to late fibroatheroma in human coronary arteries: A pathology study. *Atherosclerosis, 241*(2), 772–782. https://doi.org/10.1016/j.atherosclerosis.2015.05.011

Otsuka, F., Sakakura, K., Yahagi, K., Joner, M., & Virmani, R. (2014). Has our understanding of calcification in human coronary atherosclerosis progressed? *Arteriosclerosis, Thrombosis, and Vascular Biology, 34*(4), 724–736. https://doi.org/10.1161/atvbaha.113.302642

Otsuka, F., Yasuda, S., Noguchi, T., & Ishibashi-Ueda, H. (2016). Pathology of coronary atherosclerosis and thrombosis. *Cardiovascular Diagnosis and Therapy, 6*(4), 396–408. https://doi.org/10.21037/cdt.2016.06.01

Roth, G. A., Johnson, C., Abajobir, A., Abd-Allah, F., Abera, S. F., Abyu, G., Ahmed, M., Aksut, B., Alam, T., Alam, K., Alla, F., Alvis-Guzman, N., Amrock, S., Ansari, H., Ärnlöv, J., Asayesh, H., Atey, T. M., Avila-Burgos, L., Awasthi, A., … Murray, C. (2017). Global, regional, and national burden of cardiovascular diseases for 10 causes, 1990 to 2015. *Journal of the American College of Cardiology, 70*(1), 1–25. https://doi.org/10.1016/j.jacc.2017.04.052

Sakakura, K., Nakano, M., Otsuka, F., Ladich, E., Kolodgie, F. D., & Virmani, R. (2013). Pathophysiology of atherosclerosis plaque progression. *Heart Lung & Circulation, 22*(6), 399–411. https://doi.org/10.1016/j.hlc.2013.03.001

Sakakura, K., Nakano, M., Otsuka, F., Yahagi, K., Kutys, R., Ladich, E., Finn, A. V., Kolodgie, F. D., & Virmani, R. (2014). Comparison of pathology of chronic total occlusion with and without coronary artery bypass graft. *European Heart Journal, 35*(25), 1683–1693. https://doi.org/10.1093/eurheartj/eht422

Sakamoto, A., Jinnouchi, H., Torii, S., Virmani, R., & Finn, A. V. (2019). Coronary calcification and atherosclerosis progression. *Coronary Calcium: A Comprehensive Understanding of Its Biology, Use in Screening, and Interventional Management, 27–45.* https://doi.org/10.1016/B978-0-12-816389-4.00002-5

Sakamoto, A., Torii, S., Jinnouchi, H., Finn, A. V., Virmani, R., & Kolodgie, F. D. (2018). Pathologic intimal thickening: Are we any closer to understand early transitional plaques that lead to symptomatic disease? *Atherosclerosis, 274,* 227–229. https://doi.org/10.1016/j.atherosclerosis.2018.04.033

Sampson, U. K., Fowkes, F. G., & McDermott, M. (1990). 1990 global and regional burden of death and disability from peripheral artery disease: 21 world regions. *Global Heart, 9,* 145–158.

Sluimer, J. C., Kolodgie, F. D., Bijnens, A. P. J. J., Maxfield, K., Pacheco, E., Kutys, B., Duimel, H., Frederik, P. M., van Hinsbergh, V. W. M., Virmani, R., & Daemen, M. J. A. P. (2009). Thin-walled microvessels in human coronary atherosclerotic plaques show incomplete endothelial junctions. Relevance of compromised structural integrity for intraplaque microvascular leakage. *Journal of the American College of Cardiology, 53*(17), 1517–1527. https://doi.org/10.1016/j.jacc.2008.12.056

Song, P., Fang, Z., Wang, H., Cai, Y., Rahimi, K., Zhu, Y., Fowkes, F. G. R., Fowkes, F. J. I., & Rudan, I. (2020). Global and regional prevalence, burden, and risk factors for carotid atherosclerosis: A systematic review, meta-analysis, and modelling study. *Lancet Global Health, 8*(5), e721–e729. https://doi.org/10.1016/s2214-109x(20)30117-0

Soor, G. S., Vukin, I., Leong, S. W., Oreopoulos, G., & Butany, J. (2008). Peripheral vascular disease: Who gets it and why? A histomorphological analysis of 261 arterial segments from 58 cases. *Pathology, 40*(4), 385–391. https://doi.org/10.1080/00313020802036764

Sukhova, G. K., Schönbeck, U., Rabkin, E., Schoen, F. J., Poole, A. R., Billinghurst, R. C., & Libby, P. (1999). Evidence for increased collagenolysis by interstitial collagenases-1 and -3 in vulnerable human atheromatous plaques. *Circulation, 99*(19), 2503–2509. https://doi.org/10.1161/01.CIR.99.19.2503

Tabas, I. (2000). Cholesterol and phospholipid metabolism in macrophages. *Biochimica et Biophysica Acta (BBA) - Molecular and Cell Biology of Lipids, 1529*(1–3), 164–174. https://doi.org/10.1016/s1388-1981(00)00146-3

Tabas, I., Marathe, S., Keesler, G. A., Beatini, N., & Shiratori, Y. (1996). Evidence that the initial up-regulation of phosphatidylcholine biosynthesis in free cholesterol-loaded macrophages is an adaptive response that prevents cholesterol-induced cellular necrosis. Proposed role of an eventual failure of this response in foam cell necrosis in advanced atherosclerosis. *Journal of Biological Chemistry, 271*(37), 22773–22781. https://doi.org/10.1074/jbc.271.37.22773

Tabas, I. (2010). Macrophage death and defective inflammation resolution in atherosclerosis. *Nature Reviews Immunology, 10*(1), 36–46. https://doi.org/10.1038/nri2675

Torii, S., Sato, Y., Otsuka, F., Kolodgie, F. D., Jinnouchi, H., Sakamoto, A., Park, J., Yahagi, K., Sakakura, K., Cornelissen, A., Kawakami, R., Mori, M., Kawai, K., Amoa, F., Guo, L., Kutyna, M., Fernandez, R., Romero, M. E., Fowler, D., Finn, A. V., & Virmani, R. (2021). Eruptive calcified nodules as a potential mechanism of acute coronary thrombosis and sudden death. *Journal of the*

American College of Cardiology, 77(13), 1599–1611. https://doi.org/10.1016/j.jacc.2021.02.016

Torii, S., Mustapha, J. A., Narula, J., Mori, H., Saab, F., Jinnouchi, H., Yahagi, K., Sakamoto, A., Romero, M. E., Narula, N., Kolodgie, F. D., Virmani, R., & Finn, A. V. (2019). Histopathologic characterization of peripheral arteries in subjects with abundant risk factors: Correlating imaging with pathology. *Journal of the American College of Cardiology: Cardiovascular Imaging, 12*(8), 1501–1513. https://doi.org/10.1016/j.jcmg.2018.08.039

van der Wal, A. C., Becker, A. E., van der Loos, C. M., & Das, P. K. (1994). Site of intimal rupture or erosion of thrombosed coronary atherosclerotic plaques is characterized by an inflammatory process irrespective of the dominant plaque morphology. *Circulation, 89*(1), 36–44. https://doi.org/10.1161/01.cir.89.1.36

Van Oostrom, O., Velema, E., Schoneveld, A. H., De Vries, J. P. P. M., De Bruin, P., Seldenrijk, C. A., De Kleijn, D. P. V., Busser, E., Moll, F. L., Verheijen, J. H., Virmani, R., & Pasterkamp, G. (2005). Age-related changes in plaque composition: A study in patients suffering from carotid artery stenosis. *Cardiovascular Pathology, 14*(3), 126–134. https://doi.org/10.1016/j.carpath.2005.03.002

Velican, C. (1981). A dissecting view on the role of the fatty streak in the pathogenesis of human atherosclerosis: Culprit or bystander? *Revue Roumaine de Medecine - Serie Medecine Interne, 19*(4), 321–337.

Velican, C. (1969). Relationship between regional aortic susceptibility to atherosclerosis and macromolecular structural stability. *Journal of Atherosclerosis Research, 9*(2), 193–201. https://doi.org/10.1016/s0368-1319(69)80054-2

Vengrenyuk, Y., Carlier, S., Xanthos, S., Cardoso, L., Ganatos, P., Virmani, R., Einav, S., Gilchrist, L., & Weinbaum, S. (2006). A hypothesis for vulnerable plaque rupture due to stress-induced debonding around cellular microcalcifications in thin fibrous caps. *Proceedings of the National Academy of Sciences, 103*(40), 14678–14683. https://doi.org/10.1073/pnas.0606310103

Virani, S. S., Alonso, A., Benjamin, E. J., Bittencourt, M. S., Callaway, C. W., Carson, A. P., Chamberlain, A. M., Chang, A. R., Cheng, S., Delling, F. N., Djousse, L., Elkind, M. S. V., Ferguson, J. F., Fornage, M., Khan, S. S., Kissela, B. M., Knutson, K. L., Kwan, T. W., Lackland, D. T., … Tsao, C. W. (2020). Heart disease and stroke statistics—2020 update a report from the American Heart Association. *Circulation, 141*(9), E139–E596. https://doi.org/10.1161/CIR.0000000000000757

Virmani, R., Joner, M., & Sakakura, K. (2014). Recent highlights of ATVB: Calcification. *Arteriosclerosis, Thrombosis, and Vascular Biology, 34*(7), 1329–1332. https://doi.org/10.1161/ATVBAHA.114.304000

Virmani, R., Kolodgie, F. D., Burke, A. P., Farb, A., & Schwartz, S. M. (2000). Lessons from sudden coronary death: A comprehensive morphological classification scheme for atherosclerotic lesions. *Arteriosclerosis, Thrombosis, and Vascular Biology, 20*(5), 1262–1275. https://doi.org/10.1161/01.ATV.20.5.1262

Vos, A., Kockelkoren, R., de Vis, J. B., van der Schouw, Y. T., van der Schaaf, I. C., Velthuis, B. K., Mali, W. P. T. M., de Jong, P. A., Majoie, C. B., Roos, Y. B., Duijm, L. E., Keizer, K., van der Lugt, A., Dippel, D. W., Droogh-de Greve, K. E., Bienfait, H. P., van Walderveen, M. A., Wermer, M. J. H., Lycklama à Nijeholt, G. J., … van der Graaf, Y. (2018). Risk factors for atherosclerotic and medial arterial calcification of the intracranial internal carotid artery. *Atherosclerosis, 276*, 44–49. https://doi.org/10.1016/j.atherosclerosis.2018.07.008

Yahagi, K., Zarpak, R., Sakakura, K., Otsuka, F., Kutys, R., Ladich, E., Fowler, D. R., Joner, M., & Virmani, R. (2014). Multiple simultaneous plaque erosion in 3 coronary arteries. *Journal of the American College of Cardiology: Cardiovascular Imaging, 7*(11), 1172–1174. https://doi.org/10.1016/j.jcmg.2014.08.005

Yahagi, K., Davis, H. R., Arbustini, E., & Virmani, R. (2015). Sex differences in coronary artery disease: Pathological observations. *Atherosclerosis, 239*(1), 260–267. https://doi.org/10.1016/j.atherosclerosis.2015.01.017

Yahagi, K., Kolodgie, F. D., Otsuka, F., Finn, A. V., Davis, H. R., Joner, M., & Virmani, R. (2016). Pathophysiology of native coronary, vein graft, and in-stent atherosclerosis. *Nature Reviews Cardiology, 13*(2), 79–98. https://doi.org/10.1038/nrcardio.2015.164

4

Pathology of below-the-knee occlusions and chronic limb ischemia

Arielle Bellissard[1,2]

[1]*Department of Vascular Surgery and Kidney Transplantation, Strasbourg University Hospitals, Strasbourg, France;* [2]*CVPath Institute, Gaithersburg, MD, United States*

Chapter outline

Introduction

The terminal stage of peripheral arterial disease (PAD) is chronic limb-threatening ischemia (CLTI), which is defined by ischemic rest pain or tissue loss and represents up to 10% of patients with PAD (Conte et al., 2019; Farber & Eberhardt, 2016). Patients with CLTI are at high-risk of cardiovascular morbidity and mortality. In the absence of treatment, the risk for lower-limb amputation in patients with CLTI is estimated at 20%—25% at 1 year (Aboyans et al., 2018; Abu Dabrh et al., 2015). Optimal medical and surgical management of CLTI thus remains crucial to improve limb salvage and overall survival.

CLTI most often results from a multilevel arterial disease (Lowry et al., 2018; Tummala et al., 2020). Below-the-knee (BK) occlusive disease is rarely isolated but often associated with worst severity and clinical outcomes (Anand et al., 2020; Sadek et al.,

Pathophysiology and Treatment of Atherosclerotic Disease in Peripheral Arteries. https://doi.org/10.1016/B978-0-443-13593-4.00004-4

2009). Age, chronic kidney disease, and diabetes mellitus are risk factors for BK disease (Conte et al., 2019; Mustapha et al., 2017). BK lesions often present as diffuse calcifications in the lower limbs and long chronic total occlusions (CTO) in tibial arteries, resulting in complex tandem lesions in multiples vessels. As such, revascularization of CLTI caused by BK disease remains a challenge (Chaudery et al., 2021). The unique characteristics of BK occlusive disease ask for tailored revascularization strategies, which can't just replicate what is done in coronary and femoropopliteal arteries (Moreels & Van Herzeele, 2021). To this end, better understanding of the pathology of BK arterial lesions is essential to propose effective prevention and treatment of CLTI.

Atherosclerosis in below-the-knee arteries

Until recently, little was known about the pathology of PAD. Most of the knowledge was inferred from histopathological studies of atherosclerosis in the coronary arteries (Yahagi et al., 2016). Soor et al. were the first to report on histopathological findings in lower-limb arteries, from 58 patients who underwent amputation due to PAD (56.9% BK and 43.1% above-the-knee [AK]; 89.8% suffered from CLTI and 10.3% from acute limb ischemia) (Soor et al., 2008). The most severely diseased segments of the peripheral vessels were submitted for histology. Atherosclerotic plaques were identified in 83.5% of the segments, with an average stenosis of 68.0% of the lumen. Severe stenosis (>75%) was found in 47.7% of segments and CTO was seen in 20.2% of segments. Lipid-rich core was seen in 39.0% of the plaques and 31.7% showed signs of plaque rupture. The anterior and posterior tibial arteries showed the greatest degree of stenosis (73.3% and 71.5% of average luminal narrowing, respectively), compared to peroneal (68.2%), popliteal (67.1%), and femoral (63.6%) arteries; the dorsalis pedis showed a significantly inferior burden (58.5%). Small vessel disease was seen in 65.5% patients, with arterioles in the subcutaneous tissues showing luminal narrowing, periarterial fibrosis, and occasional thrombosis.

Similarly, O'Neill and al. analyzed peripheral vessels in 60 amputations from patients with CLTI (53% AK amputations) (O'Neill et al., 2015). Once again, the most severely diseased segments were analyzed. Intimal thickening was present in >90% of the vessels and was most prevalent in anterior and posterior tibial arteries (96% and 95%, respectively) compared to femoral (88%), popliteal (84%), and dorsalis pedis (83%), although the differences were not significant. Presence of lipids (mostly intimal foam cells) was significantly lower in BK arteries (19% vs. 37%; $P = .014$). Intimal inflammation was also less frequently seen in BK arteries (28% vs. 41%). Despite less inflammation and lipid-rich lesions, the nonatheromatous intimal thickening in BK arteries still caused substantial luminal stenosis. Mean occlusion was 60% in segments with lipids and 52% in segments without.

Narula et al. reported the histopathological analysis of 239 arteries obtained from amputation specimens of 75 patients with CLTI (205 infrapopliteal arteries and 34 femoro-popliteal arteries) (Narula et al., 2018). Atherosclerotic lesions were less frequent in BK arteries (38.5% vs. 67.6%), with a predominance of fibrocalcific lesions (59.5%). Severe luminal narrowing ($>$70%) was seen in 69% arteries. Luminal stenosis in infrapopliteal arteries was more frequently associated with chronic thrombotic occlusion, in the absence of significant atherosclerotic lesions. Observation revealed layered occlusive thrombi, suggesting repeated embolic burden, whereas acute thrombi were more commonly seen in femoro-popliteal arteries. Thrombi and cholesterol emboli were also present in the distal small arteries. These findings suggest a thromboembolic etiology for BK occlusions.

More recently, we conducted a pathological analysis of lower-limb PAD lesions in 12 legs from eight cadavers with abundant risk factors (Torii et al., 2019). Atherosclerotic lesions were classified using the modified American Heart Association classification proposed for coronary atherosclerotic lesions (Yahagi et al., 2016). Atherosclerotic plaques were significantly less common in BK arteries (56.8% vs. 95.7%; $P < .0001$), with a majority of lesions being fibrous plaques, whereas AK lesions demonstrated a higher incidence of lipid-rich plaques and calcified nodules. Acute thrombi were exclusively observed in AK arteries, whereas CTO was more frequently seen in BK arteries. Half of the CTO lesions were due to atherosclerotic plaques (1 healed plaque rupture and 4 fibrocalcific plaques), whereas the other half were embolic (Fig. 4.1).

Similar findings were reported by Vos et al., who collected 24 popliteal and 24 tibial arteries from the legs of 14 cadavers aged 70–96 years (Vos et al., 2021). Patient history of cardiovascular disease and risk factors was unknown. Two segments were randomly selected from each artery and submitted for histopathology. Once again, atherosclerotic lesions were classified according to the modified American Heart Association classification. Atherosclerosis plaques were significantly more frequent in popliteal arteries compared to tibial arteries (60% vs. 34%; $P < .0005$). Most of the lesions were classified as pathological intimal thickening or fibrocalcified plaque. A lipid core was

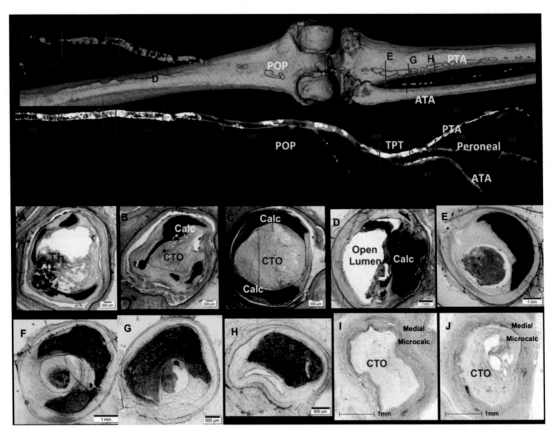

Figure 4.1 A representative case of chronic total occlusion (CTO) due to embolic phenomenon from an upstream calcified nodule. An 87-year-old woman with a history of smoking, chronic obstructive pulmonary disease, hypertension, and chronic renal failure. Radiograph of the leg arteries and CT of the leg are illustrated with line representing sites of corresponding histological sections. Calcified nodule with a nonocclusive thrombus (Th) is observed in the midsection of the superficial femoral artery (A) with distal occlusion secondary to the propagated thrombus (B, C), the vessel distal to the occlusion (D), is open (50%) and shows a fibrocalcific plaque. Sections of distal popliteal artery (POP) (E), tibioperoneal trunk (TPT) (F), posterior tibial artery (PTA) (G), and proximal part of anterior tibial artery (ATA) (H) show severely narrowed lesion with severe calcification. Proximal to midsections of ATA (I, J) were occluded from an organized embolus. From Torii, S., Mustapha, J. A., Narula, J., Mori, H., Saab, F., Jinnouchi, H., Yahagi, K., Sakamoto, A., Romero, M. E., Narula, N., Kolodgie, F. D., Virmani, R., & Finn, A. V. (2019). Histopathological characterization of peripheral arteries in subjects with abundant risk factors: Correlating imaging with pathology. *Journal of the American College of Cardiology: Cardiovascular Imaging, 12*(8), 1501–1513. https://doi.org/10.1016/j.jcmg.2018.08.039.

present in 24% of the popliteal and 17% of the tibial samples. Median luminal stenosis was 33% in the popliteal arteries and 25% in the tibial arteries; stenosis percentage was higher in samples with atherosclerotic plaques ($P < .0005$).

Medial arterial calcification

Medial arterial calcification (MAC), also known as Möncke-berg's disease, is a feature specific to PAD, for which we still lack a clear understanding of the pathophysiology (Fig. 4.2). Intimal calcification is the result of advanced atherosclerotic

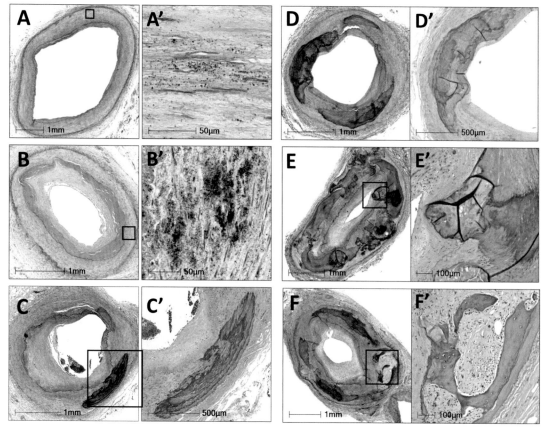

Figure 4.2 Progression of medial calcification in lower extremity peripheral arteries. (A and A') Medial microcalcification (*black dots*) of the media by von Kossa stain of nondecalcified section in an artery showing adaptive intimal thickening. (B and B') Medial punctate calcification of the media by von Kossa stain. Varying degrees (micro to punctate) of calcification are seen circumferentially involving the media. (C and C') Medial fragment of calcification is seen in Movat and Hematoxylin and eosin (H&E) stains of a decalcified section. (D and D') Medial sheet calcification involving nearly three-quarters of the circumference. (E and E') Combination of medial nodular and sheet calcification covering the circumference of the medial wall. (F and F') Bone formation in the presence of near circumferential medial sheet calcification with the presence of lacunae containing osteo-blasts and bone marrow. From Torii, S., Mustapha, J. A., Narula, J., Mori, H., Saab, F., Jinnouchi, H., Yahagi, K., Sakamoto, A., Romero, M. E., Narula, N., Kolodgie, F. D., Virmani, R., & Finn, A. V. (2019). Histopathological characterization of peripheral arteries in subjects with abundant risk factors: Correlating imaging with pathology. *Journal of the American College of Cardiology: Cardiovascular Imaging, 12*(8), 1501–1513. https://doi.org/10.1016/j.jcmg.2018.08.039.

lesions with the development of calcification within the plaque. On the other hand, MAC is developed in small- or medium-sized muscular arteries and has been shown to cause arterial stiffness, decrease in arterial elasticity, and compliance. Age, diabetes mellitus, and end-stage renal disease are known risk factors for MAC (Mustapha et al., 2017; Lanzer et al., 2021; Sato et al., 2020). MAC appears on biplane radiography and on angiography as "railroad tracks", outlining the arterial walls (Ferraresi et al., 2021).

In their study, Soor et al. described 76.2% of segments with MAC. No difference was found depending on the vessel localization. Concomitant presence of MAC and atherosclerosis was observed in 77.1% segments, but no significant relationship was found between the two. Interestingly, their cohort included seven patients who showed minimal atherosclerotic lesions but extensive MAC, with five of these patients displaying symptoms of CLTI (Soor et al., 2008).

O'Neill et al. observed calcifications mostly in the media (68% vs. 41% intimal calcification in BK arteries).Although the difference was not significant, MAC tended to be higher in AK than BK arteries; however, severity in affected vessels was greater in BK arteries ($P < .0001$). Frequent involvement of the internal elastic lamina (IEL) was observed in BK arteries (25%), where intimal calcifications were contiguous with MAC and seemed to be an extension of the calcified IEL (O'Neill et al., 2015). In the same way, Narula et al. (2018) found MAC in 71.1% of arteries, with more severity in BK arteries. Distal small arteries also showed MAC in 57.3% of cases.

Histopathological analysis of infrapopliteal arteries conducted by Mustapha et al. also described in most BK arteries a higher percentage of MAC than intimal calcification (Mustapha et al., 2017). They found more frequent and severe MAC in the anterior tibial, posterior tibial, and lateral plantar arteries (52%, 53%, and 48%, respectively) than in the femoropopliteal and tibio-peroneal segments (12% and 21%, respectively). Patterns of MAC were described as diffuse microcalcification, confluent sheet-like calcification, a combination of both, or ossification and cartilaginous metaplasia. Microcalcification would start at the early stage along the IEL, then become confluent and spread into the medial layer. No inflammation nor lipid deposition was seen in MAC areas, as opposed to atherosclerosis. Luminal narrowing >50% was found significantly more often in arteries with MAC than in arteries without (42% vs. 24%; $P < .05$), suggesting a role of MAC in luminal stenosis.

This last observation was not repeated in following studies. We found a similar degree of MAC in AK and BK arteries (2.4% and 2.3%, respectively). However, no correlation was observed between MAC and luminal stenosis (Torii et al., 2019) (Fig. 4.3)

Vos et al. described more frequent MAC in posterior tibial than in popliteal arteries (62% vs. 48%; $P = .008$) and a higher percentage of calcified medial circumference in posterior tibial arteries (34% vs. 11%; $P < .0005$). They found no relationship between atherosclerosis and MAC. No relationship was found between MAC and luminal stenosis either (Vos et al., 2021).

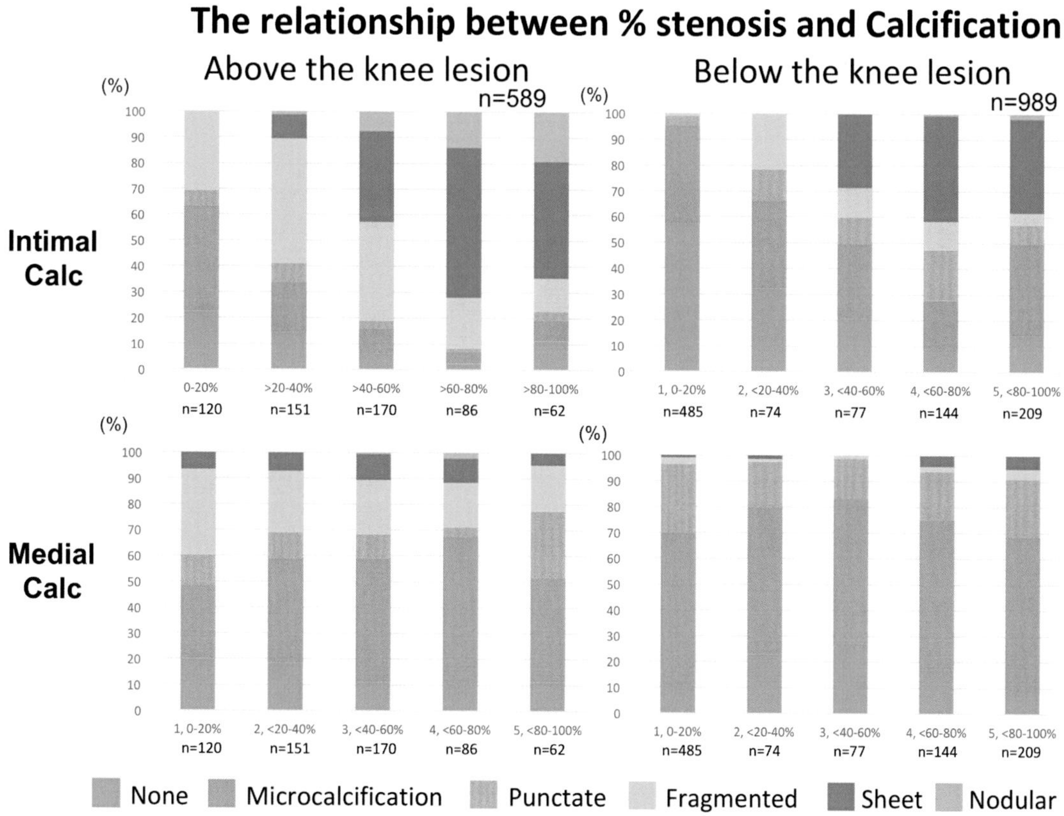

Figure 4.3 Prevalence of various types of intimal and medial calcification morphologies at 20% incremental cross-sectional area narrowing in nondecalcified lesions. Severe intimal calcification (sheet and nodular calcification) was more frequent in above (AK) than below the knee (BK), beginning as early as 10%—20% cross-sectional area narrowing. On the other hand, severe medial calcification was not as frequent in AK and BK. However, fragment calcification was more frequent in AK lesions compared with BK. From Torii, S., Mustapha, J. A., Narula, J., Mori, H., Saab, F., Jinnouchi, H., Yahagi, K., Sakamoto, A., Romero, M. E., Narula, N., Kolodgie, F. D., Virmani, R., & Finn, A. V. (2019). Histopathological characterization of peripheral arteries in subjects with abundant risk factors: Correlating imaging with pathology. *Journal of the American College of Cardiology: Cardiovascular Imaging, 12*(8), 1501—1513. https://doi.org/10.1016/j.jcmg.2018.08.039.

Summary of pathological findings in below-the-knee arteries

Conclusions from these histopathological analyses of BK arteries revealed a majority of nonsignificant atherosclerotic lesions compared to AK arteries. Intimal BK lesions are mostly composed of fibrous or fibrocalcific plaques, with minimal visualization of lipid core compared to AK (Fig. 4.4). Nonetheless, severe luminal stenosis and CTO are seen in patients with CLTI even in the absence of atherosclerosis. Little to no acute thrombus is

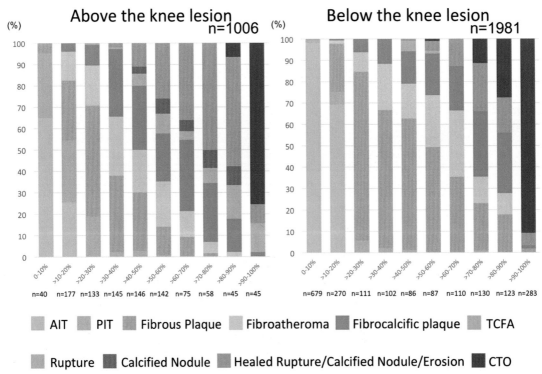

Figure 4.4 Prevalence of various types of atherosclerotic plaque morphologies at 10% incremental cross-sectional area narrowing in sections cut at 3—4 mm intervals above (AK) and below the knee (BK). Acute thrombotic lesions (plaque rupture and calcified nodule) were exclusively observed in AK lesions. AK lesions demonstrated a higher incidence of lipid-rich plaque (PIT, fibroatheroma, TCFA, rupture, and healed rupture), whereas the majority of the narrowing in BK lesions is from fibrous plaque and CTO. *AIT*, Adaptive intimal thickening; *CTO*, Chronic total occlusion; *PIT*, Pathological intimal thickening; *TCFA*, Thin-cap fibroatheroma. From Torii, S., Mustapha, J. A., Narula, J., Mori, H., Saab, F., Jinnouchi, H., Yahagi, K., Sakamoto, A., Romero, M. E., Narula, N., Kolodgie, F. D., Virmani, R., & Finn, A. V. (2019). Histopathological characterization of peripheral arteries in subjects with abundant risk factors: Correlating imaging with pathology. *Journal of the American College of Cardiology: Cardiovascular Imaging*, *12*(8), 1501—1513. https://doi.org/10.1016/j.jcmg.2018.08.039.

observed in BK vessels. Occlusion appears caused by chronic thromboembolic phenomena, suggesting an origin from upper stream plaques (Fig. 4.5).

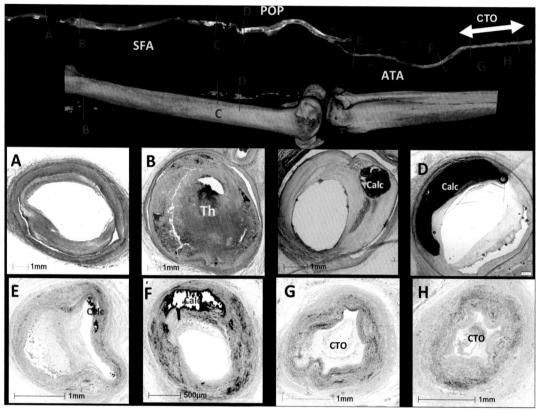

Figure 4.5 A case of chronic total occlusion (CTO) of the anterior tibial artery secondary to embolic phenomenon from an upstream plaque rupture site. An 89-year-old male with history of smoking, chronic obstructive pulmonary disease, hyperlipidemia, diabetes, and chronic renal failure. Radiograph of the leg arteries and CT of the leg are illustrated with lines representing sites of corresponding histological sections. Most proximal section of the superficial femoral artery (SFA) had mild narrowing from pathological intimal thickening (A). Plaque rupture with an occlusive thrombus (Th) was observed in the proximal section of the SFA (B). Moderate intimal calcification was observed in the distal SFA to popliteal arteries (POP). A section of proximal anterior tibial artery (ATA) demonstrates 60% narrowing from a fibroatheroma and microcalcification is observed in both intima and media (E), whereas mid-ATA section demonstrates micro- and fragment calcium in the media (F). Distal ATA lesions were occluded from an organized thrombus secondary to the propagated thrombus with medial microcalcification with negative remodeling (G and H). From Torii, S., Mustapha, J. A., Narula, J., Mori, H., Saab, F., Jinnouchi, H., Yahagi, K., Sakamoto, A., Romero, M. E., Narula, N., Kolodgie, F. D., Virmani, R., & Finn, A. V. (2019). Histopathological characterization of peripheral arteries in subjects with abundant risk factors: Correlating imaging with pathology. *Journal of the American College of Cardiology: Cardiovascular Imaging, 12*(8), 1501−1513. https://doi.org/10.1016/j.jcmg.2018.08.039.

Histopathological studies showed that MAC is associated with CLTI and is a cause of PAD independently of atherosclerosis. MAC is found in both AK and BK arteries, although it appears more severe in BK arteries. Histological observations suggest a start of MAC along the IEL, secondly spreading through the medial layer and possibly through the intimal layer also. No significant relationship is found in most studies between MAC and atherosclerosis, but MAC could still possibly impact the development of intimal lesions (Fok et al., 2018; Lanzer et al., 2021). Contrary to calcified atherosclerotic lesions, MAC occurs in the early stage of the disease and minimal calcium deposit can be found even in the arteries of younger patients (Kamenskiy et al., 2018). Complete understanding of pathways leading to arterial calcification is still lacking (St Hilaire, 2022).

Conclusion

Peripheral arteries have been lacking pathological evidence until last decades; new histopathological studies helped getting a better grasp of lesions type and morphology found in lower-limb vessels. PAD was found not to be caused exclusively by atherosclerosis. Particularly, BK arteries appear to behave differently from femoropopliteal arteries and display more chronic occlusions resulting from thromboembolic events. The important role of MAC emerged as an independent cause of PAD, with increased severity in BK arteries. For a while, MAC was thought to hold no clinical significance. It has been demonstrated since then that MAC in BK arteries is strongly associated with lower-limb amputation (Losurdo et al., 2021). These data need to be taken into consideration when choosing treatment options for CLTI (Chaudery et al., 2021; Steiner & Schmidt, 2021). As a key player in PAD pathogenesis, MAC must also be considered when devising revascularization strategies. A greater understanding of the pathology of BK vessels is still needed, particularly of the consequences of revascularization, in order to improve both prevention and management of CLTI (Mori et al., 2021).

References

Aboyans, V., Ricco, J. B., Bartelink, M. L. E. L., Björck, M., Brodmann, M., Cohnert, T., Collet, J. P., Czerny, M., De Carlo, M., Debus, S., Espinola-Klein, C., Kahan, T., Kownator, S., Mazzolai, L., Naylor, A. R., Roffi, M., Röther, J., Sprynger, M., Tendera, M., … Obiekezie, A. (2018). 2017 ESC guidelines on the diagnosis and treatment of peripheral arterial diseases, in collaboration with the European Society for Vascular Surgery (ESVS).

European Heart Journal, 39(9), 763–816. https://doi.org/10.1093/eurheartj/ehx095

Abu Dabrh, A. M., Steffen, M. W., Undavalli, C., Asi, N., Wang, Z., Elamin, M. B., Conte, M. S., & Murad, M. H. (2015). The natural history of untreated severe or critical limb ischemia. *Journal of Vascular Surgery, 62*(6), 1642–1651.e3. https://doi.org/10.1016/j.jvs.2015.07.065

Anand, G. M., Conway, A. M., & Giangola, G. (2020). Single versus multiple vessel endovascular tibial artery revascularization for critical limb ischemia: A review of the literature. *International Journal of Angiology, 29*(3), 175–179. https://doi.org/10.1055/s-0040-1714662

Chaudery, M. A., Patel, S. D., & Zayed, H. (2021). Outcomes of open and hybrid treatments in below the knee pathology for critical limb threatening ischemia. *The Journal of Cardiovascular Surgery, 62*(2), 111–117. https://doi.org/10.23736/S0021-9509.21.11654-4

Conte, M. S., Bradbury, A. W., Kolh, P., White, J. V., Dick, F., Fitridge, R., Mills, J. L., Ricco, J. B., Suresh, K. R., Murad, M. H., Forbes, T. L., AbuRahma, A., Anankwah, K., Barshes, N., Bush, R., Dalman, R. L., Davies, M., Farber, A., Hingorani, A., … Diamant, M. (2019). Global vascular guidelines on the management of chronic limb-threatening ischemia. *Journal of Vascular Surgery, 69*(6), 3–125S.e40. https://doi.org/10.1016/j.jvs.2019.02.016

Farber, A., & Eberhardt, R. T. (2016). The current state of critical limb ischemia: A systematic review. *JAMA Surgery, 151*(11), 1070–1077. https://doi.org/10.1001/jamasurg.2016.2018

Ferraresi, R., Ucci, A., Pizzuto, A., Losurdo, F., Caminiti, M., Minnella, D., Casini, A., Clerici, G., Montero-Baker, M., & Mills, J. (2021). A novel scoring system for small artery disease and medial arterial calcification is strongly associated with major adverse limb events in patients with chronic limb-threatening ischemia. *Journal of Endovascular Therapy, 28*(2), 194–207. https://doi.org/10.1177/1526602820966309

Fok, P.-W., Lanzer, P., & Vinci, M. C. (2018). Media sclerosis drives and localizes atherosclerosis in peripheral arteries. *PLoS One, 13*(10), e0205599. https://doi.org/10.1371/journal.pone.0205599

Kamenskiy, A., Poulson, W., Sim, S., Reilly, A., Luo, J., & Mactaggart, J. (2018). Prevalence of calcification in human femoropopliteal arteries and its association with demographics, risk factors, and arterial stiffness. *Arteriosclerosis, Thrombosis, and Vascular Biology, 38*(4), e48–e57. https://doi.org/10.1161/ATVBAHA.117.310490

Lanzer, P., Hannan, F. M., Lanzer, J. D., Janzen, J., Raggi, P., Furniss, D., Schuchardt, M., Thakker, R., Fok, P. W., Saez-Rodriguez, J., Millan, A., Sato, Y., Ferraresi, R., Virmani, R., & St Hilaire, C. (2021). Medial arterial calcification: JACC state-of-the-art review. *Journal of the American College of Cardiology, 78*(11), 1145–1165. https://doi.org/10.1016/j.jacc.2021.06.049

Losurdo, F., Ferraresi, R., Ucci, A., Zanetti, A., Clerici, G., & Zambon, A. (2021). Association of infrapopliteal medial arterial calcification with lower-limb amputations in high-risk patients: A systematic review and meta-analysis. *Vascular Medicine, 26*(2), 164–173. https://doi.org/10.1177/1358863X20979738

Lowry, D., Saeed, M., Narendran, P., & Tiwari, A. (2018). A review of distribution of atherosclerosis in the lower limb arteries of patients with diabetes mellitus and peripheral vascular disease. *Vascular and Endovascular Surgery, 52*(7), 535–542. https://doi.org/10.1177/1538574418791622

Moreels, N., & Van Herzeele, I. (2021). The current state of below the knee revascularization in chronic limb threatening ischemia. *The Journal of Cardiovascular Surgery, 62*(2), 95–97. https://doi.org/10.23736/S0021-9509.21.11839-7

Mori, M., Sakamoto, A., Kawakami, R., Sato, Y., Jinnouchi, H., Kawai, K., Cornelissen, A., Virmani, R., & Finn, A. V. (2021). Paclitaxel- and sirolimus-coated balloons in peripheral artery disease treatment: Current perspectives and concerns. *Vascular and Endovascular Review, 4.* https://doi.org/10.15420/ver.2020.16

Mustapha, J. A., Diaz-Sandoval, L. J., & Saab, F. (2017). Infrapopliteal calcification patterns in critical limb ischemia: Diagnostic, pathologic and therapeutic implications in the search for the endovascular holy grail. *The Journal of Cardiovascular Surgery, 58*(3), 383–401. https://doi.org/10.23736/S0021-9509.17.09878-0

Narula, N., Dannenberg, A. J., Olin, J. W., Bhatt, D. L., Johnson, K. W., Nadkarni, G., Min, J., Torii, S., Poojary, P., Anand, S. S., Bax, J. J., Yusuf, S., Virmani, R., & Narula, J. (2018). Pathology of peripheral artery disease in patients with critical limb ischemia. *Journal of the American College of Cardiology, 72*(18), 2152–2163. https://doi.org/10.1016/j.jacc.2018.08.002

O'Neill, W. C., Han, K. H., Schneider, T. M., & Hennigar, R. A. (2015). Prevalence of nonatheromatous lesions in peripheral arterial disease. *Arteriosclerosis, Thrombosis, and Vascular Biology, 35*(2), 439–447. https://doi.org/10.1161/ATVBAHA.114.304764

Sadek, M., Ellozy, S. H., Turnbull, I. C., Lookstein, R. A., Marin, M. L., & Faries, P. L. (2009). Improved outcomes are associated with multilevel endovascular intervention involving the tibial vessels compared with isolated tibial intervention. *Journal of Vascular Surgery, 49*(3), 638–644. https://doi.org/10.1016/j.jvs.2008.10.021

Sato, Y., Jinnouchi, H., Sakamoto, A., Cornelissen, A., Mori, M., Kawakami, R., Kawai, K., Virmani, R., & V. Finn, A. (2020). Calcification in human vessels and valves: From pathological point of view. *AIMS Molecular Science, 7*(3), 183–210. https://doi.org/10.3934/molsci.2020009

Soor, G. S., Vukin, I., Leong, S. W., Oreopoulos, G., & Butany, J. (2008). Peripheral vascular disease: Who gets it and why? A histomorphological analysis of 261 arterial segments from 58 cases. *Pathology, 40*(4), 385–391. https://doi.org/10.1080/00313020802036764

St Hilaire, C. (2022). Medial arterial calcification: A significant and independent contributor of peripheral artery disease. *Arteriosclerosis, Thrombosis, and Vascular Biology, 42*(3), 253–260. https://doi.org/10.1161/ATVBAHA.121.316252

Steiner, S., & Schmidt, A. (2021). Repeat BTK revascularization: When, how and what are the results? *The Journal of Cardiovascular Surgery, 62*(2), 118–123. https://doi.org/10.23736/S0021-9509.21.11679-9

Torii, S., Mustapha, J. A., Narula, J., Mori, H., Saab, F., Jinnouchi, H., Yahagi, K., Sakamoto, A., Romero, M. E., Narula, N., Kolodgie, F. D., Virmani, R., & Finn, A. V. (2019). Histopathologic characterization of peripheral arteries in Subjects with abundant risk factors: Correlating imaging with pathology. *Journal of the American College of Cardiology: Cardiovascular Imaging, 12*(8), 1501–1513. https://doi.org/10.1016/j.jcmg.2018.08.039

Tummala, S., Amin, A., & Mehta, A. (2020). Infrapopliteal artery occlusive disease: An overview of vessel preparation and treatment options. *Journal of Clinical Medicine, 9*(10), 3321. https://doi.org/10.3390/jcm9103321

Vos, A., de Jong, P. A., Verdoorn, D., Mali, W. P. T. M., Bleys, R. L. A. W., &
Vink, A. (2021). Histopathological characterization of intimal lesions and
arterial wall calcification in the arteries of the leg of elderly cadavers. *Clinical
Anatomy, 34*(6), 835–841. https://doi.org/10.1002/ca.23701

Yahagi, K., Kolodgie, F. D., Otsuka, F., Finn, A. V., Davis, H. R., Joner, M., &
Virmani, R. (2016). Pathophysiology of native coronary, vein graft, and in-
stent atherosclerosis. *Nature Reviews Cardiology, 13*(2), 79–98. https://
doi.org/10.1038/nrcardio.2015.164

5

Calcium and atherosclerosis in lower extremities

Ji-Eun Park[1], Aloke V. Finn[1,2] and Renu Virmani[2]

[1]Division of Cardiovascular Medicine, Department of Medicine, University of Maryland Medical Center, Baltimore, MD, United States; [2]CVPath Institute, Gaithersburg, MD, United States

Introduction

Arterial calcification is frequently found in atherosclerotic plaque and has been associated with traditional risk factors for atherosclerosis, including hypertension, hyperlipidemia, diabetes mellitus, chronic kidney disease, and smoking. This has been true for coronary and carotid arterial calcification, as well as peripheral arterial calcification (Berger et al., 2013; Gallino et al., 2014; Joosten et al., 2012). The extent of calcification, or calcium burden, has been used as a surrogate for clinical outcome (Bourantas et al., 2015; Généreux et al., 2014; Misare et al., 1996). However, although they frequently coexist, there are important differences between calcification types, which have implications for therapy.

Pathophysiology and Treatment of Atherosclerotic Disease in Peripheral Arteries. https://doi.org/10.1016/B978-0-443-13593-4.00005-6

Generally speaking, the two types of calcification found in the vasculature can be differentiated by their location, intimal versus medial. Once thought to be a single type of calcification, studies have shown that this is not the case, and which in fact, the two types of calcification are likely to have different pathophysiological origins. However, studies of peripheral arterial disease (PAD) have been limited by the silent nature of the disease until it gets to the end stage; thus, most studies have been performed in patients undergoing interventions such as open endarterectomy or amputation or are postmortem. Imaging studies have been limited in their ability to differentiate different types of calcification.

Intimal calcification is the type of calcification that is generally assumed when calcification is discussed in the context of arterial disease. Intimal calcification arises due to advanced atherosclerotic plaque, enhanced by lipid deposition and inflammation in association with macrophages and vascular smooth muscle cells (VSMCs). Whether calcification plays an active role in plaque rupture is not clear (with the exception of calcific nodules in coronary arteries), but it is possible that calcification destabilizes plaque during hemodynamic stress and acts as a nidus of inflammation, promoting disruption of the fibrous cap in an unstable plaque (Ho & Shanahan, 2016).

While initial studies of calcification did not differentiate intimal versus medial calcification, further studies have led to two distinct but overlapping entities, with findings overall that are consistent with higher prevalence of medial vascular calcification in the lower extremity arterial beds as compared to carotid or coronary arteries and a difference in the pathogenesis of lower extremity arterial disease as compared with coronary artery disease. Medial arterial calcification (MAC) is seen frequently in small- to medium-sized peripheral arteries and is an independent predictor of poorer outcomes, both mortality and amputation, in patients with PAD. However, the pathophysiology of medial calcification is less well understood.

Prevalence of calcification

Arterial calcification is quite common with aging. In one study of 650 asymptomatic patients (mean age 57.6 years), 61% had some form of calcification in the carotid, coronary, proximal aorta, distal aorta, or iliac vessels by electronic beam computed tomography (CT), speaking to the high prevalence of vascular calcification (Allison et al., 2004). There was an exponential increase in calcification with aging, such that 91% of women and 98% of men between ages 60 and 70 had arterial calcification, an increase from 47% of women and 70% of men who were less than 50 years old (Allison et al., 2004).

The population-wide prevalence of peripheral arterial calcification, and specifically MAC, also known as Monckeberg's sclerosis, is unknown, as it is frequently noted as a concomitant process with atherosclerotic disease and subsequently, intimal calcification. In a study of 431 femoropopliteal arteries from those aged 13–82, with a mean age of 53 years, 46% had medial calcification, with increasing calcification with age, similar to general trends of calcification with aging (Kamenskiy et al., 2018). Medial calcification is not uncommon, with higher prevalence of greater than 60% in patients with diabetes mellitus and chronic kidney disease, and is quite frequent, up to 72%, in those with chronic limb-threatening ischemia (CLTI) (Narula et al., 2018; O'Neill et al., 2015).

An earlier study of upper and lower leg arterial sections of 58 patients who underwent amputation for CLTI showed medial calcification in 76% with concomitant atherosclerosis in 77% (Soor et al., 2008). Interestingly, there was no relationship between extent of medial calcification and atherosclerosis (Soor et al., 2008). A study of 176 upper and lower leg arterial sections from 60 patients who underwent amputations for critical limb ischemia (CLI) showed medial calcification in 72% and intimal calcification in 43%, which tended to be less extensive than the medial calcification (O'Neill et al., 2015). Notable was low frequency of atherosclerotic disease, with only 23% of the sample demonstrating atheroma. In fact, contiguous intimal to medial calcification without atheroma was very common in the infrapopliteal arteries, which made up 74% of the sample (Of note, contiguous intimal to medial calcification was considered medial calcification due to the lack of atherosclerotic disease.). Medial calcification in the infrapopliteal arteries was more severe than in the femoropopliteal arteries (O'Neill et al., 2015). Intimal calcification did not commonly occur with medial calcification, with only 6% displaying both (O'Neill et al., 2015).

In a study of 239 arteries with 70% or more luminal stenosis from patients who had undergone amputation for CLI, significant atherosclerotic disease was more common in femoropopliteal arteries compared to infrapopliteal arteries, 67.6% versus 38.5% ($P < .05$), similar to the findings above (Narula et al., 2018). Calcification was found in 80% of femoropopliteal arteries and 70.6% of infrapopliteal arteries, with medial calcification in 58.5% and 72.4%, respectively ($P = .16$), confirming findings from previous studies (Narula et al., 2018; O'Neill et al., 2015; Soor et al., 2008). Thrombotic occlusion in the absence of significant atherosclerosis was more likely in the infrapopliteal arteries, suggesting that the predominant pathophysiology of luminal stenosis in these arteries is thromboembolic disease from an upstream source (Narula et al., 2018). Layering thrombi were also observed, suggesting repeated embolic phenomena (Narula et al., 2018).

A particularly detailed study of 12 limbs from eight subjects (median age 82 years) with abundant cardiovascular risk factors by Torii et al. extended the previous findings in patients with end-stage PAD (Torii et al., 2019). Arteries from these limbs were serially sectioned (2987 sections) and examined. Femoropopliteal arteries were more frequently found to have atherosclerotic disease (95.7% vs. 56.8 in infrapopliteal arteries, $P < .0001$), as well as luminal occlusion due to plaque rupture or calcified nodule (63%), as compared to the infrapopliteal arteries. However, the infrapopliteal arteries, similar to the above study by Narula et al., were far more likely to have vessel occlusion in the absence of atherosclerotic disease, with only half of chronic total occlusions (CTOs) having occlusion due to atherosclerosis. The other half of CTOs were due to distal embolization. Calcification, again, was quite common with intimal calcification in 73% of sections and medial calcification in 86%, with a higher degree of intimal calcification in femoropopliteal as compared to infrapopliteal arteries (15.1% vs. 1.6%, respectively, $P = .04$) (Torii et al., 2019). However, in this study, the amount of medial calcification was similar in femoropopliteal and infrapopliteal arteries (2.4% vs. 2.3%, respectively, $P = .71$), in contrast to the above studies performed in CLI (Narula et al., 2018; O'Neill et al., 2015; Torii et al., 2019). This difference may be accounted for by the fact that the subjects in the aforementioned studies had advanced disease as compared to the study by Torii et al., who did not carry a formal diagnosis of PAD (Torii et al., 2019). The arteries of diabetic patients had higher degrees of both intimal and medial calcification as compared to those of nondiabetics, confirming a prior similar finding (Soor et al., 2008; Torii et al., 2019). Bone formation was found more commonly in femoropopliteal arteries than in infrapopliteal arteries (83% vs. 33%, respectively, $P = .02$) (Torii et al., 2019).

Taken together, these studies show a high prevalence of both medial and intimal calcification, with a trend toward higher degrees of atherosclerotic disease with intimal calcification in the femoropopliteal arteries and high degrees of medial calcification throughout. Patients with end-stage renal disease and diabetes mellitus have higher calcification burden.

Development of intimal and medial calcification and its contribution to PAD

Calcification of the arteries can be seen in the intima and/or the media (see Table 5.1, Fig. 5.1). Although these locations have not always been differentiated in prior studies due to the

Table 5.1 Stages of calcification.

	Medial calcification	Intimal calcification	
I	Calcification of the internal elastic membrane with or without extension into the media (A and G in Fig. 5.1)	Microcalcification (includes micro and punctate) is identified by calcium particles ranging from >0.5 μm to <1 mm in diameter (M and S)	Micro- and punctate calcification
II	Calcification coalescence and becomes confluent (varying in size from 1 to 3 mm), forming fragments of calcification (B and H)	Small calcification is often accompanied by inflammation, areas of microcalcification coalescence forming fragments of calcification that are >1 mm but <3 mm in diameter (N and T)	Fragment calcification
III	Calcification length >3 mm and/or extending to involve >90° of the circumference (C and I)	Calcification of the intima >3 mm or >90° (O and U)	Sheet calcification
IV	Calcifications of the media, spanning the entire circumference (D and J)	Calcification can extend and become circumferential (P and V)	Sheet calcification (circumferential)
Nodular calcification	Nodular calcification is rarely seen in medial wall, which is composed of nodules of calcification often accompanied by fibrin (E and K)	Nodular calcification is composed of nodules of calcification often accompanied by fibrin with a fibrous cap (Q and W)	Nodular calcification
Bone formation	Bone formation may be observed in fragmented and areas of sheet calcification (F and L) bone formation and rarely cartilaginous metaplasia may be seen in late stages, most frequently in stages III and IV, but rarely also in stage II	Bone formation can be observed within the regions of calcification (R and X)	Bone formation

From Lanzer, P., Hannan, F. M., Lanzer, J. D., Janzen, J., Raggi, P., Furniss, D., Schuchardt, M., Thakker, R., Fok, P.-W., Saez-Rodriguez, J., Millan, A., Sato, Y., Ferraresi, R., Virmani, R., & St. Hilaire, C. (2021). Journal of the American College of Cardiology, 78(11), 1145–1165. https://doi.org/10.1016/j.jacc.2021.06.049

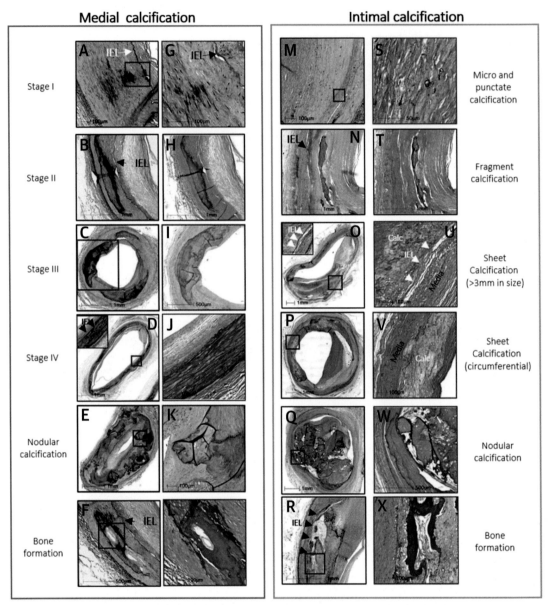

Figure 5.1 Histology of medial and intimal calcification. The legends to each medial and intimal calcification pattern are summarized in Table 5.1. The histological sections shown in the **left** and **right** columns of the medial and intimal calcifications were stained with (**A–F** and **M–R**) Movat pentachrome and (**G–L** and **S–X**) hematoxylin and eosin. The *red boxes* in the Movat pentachrome sections indicate areas of magnifications shown in the hematoxylin sections and in stage IV (medial) and sheet (intimal) Movat pentachrome sections. *IEL*, internal elastic lamina (*black arrows, black and white arrowheads*). From Lanzer, P., Hannan, F. M., Lanzer, J. D., Janzen, J., Raggi, P., Furniss, D., Schuchardt, M., Thakker, R., Fok, P.-W., Saez-Rodriguez, J., Millan, A., Sato, Y., Ferraresi, R., Virmani, R., & St. Hilaire, C. (2021). *Journal of the American College of Cardiology, 78*(11), 1145–1165. https://doi.org/10.1016/j.jacc.2021.06.049

limitations of imaging, distinguishing one from the other may have important clinical implications for treatment (Jinnouchi Hiroyuki et al., 2021). Because intimal versus medial calcification arise from different etiologies, the therapeutic targets for prevention may also differ.

Intimal calcification is a process that begins with microcalcifications (0.5 μm to 1 mm in diameter, Table 5.1), representing early-stage calcification. During initial lipid deposition during the development of atherosclerosis, debris within the atherosclerotic lesion resulting from smooth muscle cell and macrophage apoptosis acts as the nidus for the deposition of hydroxyapatite (Mori et al., 2018). These microcalcifications, seen frequently in deeper areas of necrotic core close to the internal elastic lamina (IEL), further initiate an inflammatory response. Small calcific fragments (1–3 mm in diameter) form where areas of microcalcification coalesce, progressing from the outer rim of the necrotic core to the extracellular matrix (Mori et al., 2018). As calcification extends and progresses, it develops into larger macrocalcifications (>3 mm) and sheets, representing late-stage calcification and a more stable plaque phenotype and can become circumferential. When calcified sheets fracture, they can lead to nodular calcification, which can extend into the lumen or media and become associated with fibrin with a fibrous cap. This may have particular relevance as the femoral artery is subject to bending, torsion, and compressive forces unique to its location in the body (MacTaggart et al., 2014). As atherosclerotic disease progresses, intimal calcification leads to further luminal narrowing and stenosis, which can reduce blood flow and tissue perfusion.

Key Point Medial calcification, on the other hand, arises independent of atherosclerotic disease, as it is not affected by lipid deposition and ensuing inflammation and generally does not cause luminal stenosis until the very advanced stages.

In medial calcification, calcium phosphate arises as a disseminated process in or near the IEL, developing into hydroxyapatite crystals and then extending into the media, increasing in size and distribution, leading to a decrease in wall elasticity and compliance (Table 5.1). Histological studies have shown the IEL is thinner, with discontinuous elastic fibers in this setting (Kamenskiy et al., 2018). In severe forms, ectopic vascular osteogenesis may also occur (Jinnouchi Hiroyuki et al., 2021). As disease progresses, tissue perfusion becomes impaired, likely due to disturbances in arterial stiffness and compliance. Typically over a long and clinically silent course, impaired perfusion of the tissues can lead to decreased flow, stasis, and thrombus formation, as seen in chronic limb ischemia. It is not known whether medial calcification directly or indirectly (or both) results in PAD. In calciphylaxis, in the setting of end-stage renal disease with dialysis, medial calcification of the arteries of the skin can result in ischemia and gangrene of the skin; a similar, direct process could occur with medial calcification in PAD (Ho & Shanahan, 2016). Because medial calcification causes arterial stiffening, its indirect hemodynamic effects are likely to impact the development of PAD. That is, with increased arterial stiffness comes impaired Windkessel effect (the ability of arterial system to distend during ventricular systole to accommodate additional blood volume, then recoil during diastole) due to its loss of elasticity, increase in left ventricular afterload, increase in pulsatility, all of which are likely to impair peripheral blood flow (Lanzer et al., 2021). However, it is likely that both direct and indirect processes interplay in the effects of medial calcification in PAD.

Thus, the way by which intimal calcification contributes to the progression of PAD as compared to that by which medial calcification leads to PAD and limb ischemia differ. This is important as it will affect the targets of therapies for PAD.

Mechanisms of medial arterial calcification

The molecular mechanisms of MAC are poorly understood. At its core, it seems to involve VSMCs developing an osteogenic phenotype, resulting in the accumulation of calcium. Bone morphogenetic protein (BMP), a potent inducer of bone formation through osteoblast differentiation, has been found in calcified atherosclerotic disease in human carotid arteries and has been the subject of study (Boström et al., 1993). Further research in arterial calcification is hindered by a lack of experimental models of arterial calcification and understanding of its pathogenesis, including the precipitation of calcium phosphate to hydroxyapatite (Lanzer et al., 2021; Millán et al., 2021). Currently, models have relied on surgical intervention to induce lower extremity occlusion. While investigation is underway on a number of pathways and mechanisms, we will discuss general overarching principles in the development of medial vascular calcification.

Accelerated vascular aging is thought to be at the core of medial calcification, with chronic kidney disease and diabetes mellitus as accelerating factors. Because aged VSMCs can also be seen in atherosclerotic plaque, they are thought to link calcification in PAD and atherosclerotic disease. An active, cell-mediated process, VSMCs begin the process of medial calcification, displaying an aged phenotype in disease. When VSMCs become damaged, they lose important defensive mechanisms and display an osteogenic phenotype, further promoting osteogenic differentiation (Ho & Shanahan, 2016). The initial stage involves altered phosphate homeostasis with sites of formation of hydroxyapatite crystals from calcium-rich matrix vesicles and apoptotic bodies released during apoptosis. Specific calcification inhibitors such as matrix Gla protein and pyrophosphate can downregulate this process; however, in the setting of prolonged exposure to procalcific conditions, loss of these inhibitors can occur, resulting in the onset of calcification (Ho & Shanahan, 2016; Rutsch et al., 2011; Tyson et al., 2003). In a procalcific environment, VSMCs exhibit loss of contractile markers and increased expression of bone-related genes, such as BMP and Cbfa1/Runx2, which has been shown in human peripheral arteries (Boström et al., 1993; Ho & Shanahan, 2016; Shanahan et al., 1999). It makes sense, then, in patients with chronic kidney disease, that altered phosphate homeostasis accelerates vascular calcification. In patients with diabetes, multiple mechanisms are thought to be at play, including decreased levels of matrix Gla protein, which is a known inhibitor of arterial calcification. Medications known to decrease levels of matrix Gla protein such as warfarin have been shown to increase MAC, which is further accelerated in the presence of chronic kidney disease (Alappan et al., 2020). Pyrophosphate, a strong inhibitor of calcification, is a breakdown product of adenosine triphosphate by the *ENPP1-NT5E* purine pathway. When this pathway is perturbed, extensive calcification is seen; *ENPP1* and *NTFE* mutations have been implicated in systemic and PAD (Ho & Shanahan, 2016; Kawai et al., 2022; Kim & Guzman, 2023). Because both chronic kidney disease and diabetes mellitus result in oxidative stress, one of the drivers for VSMC aging has been thought to be telomere shortening and DNA damage and mutations caused by reactive oxygen species (Madamanchi & Runge, 2007; Salpea & Humphries, 2010).

Tissue-specific mechanisms may contribute to VSMC aging. This is alluded to in the syndrome caused by *LMNA gene* mutation, progeria, also known as Hutchinson–Gilford Syndrome, in which children display premature, accelerated aging with vascular calcification. The *LMNA gene* encodes for lamins A/C, which are typically scaffolding proteins but also play a regulatory role in signaling pathways. VSMCs of children with this syndrome display loss of VSMCs in large arteries with MAC (Ho & Shanahan, 2016). A precursor protein called prelamin A is typically carboxylated and farnesylated; however, in progeria, a permanently farnesylated form of prelamin A called progerin exists due to a deletion of the cleavage site (Scaffidi & Misteli, 2006). Both prelamin A and progerin can be detected in normal, aged vasculature, so this is promising step toward revealing the mechanism of accelerated medial calcification (Scaffidi & Misteli, 2006).

Additionally, genome-wide association studies have started to allude to possible genetic contributions to arterial calcification (Lanzer et al., 2021). These multitudes of studies allude to a complex pathophysiology of arterial calcification leading to PAD. At the core of this is VMSC aging to an osteogenic phenotype, influenced by phosphate homeostasis, inflammation, oxidative stress, and tissue-specific mechanisms.

Clinical implications

Risk

Calcification of the lower extremities predicts a worse prognosis; this has been true of both intimal and medial calcification, although not all studies differentiated the two. As stated previously, arterial calcification, as well as medial calcification, is an independent predictor of poorer outcomes, both mortality and amputation, in patients with PAD. We know from previous studies that medial calcification is accelerated in patients with chronic kidney disease and with diabetes mellitus (Lanzer et al., 2021). In the study by O'Neill et al. mentioned previously, MAC was more severe and more prevalent in patients with end-stage renal disease (O'Neill et al., 2015).

The typical course of PAD is silent early in the disease and only when the disease is advanced do patients present for treatment. Thus, it becomes imperative that we use the tools that we have to risk stratify patients and use tools to help predict the course of their disease. The association between calcification and poor outcomes can be used to risk stratify patients for adverse limb events. One proposed scoring called the peripheral arterial calcium scoring system (PACSS) uses fluoroscopy and digital subtraction angiography to assess intimal and medial calcification ≥ 5 cm (Rocha-Singh et al., 2014). However, the regular use of such scoring systems has been hampered by poor diagnostic accuracy and less-than-optimal reliability (Allan et al., 2023). A scoring system for medial calcification, named the MAC (MAC) score, based on two projections of the foot by X-ray, uses the length (≥ 1 vs. 2 cm) of tram-tracking at five vascular sites, resulting in three categories of medial calcification (absent, moderate, and severe) (Ferraresi et al., 2020). It has been shown to correlate with major adverse limb events in patients with CLTI

(Ferraresi et al., 2020). These efforts highlight a need for validated risk stratification methods, and since the detection of calcium is reliant on imaging, a need for noninvasive imaging modalities to accurately and reliably detect both medial and intimal calcification.

Imaging

Since calcification type has different implications for therapy, it will become important to identify the type of calcification contributing to PAD. Due to the physical overlap of intimal and medial calcification in advanced disease, imaging has not been consistently used as the primary modality to differentiate the two; rather, it has been pathology specimens that have contributed to this differentiation. However, in specific circumstances, and particularly in interventions, imaging of calcification can be used to guide therapeutic modalities.

Transcutaneous ultrasound imaging can allow for differentiation between intimal and medial calcification. Medial calcification is typically seen on longitudinal views as echogenic abluminal bands, while intimal calcification is granular and spotty (Lanzer et al., 2021). By plain x-ray, medial calcification appears to have tram-tracking, while intimal calcification appears more plaque-like, spotty, and irregular. A novel scoring system has been proposed based on two projections of the foot by x-ray (Ferraresi et al., 2020). By evaluating the length (≥ 1 vs. 2 cm) of tram-tracking at five vascular sites, three categories of medial calcification (absent, moderate, and severe) were shown to correlate with major adverse limb events in patients with CLTI (Ferraresi et al., 2020). CT can identify calcium burden but due to resolution, it is difficult to differentiate medial from intimal calcification, especially in cases of advanced disease with heavy calcium burden (Lanzer et al., 2021). Thus, this indicates the need for further development and modification of current noninvasive imaging technologies for calcium differentiation.

Distinguishing intimal versus medial calcification was difficult to detect by intravascular ultrasound (IVUS) and optimal frequency domain imaging (OFDI, analogous to optical coherence tomography, or OCT), mostly due to overlapped calcification, without clear delineation of intima versus media (Jinnouchi Hiroyuki et al., 2021). While IVUS and OCT may help differentiate intimal from medial calcification in some cases, there are situations where the border of intima versus media may be disrupted; in these cases, it may be impossible to distinguish with imaging alone (Jinnouchi Hiroyuki et al., 2021). Additionally, because intravascular imaging is an invasive modality, it is typically reserved to situations where an invasive therapy has been decided. In an ex vivo study of intravascular imaging and histology of the vessels 12 cadaver legs, medial calcification was significantly more common than intimal calcification in below-the-knee vessels than above-the-knee (ATK), with 20% having both medial and intimal calcification, consistent with histological studies of amputated limbs (Jinnouchi Hiroyuki et al., 2021). Bone formation was more common in ATK vessels (Jinnouchi Hiroyuki et al., 2021).

Targeting therapies

Traditional medical therapies for reducing atherosclerotic burden would be the likely tools for reduction of intimal calcification. However, no specific medical treatments targeted to medial calcification pathways exist. Antithrombotic therapies have shown promise for reducing acute limb events (Eikelboom et al., 2017; Krantz et al., 2021). Further studies of the molecular mechanisms and pathways of arterial calcification will reveal therapeutic targets for both prevention and treatment.

During invasive endovascular therapies, aggressive balloon predilatation of medial calcification may not be warranted as it is for intimal calcification for calcium fracture. On the contrary, aggressive balloon predilatation may cause vascular injury, including perforation, and medial dissection resulting in intramural hematoma, along with fracture of medial calcification. Dissection occurs when excessive tensile stress has been delivered to areas where elastic and calcified media meet; it is also in these areas after dissection where neointimal hyperplasia will occur (Otsuka et al., 2014). Calcification is associated with an increased risk of complications during surgical and percutaneous procedures. Tools to modify calcium prior to endovascular intervention, such as cutting balloons, rotational and orbital atherectomy, intravascular lithotripsy, can facilitate stent delivery and placement. In particular, intravascular lithotripsy has increasingly been identified as useful tool in cases of deep calcium sheets, although randomized studies are lacking. These methods will be discussed further in later chapters.

References

Alappan, H. R., Kaur, G., Manzoor, S., Navarrete, J., & O'Neill, W. C. (2020). Warfarin accelerates medial arterial calcification in humans. *Arteriosclerosis,*

Thrombosis, and Vascular Biology, 40(5), 1413−1419. https://doi.org/10.1161/ATVBAHA.119.313879

Allan, R. B., Wise, N. C., Wong, Y. T., & Delaney, C. L. (2023). Accuracy and reliability of peripheral artery calcium scoring systems using an intravascular ultrasound reference standard. *Annals of Vascular Surgery, 91*, 233−241. https://doi.org/10.1016/j.avsg.2022.11.014, 0890-5096.

Allison, M. A., Criqui, M. H., & Wright, C. M. (2004). Patterns and risk factors for systemic calcified atherosclerosis. *Arteriosclerosis, Thrombosis, and Vascular Biology, 24*(2), 331−336. https://doi.org/10.1161/01.ATV.0000110786.02097.0c

Berger, J. S., Hochman, J., Lobach, I., Adelman, M. A., Riles, T. S., & Rockman, C. B. (2013). Modifiable risk factor burden and the prevalence of peripheral artery disease in different vascular territories. *Journal of Vascular Surgery, 58*(3), 673−681.e1. https://doi.org/10.1016/j.jvs.2013.01.053, 0741-5214.

Boström, K., Watson, K. E., Horn, S., Wortham, C., Herman, I. M., & Demer, L. L. (1993). Bone morphogenetic protein expression in human atherosclerotic lesions. *The Journal of Clinical Investigation, 91*(4), 1800−1809, 0021-9738.

Bourantas, C. V., Zhang, Y.-J., Garg, S., Mack, M., Dawkins, K. D., Kappetein, A. P., Mohr, F. W., Colombo, A., Holmes, D. R., Ståhle, E., Feldman, T., Morice, M.-C., de Vries, T., Morel, M.-A., & Serruys, P. W. (2015). Prognostic implications of severe coronary calcification in patients undergoing coronary artery bypass surgery: An analysis of the SYNTAX Study. *Catheterization and Cardiovascular Interventions, 85*(2), 199−206. https://doi.org/10.1002/ccd.25545, 1522-1946.

Eikelboom, J. W., Connolly, S. J., Bosch, J., Dagenais, G. R., Hart, R. G., Shestakovska, O., Diaz, R., Alings, M., Lonn, E. M., Anand, S. S., Widimsky, P., Hori, M., Avezum, A., Piegas, L. S., Branch, K. R. H., Probstfield, J., Bhatt, D. L., Zhu, J., Liang, Y., … Yusuf, S. (2017). Rivaroxaban with or without aspirin in stable cardiovascular disease. *New England Journal of Medicine, 377*(14), 1319−1330. https://doi.org/10.1056/NEJMoa1709118, 0028-4793.

Ferraresi, R., Ucci, A., Pizzuto, A., Losurdo, F., Caminiti, M., Minnella, D., Casini, A., Clerici, G., Montero-Baker, M., & Mills, J. (2020). A novel scoring system for small artery disease and medial arterial calcification is strongly associated with major adverse limb events in patients with chronic limb-threatening ischemia. *Journal of Endovascular Therapy, 28*(2), 194−207. https://doi.org/10.1177/1526602820966309, 1526-6028.

Généreux, P., Madhavan Mahesh, V., Mintz Gary, S., Maehara, A., Palmerini, T., LaSalle, L., Xu, K., McAndrew, T., Kirtane, A., Lansky Alexandra, J., Brener Sorin, J., Mehran, R., & Stone Gregg, W. (2014). Ischemic outcomes after coronary intervention of calcified vessels in acute coronary syndromes. *Journal of the American College of Cardiology, 63*(18), 1845−1854. https://doi.org/10.1016/j.jacc.2014.01.034

Gallino, A., Aboyans, V., Diehm, C., Cosentino, F., Stricker, H., Falk, E., Schouten, O., Lekakis, J., Amann-Vesti, B., Siclari, F., Poredos, P., Novo, S., Brodmann, M., Schulte, K.-L., Vlachopoulos, C., De Caterina, R., Libby, P., Baumgartner, I., & On behalf of the European Society of Cardiology Working Group on Peripheral Circulation. (2014). Non-coronary atherosclerosis. *European Heart Journal, 35*(17), 1112−1119. https://doi.org/10.1093/eurheartj/ehu071, 0195-668X.

Ho, C. Y., & Shanahan, C. M. (2016). Medial arterial calcification. *Arteriosclerosis, Thrombosis, and Vascular Biology, 36*(8), 1475−1482. https://doi.org/10.1161/ATVBAHA.116.306717

Jinnouchi, H., Sato, Y., Bhoite R., R., Kuntz H., S., Sakamoto, A., Kutyna, M., Torii, S., Mori, M., Kawakami, R., Amoa C., F., Kolodgie D., F., Virmani, R., & Finn V., A. (2021). Intravascular imaging and histological correlates of medial and intimal calcification in peripheral artery disease. *EuroIntervention, 17*(8), e688–e698, 1774-024X.

Joosten, M. M., Pai, J. K., Bertoia, M. L., Rimm, E. B., Spiegelman, D., Mittleman, M. A., & Mukamal, K. J. (2012). Associations between conventional cardiovascular risk factors and risk of peripheral artery disease in men. *JAMA, 308*(16), 1660–1667. https://doi.org/10.1001/jama.2012.13415, 0098-7484.

Kamenskiy, A., Poulson, W., Sim, S., Reilly, A., Luo, J., & MacTaggart, J. (2018). Prevalence of calcification in human femoropopliteal arteries and its association with demographics, risk factors, and arterial stiffness. *Arteriosclerosis, Thrombosis, and Vascular Biology, 38*(4), e48–e57. https://doi.org/10.1161/ATVBAHA.117.310490

Kawai, K., Sato, Y., Kawakami, R., Sakamoto, A., Cornelissen, A., Mori, M., Ghosh, S., Kutys, R., Virmani, R., & Finn, A. V. (2022). Generalized arterial calcification of infancy (GACI): Optimizing care with a multidisciplinary approach. *Journal of Multidisciplinary Healthcare, 15*, 1261–1276. https://doi.org/10.2147/JMDH.S251861. null.

Kim, T. I., & Guzman, R. J. (2023). Medial artery calcification in peripheral artery disease. *Frontiers in Cardiovascular Medicine, 10*, 2297-055X https://www.frontiersin.org/articles/10.3389/fcvm.2023.1093355.

Krantz, M. J., Debus, S. E., Hsia, J., Patel, M. R., Anand, S. S., Nehler, M. R., Hess, C. N., Capell, W. H., Bracken, T., Szarek, M., Mátyás, L., Krievins, D. K., Nault, P., Stefanov, S., Haskell, L. P., Berkowitz, S. D., Muehlhofer, E., Hiatt, W. R., Bauersachs, R. M., & Bonaca, M. P. (2021). Low-dose rivaroxaban plus aspirin in older patients with peripheral artery disease undergoing acute limb revascularization: Insights from the VOYAGER PAD trial. *European Heart Journal, 42*(39), 4040–4048. https://doi.org/10.1093/eurheartj/ehab408, 0195-668X.

Lanzer, P., Hannan, F. M., Lanzer, J. D., Janzen, J., Raggi, P., Furniss, D., Schuchardt, M., Thakker, R., Fok, P.-W., Saez-Rodriguez, J., Millan, A., Sato, Y., Ferraresi, R., Virmani, R., & St Hilaire, C. (2021). Medial arterial calcification: JACC state-of-the-art review. *Journal of the American College of Cardiology, 78*(11), 1145–1165. https://doi.org/10.1016/j.jacc.2021.06.049, 0735-1097.

MacTaggart, J. N., Phillips, N. Y., Lomneth, C. S., Pipinos, I. I., Bowen, R., Timothy Baxter, B., Johanning, J., Matthew Longo, G., Desyatova, A. S., Moulton, M. J., Dzenis, Y. A., & Kamenskiy, A. V. (2014). Three-dimensional bending, torsion and axial compression of the femoropopliteal artery during limb flexion. *Journal of Biomechanics, 47*(10), 2249–2256. https://doi.org/10.1016/j.jbiomech.2014.04.053, 0021-9290.

Madamanchi, N. R., & Runge, M. S. (2007). Mitochondrial dysfunction in atherosclerosis. *Circulation Research, 100*(4), 460–473. https://doi.org/10.1161/01.RES.0000258450.44413.96

Millán, Á., Lanzer, P., & Sorribas, V. (2021). The thermodynamics of medial vascular calcification. *Frontiers in Cell and Developmental Biology, 9*, 2296-634X https://www.frontiersin.org/articles/10.3389/fcell.2021.633465.

Misare, B. D., Pomposelli, F. B., Jr., Gibbons, G. W., Campbell, D. R., Freeman, D. V., & LoGerfo, F. W. (1996). Infrapopliteal bypasses to severely calcified, unclampable outflow arteries: Two-year results. *Journal of Vascular Surgery, 24*(1), 6–16. https://doi.org/10.1016/S0741-5214(96)70139-8, 0741-5214.

Mori, H., Torii, S., Kutyna, M., Sakamoto, A., Finn, A. V., & Virmani, R. (2018). Coronary artery calcification and its progression: What does it really mean? *Journal of the American College of Cardiology: Cardiovascular Imaging, 11*(1), 127–142. https://doi.org/10.1016/j.jcmg.2017.10.012, 1936-878X.

Narula, N., Dannenberg, A. J., Olin, J. W., Bhatt, D. L., Johnson, K. W., Nadkarni, G., Min, J., Torii, S., Poojary, P., Anand, S. S., Bax, J. J., Yusuf, S., Virmani, R., & Narula, J. (2018). Pathology of peripheral artery disease in patients with critical limb ischemia. *Journal of the American College of Cardiology, 72*(18), 2152–2163. https://doi.org/10.1016/j.jacc.2018.08.002, 0735-1097.

O'Neill, W. C., Han, K. H., Schneider, T. M., & Hennigar, R. A. (2015). Prevalence of nonatheromatous lesions in peripheral arterial disease. *Arteriosclerosis, Thrombosis, and Vascular Biology, 35*(2), 439–447. https://doi.org/10.1161/ATVBAHA.114.304764

Otsuka, F., Joner, M., Prati, F., Virmani, R., & Narula, J. (2014). Clinical classification of plaque morphology in coronary disease. *Nature Reviews Cardiology, 11*(7), 379–389. https://doi.org/10.1038/nrcardio.2014.62, 1759-5010.

Rocha-Singh, K. J., Zeller, T., & Jaff, M. R. (2014). Peripheral arterial calcification: Prevalence, mechanism, detection, and clinical implications. *Catheterization and Cardiovascular Interventions, 83*(6), E212–E220. https://doi.org/10.1002/ccd.25387, 1522-1946.

Rutsch, F., Nitschke, Y., Terkeltaub, R., & Towler, D. A. (2011). Genetics in arterial calcification. *Circulation Research, 109*(5), 578–592. https://doi.org/10.1161/CIRCRESAHA.111.247965

Salpea, K. D., & Humphries, S. E. (2010). Telomere length in atherosclerosis and diabetes. *Atherosclerosis, 209*(1), 35–38. https://doi.org/10.1016/j.atherosclerosis.2009.12.021, 0021-9150.

Scaffidi, P., & Misteli, T. (2006). Lamin A-dependent nuclear defects in human aging. *Science, 312*(5776), 1059–1063. https://doi.org/10.1126/science.1127168

Shanahan, C. M., Cary, N. R. B., Salisbury, J. R., Proudfoot, D., Weissberg, P. L., & Edmonds, M. E. (1999). Medial localization of mineralization-regulating proteins in association with Mönckeberg's sclerosis. *Circulation, 100*(21), 2168–2176. https://doi.org/10.1161/01.CIR.100.21.2168

Soor, G. S., Vukin, I., Leong, S. W., Oreopoulos, G., & Butany, J. (2008). Peripheral vascular disease: Who gets it and why? A histomorphological analysis of 261 arterial segments from 58 cases. *Pathology, 40*(4), 385–391. https://doi.org/10.1080/00313020802036764, 0031-3025.

Torii, S., Mustapha, J. A., Narula, J., Mori, H., Saab, F., Jinnouchi, H., Yahagi, K., Sakamoto, A., Romero, M. E., Narula, N., Kolodgie, F. D., Virmani, R., & Finn, A. V. (2019). Histopathologic characterization of peripheral arteries in subjects with abundant risk factors: Correlating imaging with pathology. *Journal of the American College of Cardiology: Cardiovascular Imaging, 12*(8, Part 1), 1501–1513. https://doi.org/10.1016/j.jcmg.2018.08.039, 1936-878X.

Tyson, K. L., Reynolds, J. L., McNair, R., Zhang, Q., Weissberg, P. L., & Shanahan, C. M. (2003). Osteo/chondrocytic transcription factors and their target genes exhibit distinct patterns of expression in human arterial calcification. *Arteriosclerosis, Thrombosis, and Vascular Biology, 23*(3), 489–494. https://doi.org/10.1161/01.ATV.0000059406.92165.31

6

Current molecular understanding of peripheral arterial disease

Shaunak Adkar[1] and Nicholas Leeper[2]

[1]*Division of Vascular Surgery, Department of Surgery, Stanford University, Palo Alto, CA, United States;* [2]*Stanford University, Palo Alto, CA, United States*

Introduction

Peripheral arterial disease (PAD) encompasses a wide variety of vascular pathology, both atherosclerotic and nonatherosclerotic, affecting the extrathoracic and extracranial arteries. In this chapter, we will focus on lower extremity atherosclerotic arterial disease. Lower extremity atherosclerotic peripheral arterial disease (henceforth referred to as PAD) is a subset of atherosclerotic cardiovascular disease (ASCVD), describing the accumulation of atherosclerosis in the lower extremity peripheral vasculature. PAD affects over 230 million people worldwide, with increased prevalence among patients within lower socioeconomic strata

Pathophysiology and Treatment of Atherosclerotic Disease in Peripheral Arteries. https://doi.org/10.1016/B978-0-443-13593-4.00006-8

(Aday & Matsushita, 2021; Pande & Creager, 2014). The specific anatomic distribution encompassed by PAD includes the aortoiliac segment proximally to the pedal arteries distally (Gerhard-Herman et al., 2017). Compared to its counterpart in the coronary bed, the basic molecular and cellular biology of PAD has been relatively understudied. The challenges in understanding the molecular basis of PAD can be appreciated by recognizing the heterogeneity of its clinical presentation, in terms of subanatomic distribution, morphology, and symptomatology. In fact, the clinical risk factors that predispose patients to PAD, including hypercholesterolemia, smoking, and diabetes, often present in distinct patterns. Smokers tend to develop aortoiliac and infrainguinal disease, whereas patients with poorly controlled diabetes often present with extensive calcified tibial disease (Fig. 6.1). While the molecular orchestration of atherosclerotic disease in the peripheral vasculature shares similarities with coronary artery disease (CAD), recent developments in the field of vascular biology highlight several of the unique molecular and cellular underpinnings of PAD.

Advances in genomics and sequencing technologies coupled with in vitro and animal model validation have afforded several mechanistic insights potentially explaining these clinical

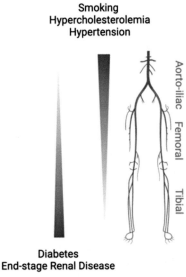

Figure 6.1 Distribution of lower extremity PAD in patients with various comorbidities. Hypertensive, hypercholesterolemic, and hypertensive patients tend to have more proximal aortoiliac and femoral disease, while patients with diabetes and end-stage renal disease often present with tibial disease.

observations in patients with PAD. Genome-wide association studies (GWAS) shed light on the shared and distinct susceptibility loci that increase the risk of PAD compared to CAD (Klarin et al., 2021). Sequencing of RNA and regions of open chromatin at the single-cell level can further allow prioritization of causal genes and cell types.

Traditionally, atherosclerotic plaque has been ascribed to the accumulation of lipid-laden foam cells in the vessel wall. Yet, this broad characterization overlooks the wide phenotypic variation noted within the peripheral vasculature, from focal ulcerated atherosclerotic lesions to diffusely calcified arteriosclerosis. This can be explained by the differential contribution of multiple interconnected pathophysiological processes affecting various cell types, including the vascular stromal cells and immune cells (Fig. 6.2). In this chapter, we will discuss the insight genetic

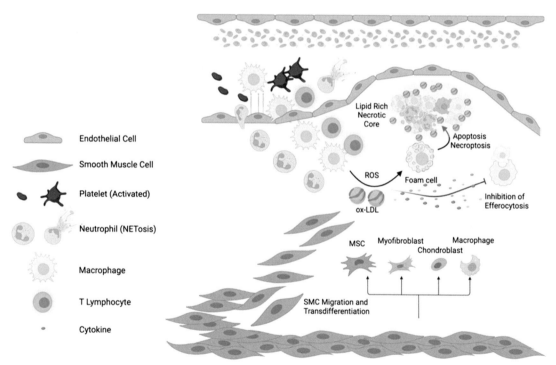

Figure 6.2 Cell-type involvement in atherosclerosis. Activation of the endothelial cells allows diapedesis, or migration, of innate immune cells (neutrophils, macrophages) as well as T-lymphocytes into the vessel wall. Macrophages accumulate lipid and become proinflammatory foam cells, which secrete inflammatory cytokines. Activation of neutrophils results in the release of prothrombotic and proinflammatory neutrophil extracellular traps (NETs). Platelets are activated by activated endothelium further contributing to thrombosis. Smooth muscle cells respond by migrating to the lesion and differentiating to multiple cell types, including mesenchymal stem cells (MSCs), myofibroblasts, chondroblasts or fibrochondrocytes, as well as macrophages.

studies have provided in our understanding of PAD and how mechanistic study guided by genetic insight holds enormous potential to pave the road for drug discovery. This is followed by discussion of the common pathophysiological mechanisms, including inflammation, macrophage dysfunction, thrombosis, and hyperglycemia, emphasizing their relevance and contribution to PAD.

Genomics

Although the etiology of PAD can largely be attributed to environmental exposures and comorbidities (i.e., smoking, hypercholesterolemia, diabetes mellitus), an individual's genetic susceptibility confers a substantial contribution to PAD development. The narrow-sense heritability (h^2) of PAD had initially been estimated by both twin and family-based studies. Twin studies describe heritability indices of 0.48−0.58 (Carmelli et al., 2000; Wahlgren & Magnusson, 2011), while the latter describe a modest heritability of 0.21−0.3 (Kullo et al., 2006; Murabito et al., 2006). These data suggest that genetic risk factors may influence the development of PAD though to a lesser degree than other forms of ASCVD (CAD, cerebral atherosclerosis) (Drobni et al., 2022; Vattathil et al., 2021). Early attempts at uncovering the genetic basis of PAD, including candidate association studies and linkage analysis, were limited by both methodology and power (Gudmundsson et al., 2002; Kullo et al., 2006; Leeper & Hamburg, 2021). As the cost of genotyping arrays for individual patients decreased, it became feasible to test the association of PAD with each variant within the genome. These GWAS have been pivotal in the discovery of novel genes and pathways associated with polygenic diseases, along with identification of candidate regulatory elements that modulate regulation of genes at risk loci (Evangelou et al., 2014; Evans et al., 2015; Kerkhof et al., 2010; Shah et al., 2020; Zhou et al., 2018). Indeed, as these are associative studies, validation of candidate causal variants and genes at these susceptibility loci must be accomplished through in vitro and in vivo experimentation (Alsaigh et al., 2021). Typically, these variants alter the expression of genes and more rarely directly change the protein structure and function. Early GWAS studies of atherosclerotic phenotypes including PAD have consistently shown signal at the 9p21 locus. Functional in vitro and in vivo work has demonstrated that dysregulation of Cdkn2b drives atherosclerosis through impaired TGF-β and efferocytosis (discussed later) (Kojima et al., 2014; Nanda et al., 2016).

Recently, the first large GWAS of PAD was performed using data from the Million Veterans Program (MVP), a large prospective cohort established by the United States Department of Veterans Affairs. This study revealed several loci overlapping with CAD and hypertension, including genes involved in cholesterol and lipid biosynthesis (Klarin et al., 2019). Surprisingly, another set of variants were found near genes involved in coagulation (*F5* encoding Factor V Leiden) and smoking (*CHRNA3*), suggesting a stronger contribution of thrombosis/smoking in the development of PAD. Factor V Leiden is a crucial component of the extrinsic pathway of the coagulation cascade, and mutations within *F5* result in hypercoagulable phenotypes including deep vein thrombosis and pulmonary embolism. Causal inference to the role of thrombosis in PAD has been performed through Mendelian randomization (MR), which uses genetic variants as instrumental variables to assess the causal relationship between an exposure and outcome, independent of confounders. This analysis found increased Factor VIII and VWF to be associated with PAD risk (FVIII: OR, 1.41 [95% CI, 1.23−1.62], $P = 6.0 \times 10-7$, VWF [von Willebrand factor]: OR, 1.28 [95% CI, 1.07−1.52], $P = .0073$) (Small et al., 2021).

As the variants identified through GWAS are not necessarily the causal variants, several techniques have been applied to help identify variants and genes that are highly likely to be causal. Commonly used approaches included assessment of the expression quantitative trait loci (eQTLs) in high linkage disequilibrium (LD) with the tagged variant (Hormozdiari et al., 2016). Perhaps the most powerful approach in prioritizing causal variants is the identification of variants in regulatory domains identified with ATAC-seq (Li et al., 2019). ATAC-seq is a functional genomics technique that identifies the open regions of chromatin within the genome (Mansisidor & Risca, 2022). Functional candidate variants are likely to be enriched in these open regions of chromatin. While this has been applied to CAD to identify regulatory elements at GWAS loci, it remains to be assessed for PAD susceptibility variants (Miller et al., 2016; Turner et al., 2022; Wang et al., 2022). In the context of CAD, single-cell ATAC-seq has been used to resolve the cell type-specific regulatory domains of CAD GWAS loci. For example, *NOS3* regulatory regions are open only in endothelial cells, and *CDH13* shows accessibility only in smooth muscle cells (Turner et al., 2022). Single-cell RNA sequencing of healthy and diseased tissue can lend further evidence to support candidate causal genes and cell types. The majority of CAD risk loci including *EDNRA*, *COL4A1*, and *SORT1* are differentially expressed in the smooth muscle cell population, suggesting that this cell type hold the most "disease relevance" (Slenders et al., 2021). As gene expression and chromatin accessibility data from the peripheral vasculature becomes available, its integration with PAD GWAS data will identify novel mechanisms and pathways involved in its pathogenesis.

Clinical correlation

Advances in genomics facilitate drug development by permitting prioritization of candidate causal genes and pathways. Recent genetics studies validate targeting hyperlipidemia. In GWAS of atherosclerotic phenotypes, including CAD and stroke, we find enrichment of candidate causal genes affecting lipid metabolism, thereby validating drugs targeting this pathway (Mishra et al., 2022; Tcheandjieu et al., 2022). In addition, the recent association of F5 with PAD through GWAS, lends mechanistic support to the COMPASS and VOYAGER PAD trials, which found that treatment with low-dose Rivaroxaban (2.5 mg twice daily) and Aspirin together reduced the risk of major adverse limb loss (MALE) and major adverse cardiac events (MACE) (Bonaca et al., 2020; Eikelboom et al., 2017; Fukaya & Leeper, 2020; Steffel et al., 2020). Although the precise mechanism by which Factor 5 contributes to PAD is unknown, a hypercoagulable state through genetic predisposition may explain histopathological findings of tibial arteries from patients with critical limb-threatening ischemia (CLTI), a severe form of PAD characterized by pain at rest or tissue loss. These samples demonstrate occlusion caused by a high burden of thrombus in addition to atherosclerotic disease (Narula et al., 2018).

Genetic susceptibility to aberrant lipid metabolism has also garnered novel treatments for atherosclerosis. The seminal finding that low-frequency loss-of-function mutations in human *PCSK9* cause decreased LDL and protect against CAD spurred the development of evolocumab and alirocumab, monoclonal antibodies inhibiting PCSK-9 (Bonaca et al., 2018; Cohen et al., 2005; Cohen et al., 2006; Deedwania et al., 2021; McKenney et al., 2012; Robinson et al., 2015; Sabatine et al., 2017). The FOURIER trial demonstrated the efficacy of evolocumab to lower the risk of MACE in patients with PAD (HR 0.79; 95%; CI, 0.66−0.94; $P = .0098$) and without PAD (HR 0.86; 95% CI, 0.80−0.93; $P = .0003$) (Bonaca et al., 2018).

Currently, emerging evidence suggests the IL-6 receptor may be a therapeutic target for PAD (Levin et al., 2021). Akin to the approaches described for the discovery of PCSK9, a missense variant of IL6R was found to be associated with reduced risk of CAD, abdominal aortic aneurysm, ischemic stroke, and PAD. The missense variant, ASP358ALA, likely perturbs membrane localization of the receptor, increasing circulating levels of IL6R. MR was subsequently applied to PAD GWAS summary statistics to infer causality of decreased membrane-bound IL6R with decreased risk of PAD across multiple genetic ancestries. This supports the concept of testing drugs targeting IL6 signaling (i.e., tocilizumab, sarilumab, siltuximab) for PAD.

Cellular pathophysiology

The molecular and cellular mechanisms underlying the formation of atherosclerotic plaque involve homeostatic dysregulation of both vascular stromal cells (i.e., endothelium and smooth muscle) and immune cell types (macrophages, T-cells, and neutrophils). Here, we will highlight and elaborate upon the multiple mechanisms that contribute to the initiation and progression of atherosclerosis and, consequently, PAD.

Hypercholesterolemia

As discussed above, there are a wealth of genetic studies describing the association of hypercholesterolemia with early-onset atherosclerosis and LDL deficiency with decreased risk of atherosclerosis. Indeed, the classic series of events involved in atheroma formation involve the invasion of low-density lipoprotein cholesterol (LDL-C) into the vessel wall (Fig. 6.2). Excess LDL-C invades the endothelium leading to a subintimal accumulation of cholesterol. An innate immune response involving the uptake of these particles by macrophages results in the formation of foam cells and the gross observation of the fatty streak. Initiation of atherosclerosis has thought to require modified LDL, typically oxidized-LDL (ox-LDL), which macrophages avidly uptake through scavengers receptors. These scavenger receptors are not downregulated in the setting of increased intracellular cholesterol content, unlike LDL-R, the canonical receptor-mediating LDL-uptake. Oxidized or acetylated LDL can be formed through a number of mechanisms including ferroptosis, which involves the generation of free-radicals as a result of iron metabolism (Fenton reaction) or direct enzymatic oxidation. Consistent with ample in vitro evidence of ox-LDL's proatherogenic contribution to foam cell formation and endothelial dysfunction, targeted inhibition of ox-LDL using a natural IgM antibody (E06) in animal models can reduce atherosclerotic burden by over 50% (Que et al., 2018). The efficacy of this approach; however, remains to be evaluated in patients. On the other hand, targeted inhibition of LDL synthesis or uptake with HMG-coreductase inhibition (statin) or PCSK-9 inhibitors has yielded remarkable protection from atherosclerotic disease. In fact, plaque regression was observed in the GLAGOV and JUPITER trials, testing efficacy of PCSK9 inhibitors and rosuvastatin, respectively (Nicholls et al., 2018; Ridker et al., 2008).

Inflammation and resolution

The immune response within the atherosclerotic lesions can be characterized, albeit simply, as a battle between the initial inflammatory response and a resolution phase. Indeed, inflammation is a necessary corollary of vascular injury by LDL-C in the context of hypercholesterolemia. In response to cholesterol deposition, endothelial cells upregulate vascular cell adhesion molecule-1, allowing binding of monocytes and T-cells to the endothelium and ultimately infiltration into the subintimal space. The recruitment of monocytes to the nascent plaque plays an important role in atheroma progression, as inhibition of chemokines necessary for monocyte recruitment (CCL2/5), attenuate plaque size in animal models (Combadière et al., 2008). Furthermore, emerging evidence suggests that subpopulations of monocytes recruited to the atheromatous lesion have differing roles within the plaque. For instance, in mice $Ly6C^{hi}$ monocytes differentiate to phenotypically inflammatory macrophages, whereas $Ly6C^{low}$ monocytes differentiate to macrophages involved in angiogenesis and matrix production. Though further discussion of these nuances is beyond the scope of this chapter, this is an emerging area of research (Zhou et al., 2000).

In addition to an innate immune response mediated by monocyte-derived macrophages, the presence of T-cells was first identified through histological examination of atherosclerotic plaque, suggesting a role of the adaptive immune system in atherogenesis (Hansson et al., 1988). The advent of single RNA sequencing has refined our understanding of the distinct subpopulations of T-cells within plaque. The majority of T-cells are T_H1 cells, which potentiate the inflammatory response through IFN-γ secretion and induce classical activation of macrophages (M1). T-cells specifically appear to play a critical role in atherogenesis. In an immunodeficient $SCID/ApoE^{-/-}$ mouse, which lacks T- and B-cells, atherosclerotic lesion size decreased by

73% compared to immunocompetent controls. Conversely, transfer of T-cells from an immunocompetent mouse to SCID/ApoE$^{-/-}$ increased lesion size by 164%.

In contrast, the resolution phase is mediated by alternatively activated (M2) macrophages, which secrete antiinflammatory cytokines including transforming growth factor beta (TGF-β), IL-10, IL-4, and IL-13. In addition, a minority of T-cells are of the T_H2 and T_{REG} subtypes, which secrete antiinflammatory cytokines and promote alternative activation of macrophages (M2).

The inflammatory response has a range of consequences in vascular stromal cells. On the endothelium, inflammatory ligands stimulate early GPCR-mediated type I endothelial activation, during which P-selectin and platelet-activating factor are released from Weibel–Palade bodies (Bach et al., 1995). This facilitates binding of leukocytes to the vascular endothelium. Subsequently, type 2 endothelial activation, mediated by stimulation of inflammatory cytokine receptors, is responsible for the diapedesis, or transmigration, of leukocytes across the endothelium. While type 1 activation persists on the order of minutes, type 2 activation is a coordinated long-term process that involves downregulation of selectins and recruitment of T-helper cells populations described above. Similarly, vascular smooth muscle cells undergo a process termed "phenotype switching", through which they acquire novel cell fates (Wirka et al., 2019). Lineage tracing experiments combined with single-cell sequencing technology shows that vascular smooth muscle cells (vSMCs) dedifferentiate to a multipotent cell type, termed "SEM", in atherosclerotic lesions. These cells have the capacity to differentiate from a contractile cell-type to synthetic fibrochondrocyte- and macrophage-like cell types (Pan et al., 2020; Shankman et al., 2015; Wang et al., 2020). The proliferative fibrochondrocyte-like cell is thought to secrete a matrix rich in fibronectin, type I, and type III collagens. Imbalance of collagen matrix can lead to destabilization of the fibrous cap of the atheroma, predisposing to plaque rupture. In addition, cleavage of the aberrantly generated extracellular matrix generates matrikines, which have the capability to further potentiate inflammatory signaling (Sorokin, 2010). Macrophage-like vSMCs participate in phagocytosis of oxidized-LDL and generate foam cells, thereby contributing to the growth of the necrotic core (Pan et al., 2020).

Several lines of experimental evidence suggest the deleterious effect of IL-1B. In animal models, global knockout of IL-1B or its receptor (IL1R1) decrease plaque burden in, whereas knockout of the IL-1 decoy receptor (IL1RN) increases plaque formation

(Isoda et al., 2004; Kirii et al., 2003). However, elegant work from Gary Owen's group assessing the role of chronic inflammation in atherosclerosis has suggested a more nuanced role of IL-1 signaling. Inhibition of IL-1B or its receptor after induction of atherosclerosis results in decreased atherosclerotic burden in Apoe$^{-/-}$ mouse aorta; however, the resulting plaque was noted to have an attenuated fibrous cap, decreased collagen content, and an enrichment of macrophages within the plaque (Gomez et al., 2018). They went on to show that this process was dependent on inflammatory signaling within the vSMC population. Clinically, these findings may promote plaque instability with resulting rupture and thromboembolism.

The clinical utility of targeting inflammatory signaling has been tested in several clinical trials, the most prominent being the CANTOS trial (Ridker et al., 2017). In CANTOS, investigators tested the utility of canakinumab, a monoclonal antibody targeting IL-1B, to reduce recurrent cardiovascular events and improve mortality in patients with prior myocardial infarction and elevated C-reactive protein (a marker of systemic inflammation). Treatment with canakinumab compared to placebo protected against recurrent cardiovascular events but did not reduce all-cause mortality (Ridker et al., 2017). Reanalysis of patients who responded to the drug, as measured by CRP reduction below the median, demonstrated an even greater reduction in recurrent cardiovascular events as well as a reduction in mortality.

Macrophage dysfunction

As described above, macrophage accumulation as foam cells is a key consequence of the inflammatory milieu in atherosclerotic lesions. The mechanism by which this occurs involves (1) impaired cholesterol efflux and (2) dysregulation of a process known as programmed cell removal, or efferocytosis (Fig. 6.3) (Yoko Kojima et al., 2020).

Reverse cholesterol efflux has been shown to be mediated through multiple independent routes including ABCA-1, which conjugates cholesterol to apolipoprotein to create high-density lipoprotein (HDL). M1 polarized cells downregulate expression of ABCA-1, inhibiting the efflux of cholesterol from macrophages (Khovidhunkit et al., 2003). Conversely, CDKN2B-deficient apoptotic vSMCs fail to initiate activation of ABCA-1, and these macrophages have been shown to secrete increased proinflammatory cytokine TNF-a and decreased antiinflammatory cytokine IL-10 (Kojima et al., 2014). Taken together, these findings place dysregulation of efferocytosis in the center of a proinflammatory

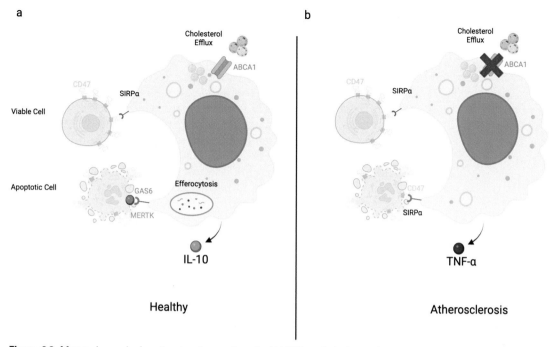

Figure 6.3 Macrophage dysfunction in atherosclerosis. (A) Efflux of cholesterol to apolipoprotein occurs via transports like ABCA1. Viable cells evade phagocytosis through binding of CD47 by SIRPα, which transduces signal inhibitory for phagocytosis. Activation of efferocytosis occurs through interaction of GAS6-MerTK pathway. Efferocytosis results in the secretion of antiinflammatory cytokine IL-10. (B) In atherosclerosis, cholesterol efflux is impaired, which supports the generation of foam cells, which secrete inflammatory cytokines. Apoptotic cells maintain expression of CD47 and evade efferocytosis, leading to accumulating debris within the necrotic core.

positive feedback mechanism. These M1 polarized cells cannot efficiently clear cholesterol, resulting in the generation of lipid-laden foam cells and their accumulation in the necrotic core.

Efferocytosis is a highly coordinated process to ensure clearance of only apoptotic cells and sparing of healthy cells. Efferocytosis involves not only phagocytosis of the target apoptotic cell but also the appropriate clearance of cellular debris and expression of antiinflammatory cytokines (TGF-β and IL-10) to promote atheroma resolution. Within the plaque, both phagocytosis of apoptotic cells and clearance of these cells/LDL are impaired. Professional phagocytes (i.e., monocyte-derived macrophages) are the primary cell type engaging in efferocytosis, though nonprofessional phagocytes, including macrophage-like vSMCs, can similarly participate in this process. Regulation of efferocytosis by macrophages is mediated through the multiple mechanisms, the CD47-SIRPa axis being one of the most prominent and well-studied to date (Jarr et al., 2021, p. 42). CD47 is a "don't eat me" signal present on all healthy cell types and binds its receptor SIRPα on macrophages to prevent phagocytosis. Conversely, during apoptosis, cell-surface expression of this protein is downregulated to cue clearance by macrophages. While SIRPα signaling usually inhibits phagocytosis, lack of this signal permits the macrophage to initiate efferocytosis. Inflammatory signaling results in retained or increased expression of CD47 on apoptotic cells, rendering them inedible by macrophages. Macrophages polarized to an M2 phenotype participate in efferocytosis to a greater degree than classically activated (M1 macrophages) in cardiovascular disease.

Thrombosis

In PAD, each component of Virchow's triad (hemostasis, hypercoagulability, and endothelial dysfunction) contributes to the thrombosis seen in the tibial vasculature of patients with CLTI (Narula et al., 2018). Thrombosis presents either as acute limb ischemia, or in the setting of chronic multifocal disease, presents in a subacute manner as the patient has had the opportunity to develop collateral flow through angiogenesis and arteriogenesis. However, as discussed above, genetic studies including GWAS and MR imply a causal and unique role of thrombosis in the development of PAD. Several prothrombotic mechanisms contribute to diminished peripheral perfusion through both mechanical obstruction and progression of atherosclerosis.

First, pathological low-flow conditions distal to an atherosclerotic lesion contribute to thrombosis. Perturbations to normal laminar flow occur both at the site of stenotic lesions, characterized by increased flow velocity and shear stress. Distal to these lesions, turbulent flow and low shear stress (below 100/s) increase blood viscosity and vascular resistance (Hathcock, 2006). In addition, these conditions promote cell–cell interactions through upregulation of intracellular adhesion molecule-4 (ICAM-4) on red blood cells and CD36 on platelets. These cell aggregates, named Rouleaux formations due to their appearance of stacked coins, further increase vascular resistance. Concomitantly, decreased shear stress drives endothelial dysfunction through inhibition of NOS3 expression and potentiation of NF-kB expression. Inflammatory signaling by the endothelium leads to expression of tissue factor (TF), which binds to circulating Factor 7 (F7). Platelets, activated during periods of high shear stress at stenotic lesions, accrue to a dysfunctional endothelium to initiate a prothrombotic cascade. Although it remains to be validated experimentally, one may speculate that the susceptibility to thrombosis increases in the lower extremity due to the length of diseased vessel.

Dysfunctional endothelium seen in areas of low shear stress not only predisposes to thrombosis but also contributes to atherogenesis. Decreased eNOS prevents vasorelaxation through the NO-cGMP axis, and results in eNOS uncoupling, a process by which eNOS produces superoxide radicals rather than NO. Low shear stress is thought to activate the angiotensin II type-1 receptor (AT1R), which uncouples eNOS through aberrant phosphorylation (Chao et al., 2018). Interestingly, eNOS uncoupling induced through low shear stress can be reversed with administration of Losartan, which inhibits AT1R. As discussed above, the presence of free radicals can accelerate accumulation of foam cells through generation of ox-LDL.

Second, oxidized LDL, cholesterol crystals, and ROS stimulate release of thrombotic components from plaque neutrophils as well as macrophages. Activated neutrophils release prothrombotic webs of decondensed chromatin termed neutrophil extracellular traps (NETs). This process, termed NETosis, was initially thought to capture and remove pathogenic organisms, such as bacteria, fungi, and protozoa (Brinkmann et al., 2004). Over the past decade, NETs have been implicated in a plethora of inflammatory pathophysiologies, including Alzheimer's disease (Zenaro et al., 2015), diabetes mellitus (Wong et al., 2015), autoimmune vasculitis (Kessenbrock et al., 2009), as well as atherosclerosis (Awasthi et al., 2016; Liu et al., 2018; Megens et al., 2012; Warnatsch et al., 2015). NETosis is largely mediated through neutrophil elastase (NE), which translocates to the nucleus to degrade histones, and peptidyl arginine deiminase 4 (PAD4), which citrullinates histones; both modifications contribute to chromatin decondensation exposing prothrombotic histones H3/H4.

This process in part drives the association of inflammation with thrombosis. Intraluminal NET scaffolds permit aggregation of platelets/RBCs and accumulation of plasma proteins, leading to a high local concentration of thrombotic factors including VWF, TF, prothrombin, and fibrinogen, the precursor of fibrin, which stabilizes thrombus (Fuchs et al., 2010). NETs and the local inflammatory milieu further stimulate circulating monocytes and tissue macrophages to secrete TF (Meisel et al., 2002, 2011; Reyes-García et al., 2019). The abundance of TF leads to thrombin production, which activate platelets, further stimulating aggregation and fibrin formation. Interestingly, NETs may provide a scaffold for thrombus independent of fibrin. Warnatsch et al. (2015) found that mice-lacking ApoE and NE (which eliminates their ability of form NETs) fed a high-fat diet (HFD) display reduced atherogenesis at 8 weeks. In this mouse model, they showed that NETs in conjunction with cholesterol-primed macrophages activate IL-1B expression, facilitating recruitment of T_H17 cells. These cells in turn recruit additional immune cells to the lesion through secretion of IL-17. Similarly, abrogation of NET formation through deletion of PAD4 yielded reduced atherosclerotic burden and vascular inflammation in ApoE$^{-/-}$ mice (Liu et al., 2018).

Finally, plaque rupture and thromboembolism are often an acute manifestation of PAD. Many of the mechanisms discussed above can predispose plaque to rupture and thrombose. An enlarging necrotic core rich with macrophages expressing TF, a thin fibrous cap caused by aberrant production of type I/III collagens by fibrochondrocyte-like vSMCs along with overexpression of MMPs, and a hypercoagulable state all contribute to the "vulnerability" of the plaque. Furthermore, the plaque is inherently thrombogenic through the expression of TF on activated macrophages within the lipid-rich core (Toschi et al., 1997).

Hyperglycemia and insulin resistance in diabetes mellitus

Diabetes mellitus is characterized by chronic hyperglycemia due to insufficient insulin production or resistance, along with chronic inflammation. The majority of these patients (90% −95%) have type 2 diabetes mellitus (T2DM), caused by insulin insufficiency and resistance due to prolonged hyperglycemia, whereas 5%−10% of patients have type 1 diabetes, which occurs due to autoimmune destruction of the pancreatic beta cells (Beckman et al., 2002). Epidemiological studies have shown that T2DM increases the risk of PAD two to four fold, and among patients with PAD, 20%−30% have diabetes (Barnes et al., 2020; Beckman et al., 2002; Marso & Hiatt, 2006). Furthermore, the risk of PAD increases proportional to diabetes severity. The UK prospective diabetes study found a 28% increase in PAD risk per 1% increase in HbA1c (Adler et al., 2002). Interestingly, the presentation of PAD in patients with diabetes is characterized by diffuse calcified atherosclerotic lesions predominant in the tibial arteries (Beckman et al., 2021; Stabley & Towler, 2017). Calcified vessels at the ankle can cause a falsely elevated arterial-brachial index (ABIs), a key measure of lower extremity perfusion, as the vessels become noncompressible.

The etiology of atherosclerosis in diabetes involves the aforementioned pathophysiological mechanisms acting in concert, ultimately driven by hyperglycemia and insulin resistance. First, hyperlipidemia is present in over 70% of patients with diabetes, who have increased LDL, VLDL, and triglycerides but decreased HDL (Harris, 1991; Hirano, 2018; Hu et al., 2022). Insulin directly suppresses both the release of free fatty acids from adipose tissue and apoB secretion from hepatocytes (Hirano, 2018; Sparks et al., 1986). Increases in serum apoB lead to increased LDL and VLDL upon cholesterol binding. Second, patients with diabetes exhibit chronic low-grade inflammation, which is caused by hyperglycemia-induced oxidative stress. Increased flux of glucose through metabolic pathways and formation of advanced glycation end products (AGEs) reduce antioxidant concentration and increases amounts of ROS (Fiorentino et al., 2013). In human monocytes, hyperglycemia-induced oxidative stress can activate the NLRP3 inflammasome to generate IL-1B and IL-18, in addition to activation of NF-kB-responsive genes, IL-6 and TNF-α (Fiorentino et al., 2013; Tseng et al., 2016; Ye et al., 2022).

This proinflammatory state caused by NLRP3 activation causes platelet activation and thrombosis. This may occur indirectly through endothelial dysfunction in an inflammatory environment as discussed above, or directly through NLRP3 activation in platelets, through downstream secretion of IL-1B and IL-18 (Vogel et al., 2019). This may explain earlier clinical findings that hyperglycemic conditions increased platelet aggregation and activation in response to high shear stress (Gresele et al., 2003).

The NLRP3 inflammasome appears to be a promising drug target for DM-mediated atherosclerosis as it contributes to both inflammation and thrombosis. Treatment with the majority of commonly used oral agents for DM attenuate activity of the NLRP3 inflammasome, likely indirectly through improvement of hyperglycemia and reduction of ROS. Sharma et al. tested the utility of a NLRP3-specific inhibitor MCC950 on mitigating atherosclerotic burden in mice treated with streptozocin, which destroys pancreatic beta-cells. MCC950 significantly reduces atherosclerotic plaque burden and the size of the necrotic core in hyperglycemic ApoE$^{-/-}$ mice. In both mouse aorta and a human monocyte cell line (THP-1), MCC950 treatment reduced the expression of IL-1B and caspase-1 (Sharma et al., 2021).

Vascular calcification

Perhaps the most distinctive feature of diabetic PAD is the preponderance of diffuse calcification, particularly within the media (Al-Aly, 2007; Snell-Bergeon et al., 2013; Stabley & Towler, 2017). Rather than focal atherosclerotic lesions, we often observe long-segment stiffening of the below-knee run-off vessels. As discussed above, a combination of endothelial dysfunction, oxidative stress, and inflammatory cascades can drive "phenotype switching" of vSMCs. After dedifferentiation to an intermediate cell type, they can become not only fibrochondrocyte-like, but also osteoblast-like. Wild-type mice treated with streptozocin for 5 days stimulates vSMCs to secrete a calcified matrix, which diminishes vascular compliance. This occurs through O-GlcNacylation of AKT, which increases its phosphorylation resulting in activation (Heath et al., 2014). Phosphorylated AKT in vSMCs upregulated the transcription factor Runx2, whose targets include osteopontin, bone sialoprotein, fibronectin, MMP13, TRAM2, and osteoprotegerin, all involved in osteogenesis and calcified matrix production (Pregizer et al., 2007). In addition to intracellular protein glycation, extracellular signals, such as AGE, can also stimulate vascular calcification through facilitating HIF-1α nuclear translocation and downstream activation of Runx2 (Zhu et al., 2018).

The db/db mouse, a leptin-deficient model of T2DM, provides further insight on the pathogenesis of calcific arteriosclerosis. The progressive hyperglycemia that develops in this model was shown to induce expression of BMP-2, an upstream regulator of Runx2 and the osteogenic program, and NF-kB. Both BMP signaling and an inflammatory program mediated by NF-kB are sufficient to activate Runx2 expression (Boström et al., 2011; Raaz et al., 2015). Human aortic endothelial cells exhibit a dose-responsive increase in BMP-2 on stimulation with increasing glucose load (Boström et al., 2011). However, Runx2 alone is not sufficient to induce vascular calcification. In a transgenic mouse model that overexpresses Runx2 specifically in smooth muscle cells, systemic arterial stiffness is increased through upregulation of type I collagen, without evidence of arterial calcification.

Systemic alterations in metabolism, specifically derangement of calcium metabolism, seen in diabetes may provide a substrate for the stiff type I collagen rich matrix. Systematic review and meta-analysis confirm the association with hypercalcemia and T2DM; hypercalcemic patients have an increased risk of incident T2DM (RR:1.25, CI: 1.1−1.25) (Zhu et al., 2019). Yet the mechanisms underlying this association remain to be illustrated.

Paradoxically, streptozocin treatment in rats inhibits intestinal absorption of calcium ion and reduces renal resorption of calcium and phosphate (Anwana & Garland, 1990; Rivoira et al., 2015). Indeed this may be a response to systemic hypercalcemia. Vascular calcification in diabetes is therefore a multifactorial process involving inflammation-driven transdifferentiation of vascular smooth muscle as well as aberrant calcium metabolism.

Conclusion

As discussed above, the convergence of multiple interconnected pathophysiological processes manifests as PAD. As we begin to dissect each of the mechanisms through genetic, molecular, and cellular approaches, we will learn the shared factors underlying PAD, as well as the driving processes in subsets of patients (e.g., diabetic PAD). This will pave the way for drug discovery and eventually personalized therapeutic approaches for PAD. As we have illustrated, genetic studies have validated the clinical utility of antithrombotics in PAD and helped pave the road for PCSK9 inhibitors for hyperlipidemia/PAD. Ongoing recruitment of patients into large biorepositories, such as the UK Biobank and MVP, will allows scientists to leverage genomics to identify and prioritize novel candidate genes and biological processes mediating various PAD phenotypes. These hypothesis-generating studies can be validated using in vitro and animal model systems prior to clinical trials. We are only at the outset of our molecular/cellular understanding of PAD, with much to learn and many treatments to be discovered.

References

Aday, A. W., & Matsushita, K. (2021). Epidemiology of peripheral artery disease and polyvascular disease. *Circulation Research, 128*(12), 1818−1832. https://doi.org/10.1161/CIRCRESAHA.121.318535, 15244571.

Adler, A. I., Stevens, R. J., Neil, A., Stratton, I. M., Boulton, A. J. M., & Holman, R. R. (2002). UKPDS 59: Hyperglycemia and other potentially modifiable risk factors for peripheral vascular disease in type 2 diabetes. *Diabetes Care, 25*(5), 894−899. https://doi.org/10.2337/diacare.25.5.894

Al-Aly, Z. (2007). Medial vascular calcification in diabetes mellitus and chronic kidney disease: The role of inflammation. *Cardiovascular and Hematological Disorders — Drug Targets, 7*(1), 1−6. https://doi.org/10.2174/187152907780059047, 1871529X.

Alsaigh, T., Bartolo, B. A. D., Mulangala, J., Figtree, G. A., & Leeper, N. J. (2021). Bench-to-Bedside in vascular medicine: Optimizing the translational pipeline for patients with peripheral artery disease. *Circulation Research, 128.*

Anwana, A. B., & Garland, H. O. (1990). Renal calcium and magnesium handling in experimental diabetes mellitus in the rat. *Acta Endocrinologica, 122*(4), 479–486. https://doi.org/10.1530/acta.0.1220479, 00015598.

Awasthi, D., Nagarkoti, S., Kumar, A., Dubey, M., Singh, A. K., Pathak, P., Chandra, T., Barthwal, M. K., & Dikshit, M. (2016). Oxidized LDL induced extracellular trap formation in human neutrophils via TLR-PKC-IRAK-MAPK and NADPH-oxidase activation. *Free Radical Biology and Medicine, 93*, 190–203. https://doi.org/10.1016/j.freeradbiomed.2016.01.004, 18734596.

Bach, F. H., Robson, S. C., Winkler, H., Ferran, C., Stuhlmeier, K. M., Wrighton, C. J., & Hancock, W. W. (1995). Barriers to xenotransplantation. *Nature Medicine, 1*(9), 869–873. https://doi.org/10.1038/nm0995-869, 1546170X.

Barnes, J. A., Eid, M. A., Creager, M. A., & Goodney, P. P. (2020). Epidemiology and risk of amputation in patients with diabetes mellitus and peripheral artery disease. *Arteriosclerosis, Thrombosis, and Vascular Biology, 40*(8), 1808–1817. https://doi.org/10.1161/ATVBAHA.120.314595, 15244636.

Beckman, J. A., Creager, M. A., & Libby, P. (2002). Diabetes and atherosclerosis epidemiology, pathophysiology, and management. *Journal of the American Medical Association, 287*(19), 2570–2581. https://doi.org/10.1001/jama.287.19.2570, 00987484.

Beckman, J. A., Schneider, P. A., & Conte, M. S. (2021). Advances in revascularization for peripheral artery disease: Revascularization in PAD. *Circulation Research, 128*(12), 1885–1912. https://doi.org/10.1161/CIRCRESAHA.121.318261, 15244571.

Bonaca, M. P., Nault, P., Giugliano, R. P., Keech, A. C., Pineda, A. L., Kanevsky, E., Kuder, J., Murphy, S. A., Jukema, J. W., Lewis, B. S., Tokgozoglu, L., Somaratne, R., Sever, P. S., Pedersen, T. R., & Sabatine, M. S. (2018). Low-density lipoprotein cholesterol lowering with evolocumab and outcomes in patients with peripheral artery disease. *Circulation, 137*(4), 338–350. https://doi.org/10.1161/circulationaha.117.032235, 0009-7322.

Bonaca, M. P., Bauersachs, R. M., Anand, S. S., Debus, E. S., Nehler, M. R., Patel, M. R., Fanelli, F., Capell, W. H., Diao, L., Jaeger, N., Hess, C. N., Pap, A. F., Kittelson, J. M., Gudz, I., Mátyás, L., Krievins, D. K., Diaz, R., Brodmann, M., Muehlhofer, E., … Hiatt, W. R. (2020). Rivaroxaban in peripheral artery disease after revascularization. *New England Journal of Medicine, 382*(21), 1994–2004. https://doi.org/10.1056/NEJMoa2000052, 15334406.

Boström, K. I., Jumabay, M., Matveyenko, A., Nicholas, S. B., & Yao, Y. (2011). Activation of vascular bone morphogenetic protein signaling in diabetes mellitus. *Circulation Research, 108*(4), 446–457. https://doi.org/10.1161/CIRCRESAHA.110.236596, 15244571.

Brinkmann, V., Reichard, U., Goosmann, C., Fauler, B., Uhlemann, Y., Weiss, D. S., Weinrauch, Y., & Zychlinsky, A. (2004). Neutrophil extracellular traps kill bacteria. *Science, 303*(5663), 1532–1535. https://doi.org/10.1126/science.1092385

Carmelli, D., Fabsitz, R. R., Swan, G. E., Reed, T., Miller, B., & Wolf, P. A. (2000). Contribution of genetic and environmental influences to Ankle-Brachial blood pressure index in the NHLBI twin study. *American Journal of Epidemiology, 151*(5), 452–458. https://doi.org/10.1093/oxfordjournals.aje.a010230, 00029262.

Chao, Y., Ye, P., Zhu, L., Kong, X., Qu, X., Zhang, J., Luo, J., Yang, H., & Chen, S. (2018). Low shear stress induces endothelial reactive oxygen species via the AT1R/eNOS/NO pathway. *Journal of Cellular Physiology, 233*(2), 1384−1395. https://doi.org/10.1002/jcp.26016, 28518223.

Cohen, J. C., Boerwinkle, E., Mosley, T. H., & Hobbs, H. H. (2006). Sequence variations in PCSK9, low LDL, and protection against coronary heart disease. *New England Journal of Medicine, 354*(12), 1264−1272. https://doi.org/10.1056/NEJMoa054013, 15334406.

Cohen, J., Pertsemlidis, A., Kotowski, I. K., Graham, R., Garcia, C. K., & Hobbs, H. H. (2005). Low LDL cholesterol in individuals of African descent resulting from frequent nonsense mutations in PCSK9. *Nature Genetics, 37*(2), 161−165. https://doi.org/10.1038/ng1509, 15461718.

Combadière, C., Potteaux, S., Rodero, M., Simon, T., Pezard, A., Esposito, B., Merval, R., Proudfoot, A., Tedgui, A., & Mallat, Z. (2008). Combined inhibition of CCL2, CX3CR1, and CCR5 abrogates Ly6Chi and Ly6Clo monocytosis and almost abolishes atherosclerosis in hypercholesterolemic mice. *Circulation, 117*(13), 1649−1657. https://doi.org/10.1161/CIRCULATIONAHA.107.745091, 00097322.

Deedwania, P., Murphy, S. A., Scheen, A., Badariene, J., Pineda, A. L., Honarpour, N., Keech, A. C., Sever, P. S., Pedersen, T. R., Sabatine, M. S., & Giugliano, R. P. (2021). Efficacy and safety of PCSK9 inhibition with evolocumab in reducing cardiovascular events in patients with metabolic syndrome receiving statin therapy. *JAMA Cardiology, 6*(2), 139. https://doi.org/10.1001/jamacardio.2020.3151, 2380-6583.

Drobni, Z. D., Kolossvary, M., Karady, J., Jermendy, A. L., Tarnoki, A. D., Tarnoki, D. L., Simon, J., Szilveszter, B., Littvay, L., Voros, S., Jermendy, G., Merkely, B., & Maurovich-Horvat, P. (2022). Heritability of coronary artery disease: Insights from a classical twin study. *Circulation: Cardiovascular Imaging, 15*(3), 133−141. https://doi.org/10.1161/CIRCIMAGING.121.013348, 19420080.

Eikelboom, J. W., Connolly, S. J., Bosch, J., Dagenais, G. R., Hart, R. G., Shestakovska, O., Diaz, R., Alings, M., Lonn, E. M., Anand, S. S., Widimsky, P., Hori, M., Avezum, A., Piegas, L. S., Branch, K. R. H., Probstfield, J., Bhatt, D. L., Zhu, J., Liang, Y., … Yusuf, S. (2017). Rivaroxaban with or without Aspirin in stable cardiovascular disease. *New England Journal of Medicine, 377*(14), 1319−1330. https://doi.org/10.1056/NEJMoa1709118, 0028-4793.

Evangelou, E., Kerkhof, H. J., Styrkarsdottir, U., Ntzani, E. E., Bos, S. D., Esko, T., Evans, D. S., Metrustry, S., Panoutsopoulou, K., Ramos, Y. F. M., Thorleifsson, G., Tsilidis, K. K., Arden, N., Aslam, N., Bellamy, N., Birrell, F., Blanco, F. J., Carr, A., Chapman, K., … Valdes, A. M. (2014). A meta-analysis of genome-wide association studies identifies novel variants associated with osteoarthritis of the hip. *Annals of the Rheumatic Diseases, 73*(12), 2130−2136. https://doi.org/10.1136/annrheumdis-2012-203114, 14682060.

Evans, D. S., Cailotto, F., Parimi, N., Valdes, A. M., Castaño-Betancourt, M. C., Liu, Y., Kaplan, R. C., Bidlingmaier, M., Vasan, R. S., Teumer, A., Tranah, G. J., Nevitt, M. C., Cummings, S. R., Orwoll, E. S., Barrett-Connor, E., Renner, J. B., Jordan, J. M., Doherty, M., Doherty, S. A., … Lane, N. E. (2015). Genome-wide association and functional studies identify a role for IGFBP3 in hip osteoarthritis. *Annals of the Rheumatic Diseases, 74*(10), 1861−1867. https://doi.org/10.1136/annrheumdis-2013-205020, 14682060.

Fiorentino, T. V., Prioletta, A., Zuo, P., & Folli, F. (2013). Hyperglycemia-induced oxidative stress and its role in diabetes mellitus related cardiovascular diseases. *Current Pharmaceutical Design, 19*(32), 5695–5703. https://doi.org/10.2174/1381612811319320005, 18734286.

Fuchs, T. A., Brill, A., Duerschmied, D., Schatzberg, D., Monestier, M., Myers, D. D., Wrobleski, S. K., Wakefield, T. W., Hartwig, J. H., & Wagner, D. D. (2010). Extracellular DNA traps promote thrombosis. *Proceedings of the National Academy of Sciences of the United States of America, 107*(36), 15880–15885. https://doi.org/10.1073/pnas.1005743107, 10916490.

Fukaya, E., & Leeper, N. J. (2020). The impact of low-dose anticoagulation therapy on peripheral artery disease: Insights from the VOYAGER trial. *Cardiovascular Research, 116*(12), E156–E158. https://doi.org/10.1093/cvr/cvaa225, 17553245.

Gerhard-Herman, M. D., Gornik, H. L., Barrett, C., Barshes, N. R., Corriere, M. A., Drachman, D. E., Fleisher, L. A., Fowkes, F. G. R., Hamburg, N. M., Kinlay, S., Lookstein, R., Misra, S., Mureebe, L., Olin, J. W., Patel, R. A. G., Regensteiner, J. G., Schanzer, A., Shishehbor, M. H., Stewart, K. J., Treat-Jacobson, D., & Walsh, M. E. (2017). 2016 AHA/ACC guideline on the management of patients with lower extremity peripheral artery disease: Executive summary: A report of the American College of Cardiology/American heart association task force on clinical practice guidelines. *Circulation, 135*(12). https://doi.org/10.1161/cir.0000000000000470, 0009-7322.

Gomez, D., Baylis, R. A., Durgin, B. G., Newman, A. A. C., Alencar, G. F., Mahan, S., St Hilaire, C., Müller, W., Waisman, A., Francis, S. E., Pinteaux, E., Randolph, G. J., Gram, H., & Owens, G. K. (2018). Interleukin-1β has atheroprotective effects in advanced atherosclerotic lesions of mice. *Nature Medicine, 24*(9), 1418–1429. https://doi.org/10.1038/s41591-018-0124-5, 1546170X.

Gresele, P., Guglielmini, G., De Angelis, M., Ciferri, S., Ciofetta, M., Falcinelli, E., Lalli, C., Ciabattoni, G., Davì, G., & Bolli, G. B. (2003). Acute, short-term hyperglycemia enhances shear stress-induced platelet activation in patients with Type II diabetes mellitus. *Journal of the American College of Cardiology, 41*(6), 1013–1020. https://doi.org/10.1016/S0735-1097(02)02972-8, 07351097.

Gudmundsson, G., Matthiasson, S. E., Arason, H., Johannsson, H., Runarsson, F., Bjarnason, H., Helgadottir, K., Thorisdottir, S., Ingadottir, G., Lindpaintner, K., Sainz, J., Gudnason, V., Frigge, M. L., Kong, A., Gulcher, J. R., & Stefansson, K. (2002). Localization of a gene for peripheral arterial occlusive disease to chromosome 1p31. *The American Journal of Human Genetics, 70*(3), 586–592. https://doi.org/10.1086/339251, 00029297.

Hansson, G. K., Jonasson, L., Lojsthed, B., Stemme, S., Kocher, O., & Gabbiani, G. (1988). Localization of T lymphocytes and macrophages in fibrous and complicated human atherosclerotic plaques. *Atherosclerosis, 72*(2–3), 135–141. https://doi.org/10.1016/0021-9150(88)90074-3, 00219150.

Harris, M. I. (1991). Hypercholesterolemia in diabetes and glucose intolerance in the U.S. population. *Diabetes Care, 14*(5), 366–374. https://doi.org/10.2337/diacare.14.5.366, 01495992.

Hathcock, J. J. (2006). Flow effects on coagulation and thrombosis. *Arteriosclerosis, Thrombosis, and Vascular Biology, 26*(8), 1729–1737, 16741150.

Heath, J. M., Sun, Y., Yuan, K., Bradley, W. E., Litovsky, S., Dell'Italia, L. J., Chatham, J. C., Wu, H., & Chen, Y. (2014). Activation of AKT by O-linked N-Acetylglucosamine induces vascular calcification in diabetes mellitus. *Circulation Research, 114*(7), 1094—1102. https://doi.org/10.1161/CIRCRESAHA.114.302968, 15244571.

Hirano, T. (2018). Pathophysiology of diabetic dyslipidemia. *Journal of Atherosclerosis and Thrombosis, 25*(9), 771—782. https://doi.org/10.5551/jat.RV17023, 18803873.

Hormozdiari, F., van de Bunt, M., Segrè, A. V., Li, X., Joo, J. W. J., Bilow, M., Sul, J. H., Sankararaman, S., Pasaniuc, B., & Eskin, E. (2016). Colocalization of GWAS and eQTL signals detects target genes. *The American Journal of Human Genetics, 99*(6), 1245—1260. https://doi.org/10.1016/j.ajhg.2016.10.003, 15376605.

Hu, X., Liu, Q., Guo, X., Wang, W., Yu, B., Liang, B., Zhou, Y., Dong, H., & Lin, J. (2022). The role of remnant cholesterol beyond low-density lipoprotein cholesterol in diabetes mellitus. *Cardiovascular Diabetology, 21*(1). https://doi.org/10.1186/s12933-022-01554-0, 14752840.

Isoda, K., Sawada, S., Ishigami, N., Matsuki, T., Miyazaki, K., Kusuhara, M., Iwakura, Y., & Ohsuzu, F. (2004). Lack of interleukin-1 receptor antagonist modulates plaque composition in apolipoprotein E-deficient mice. *Arteriosclerosis, Thrombosis, and Vascular Biology, 24*(6), 1068—1073. https://doi.org/10.1161/01.ATV.0000127025.48140.a3

Jarr, K.-U., Kojima, Y., Weissman, I. L., & Leeper, N. J. (2021). *Jeffrey M. Hoeg Award Lecture: Defining the role of efferocytosis in cardiovascular disease: A focus on the CD47 (Cluster of differentiation 47) Axis.*

Kerkhof, H. J. M., Lories, R. J., Meulenbelt, I., Jonsdottir, I., Valdes, A. M., Arp, P., Ingvarsson, T., Jhamai, M., Jonsson, H., Stolk, L., Thorleifsson, G., Zhai, G., Zhang, F., Zhu, Y., van der Breggen, R., Carr, A., Doherty, M., Doherty, S., Felson, D. T., … van Meurs, J. B. J. (2010). A genome-wide association study identifies a locus on chromosome 7q22 to influence susceptibility for osteoarthritis. *Arthritis and Rheumatism, 62*(2). https://doi.org/10.1002/art.27184, 00043591, NA-NA.

Kessenbrock, K., Krumbholz, M., Schönermarck, U., Back, W., Gross, W. L., Werb, Z., Gröne, H. J., Brinkmann, V., & Jenne, D. E. (2009). Netting neutrophils in autoimmune small-vessel vasculitis. *Nature Medicine, 15*(6), 623—625. https://doi.org/10.1038/nm.1959, 1546170X.

Khovidhunkit, W., Moser, A. H., Shigenaga, J. K., Grunfeld, C., & Feingold, K. R. (2003). Endotoxin down-regulates ABCG5 and ABCG8 in mouse liver and ABCA1 and ABCG1 in J774 murine macrophages: Differential role of LXR. *Journal of Lipid Research, 44*(9), 1728—1736. https://doi.org/10.1194/jlr.M300100-JLR200

Kirii, H., Niwa, T., Yamada, Y., Wada, H., Saito, K., Iwakura, Y., Asano, M., Moriwaki, H., & Seishima, M. (2003). Lack of interleukin-1ß decreases the severity of atherosclerosis in apoE-deficient mice. *Arteriosclerosis, Thrombosis, and Vascular Biology, 23*(4), 656—660. https://doi.org/10.1161/01.ATV.0000064374.15232.C3

Klarin, D., Lynch, J., Aragam, K., Chaffin, M., Assimes, T. L., Huang, J., Lee, K. M., Shao, Q., Huffman, J. E., Natarajan, P., Arya, S., Small, A., Sun, Y. V., Vujkovic, M., Freiberg, M. S., Wang, L., Chen, J., Saleheen, D., Lee, J. S., … Damrauer, S. M. (2019). Genome-wide association study of peripheral artery disease in the Million Veteran Program. *Nature Medicine, 25*(8), 1274—1279. https://doi.org/10.1038/s41591-019-0492-5, 31285632.

Klarin, D., Tsao, P. S., & Damrauer, S. M. (2021). Genetic determinants of peripheral artery disease. *Circulation Research, 128*(12), 1805–1817. https://doi.org/10.1161/CIRCRESAHA.121.318327, 15244571.

Kojima, Y., Downing, K., Kundu, R., Miller, C., Dewey, F., Lancero, H., Raaz, U., Perisic, L., Hedin, U., Schadt, E., Maegdefessel, L., Quertermous, T., & Leeper, N. J. (2014). Cyclin-dependent kinase inhibitor 2B regulates efferocytosis and atherosclerosis. *Journal of Clinical Investigation, 124*(3), 1083–1097. https://doi.org/10.1172/JCI70391, 15588238.

Kojima, Y., Ye, J., Nanda, V., Wang, Y., Flores, A. M., Jarr, K.-U., Tsantilas, P., Guo, L., Finn, A. V., Virmani, R., & Leeper, N. J. (2020). Knockout of the murine ortholog to the human 9p21 coronary artery disease locus leads to smooth muscle cell proliferation, vascular calcification, and advanced atherosclerosis. *Circulation, 141*(15), 1274–1276. https://doi.org/10.1161/circulationaha.119.043413, 0009-7322.

Kullo, I. J., Turner, S. T., Kardia, S. L. R., Mosley, T. H., Boerwinkle, E., & Andrade, M.d. (2006). A genome-wide linkage scan for ankle-brachial index in African American and non-hispanic white subjects participating in the GENOA study. *Atherosclerosis, 187*(2), 433–438. https://doi.org/10.1016/j.atherosclerosis.2005.10.003, 00219150.

Leeper, N. J., & Hamburg, N. M. (2021). Peripheral vascular disease in 2021. *Circulation Research, 128*(12), 1803–1804. https://doi.org/10.1161/CIRCRESAHA.121.319562, 15244571.

Levin, M. G., Klarin, D., Georgakis, M. K., Lynch, J., Liao, K. P., Voight, B. F., O'Donnell, C. J., Chang, K. M., Assimes, T. L., Tsao, P. S., & Damrauer, S. M. (2021). A missense variant in the IL-6 receptor and protection from peripheral artery disease. *Circulation Research*, 968–970. https://doi.org/10.1161/CIRCRESAHA.121.319589, 15244571.

Li, Z., Schulz, M. H., Look, T., Begemann, M., Zenke, M., & Costa, I. G. (2019). Identification of transcription factor binding sites using ATAC-seq. *Genome Biology, 20*(1). https://doi.org/10.1186/s13059-019-1642-2, 1474760X.

Liu, Y., Carmona-Rivera, C., Moore, E., Seto, N. L., Knight, J. S., Pryor, M., Yang, Z. H., Hemmers, S., Remaley, A. T., Mowen, K. A., & Kaplan, M. J. (2018). Myeloid-specific deletion of peptidylarginine deiminase 4 mitigates atherosclerosis. *Frontiers in Immunology, 9*. https://doi.org/10.3389/fimmu.2018.01680, 16643224.

Mansisidor, A. R., & Risca, V. I. (2022). Chromatin accessibility: Methods, mechanisms, and biological insights. *Nucleus, 13*(1), 236–276. https://doi.org/10.1080/19491034.2022.2143106, 19491042.

Marso, S. P., & Hiatt, W. R. (2006). Peripheral arterial disease in patients with diabetes. *Journal of the American College of Cardiology, 47*(5), 921–929. https://doi.org/10.1016/j.jacc.2005.09.065

McKenney, J. M., Koren, M. J., Kereiakes, D. J., Hanotin, C., Ferrand, A. C., & Stein, E. A. (2012). Safety and efficacy of a monoclonal antibody to proprotein convertase subtilisin/kexin type 9 serine protease, SAR236553/REGN727, in patients with primary hypercholesterolemia receiving ongoing stable atorvastatin therapy. *Journal of the American College of Cardiology, 59*(25), 2344–2353. https://doi.org/10.1016/j.jacc.2012.03.007, 15583597.

Megens, R. T. A., Vijayan, S., Lievens, D., Döring, Y., van Zandvoort, M. A. M. J., Grommes, J., Weber, C., & Soehnlein, O. (2012). Presence of luminal neutrophil extracellular traps in atherosclerosis. *Thrombosis and Haemostasis, 107*(3), 597–598. https://doi.org/10.1160/TH11-09-0650, 03406245.

Meisel, S. R., Xu, X. P., Edgington, T. S., Cercek, B., Ong, J., Kaul, S., & Shah, P. K. (2011). Dose-dependent modulation of tissue factor protein and procoagulant activity in human monocyte-derived macrophages by oxidized low density lipoprotein. *Journal of Atherosclerosis and Thrombosis, 18*(7), 596–603. https://doi.org/10.5551/jat.7179, 18803873.

Meisel, S. R., Xu, X. P., Edgington, T. S., Dimayuga, P., Kaul, S., Lee, S., Fishbein, M. C., Cercek, B., & Shah, P. K. (2002). Differentiation of adherent human monocytes into macrophages markedly enhances tissue factor protein expression and procoagulant activity. *Atherosclerosis, 161*(1), 35–43. https://doi.org/10.1016/S0021-9150(01)00616-5, 00219150.

Miller, C. L., Pjanic, M., Wang, T., Nguyen, T., Cohain, A., Lee, J. D., Perisic, L., Hedin, U., Kundu, R. K., Majmudar, D., Kim, J. B., Wang, O., Betsholtz, C., Ruusalepp, A., Franzén, O., Assimes, T. L., Montgomery, S. B., Schadt, E. E., Björkegren, J. L. M., & Quertermous, T. (2016). Integrative functional genomics identifies regulatory mechanisms at coronary artery disease loci. *Nature Communications, 7.* https://doi.org/10.1038/ncomms12092, 20411723.

Mishra, A., Malik, R., Hachiya, T., Jürgenson, T., Namba, S., Posner, D. C., Kamanu, F. K., Koido, M., Le Grand, Q., Shi, M., He, Y., Georgakis, M. K., Caro, I., Krebs, K., Liaw, Y. C., Vaura, F. C., Lin, K., Winsvold, B. S., Srinivasasainagendra, V., ... Debette, S. (2022). Stroke genetics informs drug discovery and risk prediction across ancestries. *Nature, 611*(7934), 115–123. https://doi.org/10.1038/s41586-022-05165-3, 14764687.

Murabito, J. M., Guo, C. Y., Fox, C. S., & D'Agostino, R. B. (2006). Heritability of the ankle-brachial index: The Framingham offspring study. *American Journal of Epidemiology, 164*(10), 963–968. https://doi.org/10.1093/aje/kwj295, 14766256.

Nanda, V., Downing, K. P., Ye, J., Xiao, S., Kojima, Y., Spin, J. M., DiRenzo, D., Nead, K. T., Connolly, A. J., Dandona, S., Perisic, L., Hedin, U., Maegdefessel, L., Dalman, J., Guo, L., Zhao, X. Q., Kolodgie, F. D., Virmani, R., Davis, H. R., & Leeper, N. J. (2016). CDKN2B regulates TGF β signaling and smooth muscle cell investment of hypoxic neovessels. *Circulation Research, 118*(2), 230–240. https://doi.org/10.1161/circresaha.115.307906, 0009-7330.

Narula, N., Dannenberg, A. J., Olin, J. W., Bhatt, D. L., Johnson, K. W., Nadkarni, G., Min, J., Torii, S., Poojary, P., Anand, S. S., Bax, J. J., Yusuf, S., Virmani, R., & Narula, J. (2018). Pathology of peripheral artery disease in patients with critical limb ischemia. *Journal of the American College of Cardiology, 72*(18), 2152–2163. https://doi.org/10.1016/j.jacc.2018.08.002, 15583597.

Nicholls, S. J., Puri, R., Anderson, T., Ballantyne, C. M., Cho, L., Kastelein, J. J. P., Koenig, W., Somaratne, R., Kassahun, H., Yang, J., Wasserman, S. M., Honda, S., Shishikura, D., Scherer, D. J., Borgman, M., Brennan, D. M., Wolski, K., & Nissen, S. E. (2018). Effect of evolocumab on coronary plaque composition. *Journal of the American College of Cardiology, 72*(17), 2012–2021. https://doi.org/10.1016/j.jacc.2018.06.078, 15583597.

Pan, H., Xue, C., Auerbach, B. J., Fan, J., Bashore, A. C., Cui, J., Yang, D. Y., Trignano, S. B., Liu, W., Shi, J., Ihucgbu, C. O., Bush, E. C., Worley, J., Vlahos, L., Laise, P., Solomon, R. A., Connolly, E. S., Califano, A., Sims, P. A., ... Reilly, M. P. (2020). Single-cell genomics reveals a novel cell state during smooth muscle cell phenotypic switching and potential therapeutic targets for atherosclerosis in mouse and human. *Circulation, 142*(21), 2060–2075. https://doi.org/10.1161/circulationaha.120.048378, 0009-7322.

Pande, R. L., & Creager, M. A. (2014). Socioeconomic inequality and peripheral artery disease prevalence in US adults. *Circulation: Cardiovascular Quality and Outcomes, 7*(4), 532–539. https://doi.org/10.1161/CIRCOUTCOMES.113.000618, 19417705.

Pregizer, S., Barski, A., Gersbach, C. A., García, A. J., & Frenkel, B. (2007). Identification of novel Runx2 targets in osteoblasts: Cell type-specific BMP-dependent regulation of Tram2. *Journal of Cellular Biochemistry, 102*(6), 1458–1471. https://doi.org/10.1002/jcb.21366, 10974644.

Que, X., Hung, M. Y., Yeang, C., Gonen, A., Prohaska, T. A., Sun, X., Diehl, C., Määttä, A., Gaddis, D. E., Bowden, K., Pattison, J., MacDonald, J. G., Ylä-Herttuala, S., Mellon, P. L., Hedrick, C. C., Ley, K., Miller, Y. I., Glass, C. K., Peterson, K. L., ... Witztum, J. L. (2018). Oxidized phospholipids are proinflammatory and proatherogenic in hypercholesterolaemic mice. *Nature, 558*(7709), 301–306. https://doi.org/10.1038/s41586-018-0198-8, 14764687.

Raaz, U., Schellinger, I. N., Chernogubova, E., Warnecke, C., Kayama, Y., Penov, K., Hennigs, J. K., Salomons, F., Eken, S., Emrich, F. C., Zheng, W. H., Adam, M., Jagger, A., Nakagami, F., Toh, R., Toyama, K., Deng, A., Buerke, M., Maegdefessel, L., ... Tsao, P. S. (2015). Transcription factor Runx2 promotes aortic fibrosis and stiffness in type 2 diabetes mellitus. *Circulation Research, 117*(6), 513–524. https://doi.org/10.1161/CIRCRESAHA.115.306341, 15244571.

Reyes-García, A. M.de L., Aroca, A., Arroyo, A. B., García-Barbera, N., Vicente, V., González-Conejero, R., & Martínez, C. (2019). Neutrophil extracellular trap components increase the expression of coagulation factors. *Biomedical Reports, 10*(3), 195–201. https://doi.org/10.3892/br.2019.1187, 30906549.

Ridker, P. M., Danielson, E., Fonseca, F. A. H., Genest, J., Gotto, A. M., Kastelein, J. J. P., Koenig, W., Libby, P., Lorenzatti, A. J., MacFadyen, J. G., Nordestgaard, B. G., Shepherd, J., Willerson, J. T., & Glynn, R. J. (2008). Rosuvastatin to prevent vascular events in men and women with elevated C-reactive protein. *New England Journal of Medicine, 359*(21), 2195–2207. https://doi.org/10.1056/NEJMoa0807646, 15334406.

Ridker, P. M., Everett, B. M., Thuren, T., MacFadyen, J. G., Chang, W. H., Ballantyne, C., Fonseca, F., Nicolau, J., Koenig, W., Anker, S. D., Kastelein, J. J. P., Cornel, J. H., Pais, P., Pella, D., Genest, J., Cifkova, R., Lorenzatti, A., Forster, T., Kobalava, Z., ... Zineldine, A. (2017). Antiinflammatory therapy with canakinumab for atherosclerotic disease. *New England Journal of Medicine, 377*(12), 1119–1131. https://doi.org/10.1056/NEJMoa1707914, 15334406.

Rivoira, M., Rodríguez, V., López, M. P., & Tolosa De Talamoni, N. (2015). Time dependent changes in the intestinal Ca^{2+} absorption in rats with type i diabetes mellitus are associated with alterations in the intestinal redox state. *Biochimica et Biophysica Acta - Molecular Basis of Disease, 1852*(3), 386–394. https://doi.org/10.1016/j.bbadis.2014.11.018, 1879260X.

Robinson, J. G., Farnier, M., Krempf, M., Bergeron, J., Luc, G., Averna, M., Stroes, E. S., Langslet, G., Raal, F. J., El Shahawy, M., Koren, M. J., Lepor, N. E., Lorenzato, C., Pordy, R., Chaudhari, U., & Kastelein, J. J. P. (2015). Efficacy and safety of alirocumab in reducing lipids and cardiovascular events. *New England Journal of Medicine, 372*(16), 1489–1499. https://doi.org/10.1056/NEJMoa1501031, 15334406.

Sabatine, M. S., Giugliano, R. P., Keech, A. C., Honarpour, N., Wiviott, S. D., Murphy, S. A., Kuder, J. F., Wang, H., Liu, T., Wasserman, S. M., Sever, P. S., Pedersen, T. R., Fish, M. P., Abrahamsen, T. E., Im, K., Kanevsky, E., Bonaca, M. P., Lira Pineda, A., Hanlon, K., ... Shifrin, G. (2017). Evolocumab and clinical outcomes in patients with cardiovascular disease. *New England Journal of Medicine, 376*(18), 1713–1722. https://doi.org/10.1056/NEJMoa1615664, 15334406.

Shah, S., Henry, A., Roselli, C., Lin, H., Sveinbjörnsson, G., Fatemifar, G., Hedman, Å. K., Wilk, J. B., Morley, M. P., Chaffin, M. D., Helgadottir, A., Verweij, N., Dehghan, A., Almgren, P., Andersson, C., Aragam, K. G., Ärnlöv, J., Backman, J. D., Biggs, M. L., ... Lumbers, R. T. (2020). Genome-wide association and Mendelian randomisation analysis provide insights into the pathogenesis of heart failure. *Nature Communications, 11*(1). https://doi.org/10.1038/s41467-019-13690-5, 20411723.

Shankman, L. S., Gomez, D., Cherepanova, O. A., Salmon, M., Alencar, G. F., Haskins, R. M., Swiatlowska, P., Newman, A. A. C., Greene, E. S., Straub, A. C., Isakson, B., Randolph, G. J., & Owens, G. K. (2015). KLF4-dependent phenotypic modulation of smooth muscle cells has a key role in atherosclerotic plaque pathogenesis. *Nature Medicine, 21*(6), 628–637. https://doi.org/10.1038/nm.3866, 1546170X.

Sharma, A., Choi, J. S. Y., Stefanovic, N., Al-Sharea, A., Simpson, D. S., Mukhamedova, N., Jandeleit-Dahm, K., Murphy, A. J., Sviridov, D., Vince, J. E., Ritchie, R. H., & de Haan, J. B. (2021). Specific NLRP3 inhibition protects against diabetes-associated atherosclerosis. *Diabetes, 70*(3), 772–787. https://doi.org/10.2337/DB20-0357, 1939327X.

Slenders, L., Landsmeer, L. P. L., Cui, K., Depuydt, M. A. C., Verwer, M., Mekke, J., Timmerman, N., van den Dungen, N. A. M., Kuiper, J., Winther, M. P. J., Prange, K. H. M., Ma, W. F., Miller, C. L., Aherrahrou, R., Civelek, M., de Borst, G. J., de Kleijn, D. P. V., Asselbergs, F. W., den Ruijter, H. M., ... Mokry, M. (2021). Intersecting single-cell transcriptomics and genome-wide association studies identifies crucial cell populations and candidate genes for atherosclerosis. *medRxiv*. https://doi.org/10.1101/2021.11.23.21266487

Small, A. M., Huffman, J. E., Klarin, D., Sabater-Lleal, M., Lynch, J. A., Assimes, T. L., Sun, Y. V., Miller, D., Freiberg, M. S., Morrison, A. C., Rader, D. J., Wilson, P. W. F., Cho, K., Tsao, P. S., Chang, K. M., Smith, N. L., O'Donnell, C. J., Vries, P. S. D., & Damrauer, S. M. (2021). Mendelian randomization analysis of hemostatic factors and their contribution to peripheral artery disease-brief report. *Arteriosclerosis, Thrombosis, and Vascular Biology, 41*(1), 380–386. https://doi.org/10.1161/ATVBAHA.119.313847, 15244636.

Snell-Bergeon, J. K., Budoff, M. J., & Hokanson, J. E. (2013). Vascular calcification in diabetes: Mechanisms and implications. *Current Diabetes Reports, 13*(3), 391–402. https://doi.org/10.1007/s11892-013-0379-7, 15390829.

Sorokin, L. (2010). The impact of the extracellular matrix on inflammation. *Nature Reviews Immunology, 10*(10), 712–723. https://doi.org/10.1038/nri2852, 14741733.

Sparks, C. E., Sparks, J. D., Bolognino, M., Salhanick, A., Strumph, P. S., & Amatruda, J. M. (1986). Insulin effects on apolipoprotein B lipoprotein synthesis and secretion by primary cultures of rat hepatocytes. *Metabolism, 35*(12), 1128–1136. https://doi.org/10.1016/0026-0495(86)90026-0, 00260495.

Stabley, J. N., & Towler, D. A. (2017). Arterial calcification in diabetes mellitus. *Arteriosclerosis, Thrombosis, and Vascular Biology, 37*(2), 205–217. https://doi.org/10.1161/atvbaha.116.306258, 1079-5642.

Steffel, J., Eikelboom, J. W., Anand, S. S., Shestakovska, O., Yusuf, S., & Fox, K. A. A. (2020). The compass trial. *Circulation, 142*(1), 40–48. https://doi.org/10.1161/circulationaha.120.046048, 0009-7322.

Tcheandjieu, C., Zhu, X., Hilliard, A. T., Clarke, S. L., Napolioni, V., Ma, S., Lee, K. M., Fang, H., Chen, F., Lu, Y., Tsao, N. L., Raghavan, S., Koyama, S., Gorman, B. R., Vujkovic, M., Klarin, D., Levin, M. G., Sinnott-Armstrong, N., Wojcik, G. L., ... Assimes, T. L. (2022). Large-scale genome-wide association study of coronary artery disease in genetically diverse populations. *Nature Medicine, 28*(8), 1679—1692. https://doi.org/10.1038/s41591-022-01891-3, 1546170X.

Toschi, V., Gallo, R., Lettino, M., Fallon, J. T., David Gertz, S., Fernández-Ortiz, A., Chesebro, J. H., Badimon, L., Nemerson, Y., Fuster, V., & Badimon, J. J. (1997). Tissue factor modulates the thrombogenicity of human atherosclerotic plaques. *Circulation, 95*(3), 594—599. https://doi.org/10.1161/01.CIR.95.3.594, 00097322.

Tseng, H. H. L., Vong, C. T., Kwan, Y. W., Lee, S. M. Y., & Hoi, M. P. M. (2016). TRPM2 regulates TXNIP-mediated NLRP3 inflammasome activation via interaction with p47 phox under high glucose in human monocytic cells. *Scientific Reports, 6.* https://doi.org/10.1038/srep35016, 20452322.

Turner, A. W., Hu, S. S., Mosquera, J. V., Ma, W. F., Hodonsky, C. J., Wong, D., Auguste, G., Song, Y., Sol-Church, K., Farber, E., Kundu, S., Kundaje, A., Lopez, N. G., Ma, L., Ghosh, S. K. B., Onengut-Gumuscu, S., Ashley, E. A., Quertermous, T., Finn, A. V., ... Miller, C. L. (2022). Single-nucleus chromatin accessibility profiling highlights regulatory mechanisms of coronary artery disease risk. *Nature Genetics, 54*(6), 804—816. https://doi.org/10.1038/s41588-022-01069-0, 15461718.

Vattathil, S. M., Liu, Y., Harerimana, N. V., Lori, A., Gerasimov, E. S., Beach, T. G., Reiman, E. M., De Jager, P. L., Schneider, J. A., Bennett, D. A., Seyfried, N. T., Levey, A. I., Wingo, A. P., & Wingo, T. S. (2021). A genetic study of cerebral atherosclerosis reveals novel associations with ntng1 and cnot3. *Genes, 12*(6). https://doi.org/10.3390/genes12060815, 20734425.

Vogel, S., Murthy, P., Cui, X., Lotze, M. T., Zeh, H. J., & Sachdev, U. (2019). TLR4-dependent upregulation of the platelet NLRP3 inflammasome promotes platelet aggregation in a murine model of hindlimb ischemia. *Biochemical and Biophysical Research Communications, 508*(2), 614—619. https://doi.org/10.1016/j.bbrc.2018.11.125, 10902104.

Wahlgren, C. M., & Magnusson, P. K. E. (2011). Genetic influences on peripheral arterial disease in a twin population. *Arteriosclerosis, Thrombosis, and Vascular Biology, 31*(3), 678—682. https://doi.org/10.1161/ATVBAHA.110.210385, 10795642.

Wang, Y., Gao, H., Wang, F., Ye, Z., Mokry, M., Turner, A. W., Ye, J., Koplev, S., Luo, L., Alsaigh, T., Adkar, S. S., Elishaev, M., Gao, X., Maegdefessel, L., Björkegren, J. L. M., Pasterkamp, G., Miller, C. L., Ross, E. G., & Leeper, N. J. (2022). Dynamic changes in chromatin accessibility are associated with the atherogenic transitioning of vascular smooth muscle cells. *Cardiovascular Research, 118*(13), 2792—2804. https://doi.org/10.1093/cvr/cvab347, 17553245.

Wang, Y., Nanda, V., Direnzo, D., Ye, J., Xiao, S., Kojima, Y., Howe, K. L., Jarr, K. U., Flores, A. M., Tsantilas, P., Tsao, N., Rao, A., Newman, A. A. C., Eberhard, A. V., Priest, J. R., Ruusalepp, A., Pasterkamp, G., Maegdefessel, L., Miller, C. L., ... Leeper, N. J. (2020). Clonally expanding smooth muscle cells promote atherosclerosis by escaping efferocytosis and activating the complement cascade. *Proceedings of the National Academy of Sciences of the United States of America, 117*(27), 15818—15826. https://doi.org/10.1073/pnas.2006348117, 10916490.

Warnatsch, A., Ioannou, M., Wang, Q., & Papayannopoulos, V. (2015). Neutrophil extracellular traps license macrophages for cytokine production in atherosclerosis. *Science, 349*(6245), 316–320. https://doi.org/10.1126/science.aaa8064, 10959203.

Wirka, R. C., Wagh, D., Paik, D. T., Pjanic, M., Nguyen, T., Miller, C. L., Kundu, R., Nagao, M., Coller, J., Koyano, T. K., Fong, R., Woo, Y. J., Liu, B., Montgomery, S. B., Wu, J. C., Zhu, K., Chang, R., Alamprese, M., Tallquist, M. D., Kim, J. B., & Quertermous, T. (2019). Atheroprotective roles of smooth muscle cell phenotypic modulation and the TCF21 disease gene as revealed by single-cell analysis. *Nature Medicine, 25*(8), 1280–1289. https://doi.org/10.1038/s41591-019-0512-5, 1546170X.

Wong, S. L., Demers, M., Martinod, K., Gallant, M., Wang, Y., Goldfine, A. B., Kahn, C. R., & Wagner, D. D. (2015). Diabetes primes neutrophils to undergo NETosis, which impairs wound healing. *Nature Medicine, 21*(7), 815–819. https://doi.org/10.1038/nm.3887, 1546170X.

Ye, J., Li, L., Wang, M., Ma, Q., Tian, Y., Zhang, Q., Liu, J., Li, B., Zhang, B., Liu, H., & Sun, G. (2022). Diabetes mellitus promotes the development of atherosclerosis: The role of NLRP3. *Frontiers in Immunology, 13*. https://doi.org/10.3389/fimmu.2022.900254, 16643224.

Zenaro, E., Pietronigro, E., Bianca, V. D., Piacentino, G., Marongiu, L., Budui, S., Turano, E., Rossi, B., Angiari, S., Dusi, S., Montresor, A., Carlucci, T., Nanì, S., Tosadori, G., Calciano, L., Catalucci, D., Berton, G., Bonetti, B., & Constantin, G. (2015). Neutrophils promote Alzheimer's disease-like pathology and cognitive decline via LFA-1 integrin. *Nature Medicine, 21*(8), 880–886. https://doi.org/10.1038/nm.3913, 1546170X.

Zhou, S., Gan-Or, Z., Ambalavanan, A., Lai, D., Xie, P., Bourassa, C. V., Strong, S., Ross, J. P., Dionne-Laporte, A., Spiegelman, D., Dupré, N., Foroud, T. M., Xiong, L., Dion, P. A., & Rouleau, G. A. (2018). Genome-wide association analysis identifies new candidate risk loci for familial intracranial aneurysm in the French-Canadian population. *Scientific Reports, 8*(1). https://doi.org/10.1038/s41598-018-21603-7, 20452322.

Zhou, X., Nicoletti, A., Elhage, R., & Hansson, G. K. (2000). Transfer of CD4+ T cells aggravates atherosclerosis in immunodeficient apolipoprotein E knockout mice. *Circulation, 102*(24), 2919–2922. https://doi.org/10.1161/01.CIR.102.24.2919, 00097322.

Zhu, J., Xun, P., Bae, J. C., Kim, J. H., Kim, D. J., Yang, K., & He, K. (2019). Circulating calcium levels and the risk of type 2 diabetes: A systematic review and meta-analysis. *British Journal of Nutrition, 122*(4), 376–387. https://doi.org/10.1017/S0007114519001430, 14752662.

Zhu, Y., Ma, W. Q., Han, X. Q., Wang, Y., Wang, X., & Liu, N. F. (2018). Advanced glycation end products accelerate calcification in VSMCs through HIF-1α/PDK4 activation and suppress glucose metabolism. *Scientific Reports, 8*(1). https://doi.org/10.1038/s41598-018-31877-6, 20452322.

7

Clinical presentation and diagnosis of PAD

Sonal Pruthi, Sareena George and Sahil Parikh
Division of Cardiology, Department of Medicine, Columbia University Irving Medical Center, New York, NY, United States

Introduction

Peripheral arterial disease (PAD) is the third leading cause of atherosclerotic disease following coronary disease and stroke (Criqui et al., 2021). PAD affects 8–12 million Americans aged >40 years and more than 200 million people worldwide. The prognosis of patients with lower extremity PAD is characterized by an increased risk for cardiovascular ischemic events (Conte et al., 2015; Criqui et al., 2021; Jelani et al., 2018). PAD is also associated with a reduction in functional capacity, quality of life, and in severe

Pathophysiology and Treatment of Atherosclerotic Disease in Peripheral Arteries. https://doi.org/10.1016/B978-0-443-13593-4.00007-X

cases, limb loss (Patel et al., 2015). The major cause of PAD is due to atherosclerotic disease. However, other causes include thrombo-embolic, inflammatory, aneurysmal disease and can be due to trauma, entrapment syndromes, and congenital abnormalities. Table 7.1 highlights the differential diagnosis of PAD

PAD can present with a spectrum of symptoms, which include asymptomatic, atypical symptoms, claudication, and chronic limb-

Table 7.1 Differential diagnosis of peripheral arterial disease.

Diagnosis	Location	Characteristics
Musculoskeletal		
• Baker's Cyst (symptomatic)	Pain behind the knee and down the calf	Tender to touch and maybe associated with swelling
• Arthritis	Hip and thigh pain, foot pain/ache	Varies with exertion and weight bearing, also with change in weather
• Chronic compartment syndrome	Tight, throbbing pain in calf muscles	Seen in athletes after heavy exercise. Improves with elevation
• Medial tibial stress syndrome	Anterior pain	Pain in the anterior shin post exercise, may be reproducible with palpation of posteromedial tibial border
Neurological		
• Spinal stenosis/pseudoclaudication	Low back pain radiating to bilateral lower extremities	May be associated with numbness, weakness, fatigue. Worsens with ambulation, relieves with bending forward
• Nerve root compression	Radiating pain originating in the back	May be associated with numbness, paresthesia. Worsens with ambulation, change in position. Improves with lumbar extension
• Peripheral neuropathy	Distal pain, tingling	May follow a glove-stocking distribution. May be seen in patients with diabetes/alcohol use
Vascular		
• Deep venous thrombosis	Mostly unilateral pain	May be associated with swelling/tenderness. May be associated with history of immobility/risk factors—long distance travel, surgery, cancer
• Popliteal artery entrapment	Cramping behind calf	Provoked by activity. Seen in young, active patients
• Thrombangitis obliterans/Buerger's disease	Associated with rest pain, digital ulcers, gangrene	Seen in smokers, typically in younger patients

threatening ischemia (CLTI). While it is understudied and underrecognized, it is important to identify and diagnose PAD in order to treat and modify the risk of atherothrombotic disease, decrease disability, and improve quality of life (Krawisz et al., 2021).

Who are high risk groups for PAD?

PAD is underrecognized and clinicians should be attentive to its presence. Risk factors for PAD are similar to those of atherosclerotic disease, which include advanced age, diabetes, hypertension, dyslipidemia, cardiovascular disease, and stroke. The most significant risk factor for the development of PAD is smoking, which also has the greatest impact on disease severity. Diabetes and chronic renal dysfunction also increase risk of PAD. It is important to evaluate these patients and assess for history of leg symptoms with exertion or ischemic rest pain, abnormal lower extremity pulse examination, and wounds.

Based on ACC/AHA 2016 guidelines, patients are at increased risk of PAD in the presence of one of the following risk factors (Gerhard-Herman et al., 2017):

Patients who are at increased risk of PAD include.

- Greater than 65 years of age
- 50–64 years with risk factors (diabetes mellitus, smoking, hyperlipidemia, hypertension) or family history of PAD
- Less than 50 years of age with diabetes and at least one risk factor for PAD
- Individuals with known disease in at least one other vascular bed (renal, carotid, subclavian, mesenteric, or abdominal aortic aneurysm)

Even though there are no standardized guidelines that currently recommend screening for PAD in asymptomatic patients, those at increased risk of PAD as mentioned above should have a thorough history taking for symptoms and detailed physical examination as mentioned below and noninvasive blood pressure testing in both arms at least once.

Clinical presentation

Most patients with PAD do not have typical claudication symptoms but rather subtle impairments of lower extremity function. Asymptomatic disease is defined as the absence of exertional leg symptoms in the presence of PAD (typically defined as ABI <0.9). Studies have indicated that asymptomatic patients have limited functional capacity. This is likely indicative of underlying PAD for which patients have restricted or limited their physical activity in order to avoid ischemic leg symptoms (Beckman et al., 2021; Criqui et al., 2021; Jelani et al., 2018). Atypical symptoms account for 20%—40% of the patients with PAD. It is defined by leg symptoms at rest and exercise and doesn't consistently cause the patient to stop walking. It can easily be mistaken for other comorbid conditions such as arthritis or spinal stenosis·

Claudication

Claudication is the primary symptom of lower extremity PAD, affecting about 33% of patients. It is described as a pain or muscular discomfort (aching, heaviness, burning) in the calf, thigh, or buttock muscle groups that is produced consistently by exercise and relieved with rest. Claudication is typically an atherosclerotic occlusive process and symptoms arise due to inadequate blood flow during activity. This can significantly reduce functional capacity and quality of life (Beckman et al., 2021; Krawisz et al., 2021).

Several clinical classifications exist to help to categorize symptoms and disease severity. Two of the most common are the Fontaine and Rutherford classification systems. They are used to assess information regarding lower extremity symptoms and broadly define functional limitations of patients with lower extremity PAD. The Fontaine classification includes two stages for intermittent claudication and two stages for CLTI, while the Rutherford classification further delineates with three categories for both claudication and CLTI. The severity of claudication is defined by the distance a patient is able to walk before symptoms arise and has to rest for relief of symptoms. Mild claudication is two to three blocks (900 ft), moderate is one to two blocks (600 ft), and severe is one block (300 ft). These categorizations help to determine the degree of ischemia and ultimately guide treatment options. Table 7.2 describes clinical classification of claudication.

Chronic limb-threatening Ischemia

CLTI is a severe form of PAD that presents with ischemic rest pain and/or skin changes or tissue loss (ulceration or gangrene). The discomfort is often worse when the patient is supine and improved when the limb is in a dependent position. CLTI accounts for about 1%—3% of PAD cases. The atherosclerotic

Table 7.2 Clinical classification of claudication.

Clinical classifications of PAD				
Fontaine			**Rutherford**	
Stage	**Clinical**	**Grade**	**Category**	**Clinical**
I	Asymptomatic	0	0	Asymptomatic
IIa	Mild claudication	I	1	Mild claudication
IIb	Moderate-severe claudication	I	2	Moderate claudication
		I	3	Severe claudication
III	Ischemic rest pain	II	4	Ischemic rest pain
IV	Ulceration or gangrene	III	5	Minor tissue loss
		IV	6	Ulceration or gangrene

disease is often more complex and more distal, involving more than one anatomical segment with severe and diffuse tibial and pedal artery involvement. Ulcerations are typically located on the forefoot, toes, or around the heel and occur when digital collateral flow diminishes, or arterial branch occlusions develop. These wounds can start off as skin tears, blisters, or abrasions that have difficulty healing due to insufficient local blood flow. The Wifi (wound, ischemia, and foot infection) classification helps for risk stratify patients with CLTI. The severity of the wound, ischemia, and infection is evaluated to assess risk of amputation. This subset of PAD patients have the highest morbidity and mortality due to association with high rates of myocardial infarction, ischemic stroke, and cardiovascular death. In the United States, patients with CLI have a 25% amputation rate and 25% CV mortality rate within 1 year and 50%–60% CV mortality rate over 5 years. Approximately, 5%–10% of patients with claudication or asymptomatic/atypical symptoms will progress to CLTI within 5 years (Hirsch et al., 2006; Patel et al., 2015).

Acute limb ischemia

Acute limb ischemia (ALI) is a rare and severe consequence of PAD. It occurs when there is a sudden or rapid decrease in limb/leg perfusion threatening tissue viability and causing pain, paresthesia, pulselessness, pallor, and/or paralysis likely due an

Table 7.3 Assessment of acute limb ischemia.

		Arterial Doppler	Venous Doppler	Motor loss/ muscle weakness	Sensory loss	Management
1. Viable	Not immediately threatened	+	+	None	None	Revascularization
1. Threatened	(IIa) Marginally threatened	+/−	+	None	None/ minimal(toes)	Emergent revascularization
	(IIb) immediately threatened	−	+	Mild/ moderate	More than toes/rest pain	Emergent revascularization
1. Irreversible	Major tissue loss or permanent nerve damage	−	−	Profound weakness/ paralysis	Permanent nerve damage, profound sensory loss	Amputation

atherothrombotic event. This is a vascular emergency, and the viability of the limb must be assessed immediately. If the limb is salvageable, prompt endovascular or surgical revascularization is necessary (Criqui et al., 2021). Table 7.3 highlights assessment of ALI.

Clinical evaluation of peripheral arterial disease

Taking a through history and conducting a meticulous examination play a pivotal role in the diagnosis of PAD, allowing for differentiation from other potentially confounding conditions. This in combination with diagnostic imaging findings is used for diagnosing PAD.

Individuals with an elevated risk of PAD should receive a comprehensive vascular assessment. Table 7.4 provides an overview of clinical assessment for PAD.

Patients with vascular disease can have arterial, venous, or neuropathic ulcers (Table 7.5).

Table 7.4 Clinical assessment for PAD.

Assessment	Abnormality
• Feeling for pulses in femoral, popliteal, dorsalis pedis, posterior tibial artery	Decreased pulses
• Blood pressure in both extremities	Interarm blood pressure gradient >15–20 mm Hg, suggestive of subclavian stenosis
• Auscultation of carotid, subclavian, femoral, and abdominal aorta	Bruits
• Inspection of lower extremities	• Delayed capillary refill • Cool extremities • Dependent rubor, elevation pallor • Arterial ulcers • Gangrene

Table 7.5 Evaluation of ulcers.

Characteristic	Arterial ulcers	Venous ulcers	Neuropathic ulcers
Underlying cause	Reduced blood flow	Chronic venous insufficiency	Neuropathy
Location	Distal toes, heel, or lateral malleolus	Posterior calf, medial or lateral malleolus	Pressure points—plantar surface of foot or heel
Appearance	Pale, shiny, dry skin, with well-defined borders; minimal hair growth	Swollen, red, weeping with often scaling dermatitis	Calloused or thickened skin, may have open sores
Pain	Severe, intermittent pain, especially at night	Mild to moderate pain, aching or burning sensation, worse with standing	Often painless
Edema	Minimal to no edema	Often significant edema	Usually absent or mild
Skin changes	Atrophic (thin), shiny, cold, and pale	Dermatitis, hemosiderin staining, thickened skin	Often dry, cracked, and prone to callus formation
Pulses	Diminished or absent	Normal	Normal

Laboratory diagnosis of PAD—Ankle brachial index and vascular ultrasound

Ankle brachial index (ABI)

For further assessment of arterial disease ABI is a simple procedure that can be performed in office.

First alluded in 1950, by Travis Winsor that the ankle pressure is lower if the arteries are obstructed and hence proposed ABI for noninvasive diagnosis of symptomatic PAD. In 1970, Yao from St. Mary's Hospital in London reported that the severity of PAD is correlated with decrease in ABI.

Definition

ABI is defined as the ratio of higher of the two systolic pressures in dorsalis pedis or posterior tibial artery, divided by the higher of the two systolic brachial pressures and is the preferred screening test for diagnosis of PAD in symptomatic and asymptomatic patients with atherosclerotic risk factors.

$$ABI = \text{Systolic dorsalis pedis or posterior tibialis pressure/systolic brachial pressure.}$$

Physiology

The increased systolic blood pressure in ankles compared to arms occurs due to the phenomenon of peripheral blood pressure waveform amplification. The measured systolic blood pressure at any site includes antegrade pressure waves generated from left ventricle ejection and summation of retrograde waveforms generated from reflected waves from areas of resistance in the vessel, for instance, tortuosity or branch points. Hence as the waveform travels distally, the pressure increases. In addition to this, prolonged episodes of increased hydrostatic pressure in lower extremities due to walking or running causes remodeling of lower extremity vasculature leading to increased wall thickness with unchanged luminal diameter. This remodeling has been postulated to occur in second or third year of life which is why the normal ABI in a newborn is < 1.0 compared to adult normal values. Even though ABI is expected to increase with age due to arterial stiffening, population studies have shown otherwise likely due to prevalence of PAD. Similarly, based on this, taller people should have a higher ABI, however in Multi-Ethnic Study of Atherosclerosis (MESA) study, ABI increase was nonsignificant

(<0.01 higher for every 20-cm height increase). After multivariate adjustments, ABI was 0.02 lower in women and African American than men in a subset of MESA participants free of PAD and traditional risk factors for atherosclerosis.

Measurement

ABI can be measured using a manual blood pressure cuff with a stethoscope or Doppler for pulse detection. The patient is placed in supine position, and BP cuff placed at the level of heart. The cuff is inflated to 20 mm above the expected systolic blood pressure and accompanied by disappearance of Doppler signal/ auscultatory sounds. The cuff is slowly deflated and reappearance of signal equals to systolic pressure at that site. The brachial pulse is detected in the antecubital fossa. For the ankle, the cuff is placed immediately proximal to the malleoli. The Doppler signal for Dorsalis pedis is found slightly lateral to the midline of the dorsum of the foot. The posterior tibial artery is detected posterior to the medial malleolus. Mild dorsiflexion of the foot can aid in elucidating posterior tibial artery.

Current AHA, NICE, and ESC guidelines recommend use of Doppler devices for ABI over automated measurement since they have poor correlation in those with lower ABI. To avoid fallacies while measuring ABI—the cuff should be appropriately sized. The bladder length of the cuff should be 80%, and the width should be 40% of the circumference of the extremity. The AHA suggests performing the order of measurements as follows: First arm, same side ankle (both PT and DP), opposite leg, and opposite arm. While measuring ABI, it is imperative to measure blood pressure in both arms and use the higher of the two for calculating ABI. This will prevent underestimation of the disease in case of discrepant upper extremity blood pressures due to concomitant subclavian artery stenosis. Other measures to increase the accuracy of the ABI include having the patient rest supine for at least 5 minutes to allow their blood pressure to stabilize and avoid smoking prior to the test.

Normal resting ABI = 1−1.4.

0.91−0.99 = Borderline possibility of underlying PAD.

<0.9 = Abnormal with <0.5 suggestive of severe occlusive arterial disease.

>1.4 is suggestive of noncompressible vessels mostly due to arterial calcification.

It is important to consider clinical history, examination, and pretest probability while interpreting borderline ABIs.

In patients with medial calcinosis, diabetes mellitus and end stage renal failure, utility of ABI may be limited due to vessel wall calcification and increased stiffness leading to noncompressibility. In these situations where ABI >1.4, Toe-brachial index (TBI) can be used in addition to ABI for screening asymptomatic patients with PAD and those with high cardiovascular risk. TBI ≤ 0.7 is considered an abnormal test.

Sometimes, patients with exertional or claudication symptoms may have normal resting ABI. In such cases, exercise ABI is recommended to objectively assess their functional status. Patients with borderline normal ABI (0.9—0.99) can also be worked up with exercise ABI. During exercise, there is vasoconstriction in the nonexercising limbs with increase in systolic pressure there and decreased systolic pressure in the ankles, hence there is a mild decrease in ABI immediately postexercise and returning to normal within 1—2 minutes. However, as the stenosis increases, the drop is greater leading to longer time to recovery. A 20% drop in postexercise ABI from the resting baseline indicates an abnormal test. In the absence of a treadmill, an office protocol of repeated active plantar flexion can be used as substitute and correlates well. According to 2016 ACC/AHA guidelines on management of patients with lower extremity PAD, a 6-minute walk test in a corridor can be also utilized as an alternative to treadmill ABI for functional assessment.

Apart from being a screening tool, ABI has been shown to help with risk stratification of patients. Low ABI has been shown to positively correlate with presence of CAD and cerebrovascular disease; however, the relationship has not proven to be linear. Even though an increase in ABI postrevascularization can suggest improvement, it is poorly correlated with detecting revascularization failure over time since it is not site specific and can worsen over time due to revascularization/graft failure or progression of disease in native arteries.

Vascular ultrasound

Ultrasound imaging has emerged as a powerful tool for the evaluation of vascular conditions owing to its noninvasive nature, real-time capabilities, and absence of ionizing radiation. Vascular ultrasounds provide detailed information about blood flow, vessel structure, and potential abnormalities, enabling clinicians to diagnose and monitor a wide range of vascular conditions.

Vascular ultrasounds employ various imaging modes, including B-mode, Doppler, color Doppler, and spectral Doppler.

B-mode provides grayscale images that reveal vessel morphology and surrounding structures. Doppler modes analyze blood flow patterns and velocities. Color Doppler overlays color on B-mode images to indicate the direction and speed of blood flow, while spectral Doppler displays a graph of velocity over time (Kim et al., 2020).

Waveform: Normal waveform in the lower extremities is triphasic. The three phases corresponded to cardiac cycle with the first deflection above the baseline representing systole, the first deflection below the baseline corresponds to the early diastolic flow reversal, and the third deflection above baseline corresponds to reflective wave in late diastole. Triphasic waveform is most consistently used to characterize normal blood flow. The late diastolic component is typically absent in a biphasic waveform, leaving only systolic upstroke and early diastolic flow reversal and can be seen in both normal and abnormal states. Monophasic waveforms typically do not cross the zero-flow baseline and are unidirectional. Monophasic waveforms are typically abnormal and are found distal to a hemodynamically significant arterial obstruction but sometimes can also be seen proximal to a significant obstruction.

In a normal vessel, a spectral display depicts a sharp upstroke or acceleration.

Velocity: Peak systolic velocity (PSV) and end diastolic velocity (EDV) measurements are obtained through spectral Doppler to help assess the severity of stenosis. An increased PSV and decreased EDV suggest hemodynamically significant stenosis.

Abnormal study

The severity of reduction in lumen diameter is reflected in a continuum of changes in the waveform morphology and velocity.

Mild stenosis (<50%): Slight disruption to laminar flow without significant increase in PSV. Early diastolic reverse flow is preserved, and the waveform remains multiphasic. The PSV ratio between normal and diseased segments is < 2.

Moderate stenosis (50%−74%): The PSV ratio between normal and diseased segments is 2−4. The early diastolic reverse flow is often lost.

Severe stenosis (>75%): There is disruption to laminar flow. The PSV ratio between normal and diseased segments is > 4 just prior to the stenosis, often accompanied by monophasic waveforms with prolonged upstroke and decreased PSV distally.

Beyond stenotic conditions, anomalies such as pseudoaneurysms and arteriovenous fistulas manifest distinct waveform patterns. Vascular ultrasound may be complemented by other modalities like CT angiography, MR angiography and digital sub-straction angiography to provide a more comprehensive assessment based on clinical indication.

Waveform interpretation should always be considered within the broader clinical context. Combining waveform findings with patient history, physical examination, and other imaging modalities provides a comprehensive understanding of the vascular condition.

Conclusion

In summary, a comprehensive understanding of the clinical presentation and thorough assessment of PAD with longitudinal follow-up is indispensable for physicians. Early recognition and appropriate management are pivotal in improving the quality of life and reducing the risk of limb loss and cardiovascular events in these patients.

References

Beckman, J. A., Schneider, P. A., & Conte, M. S. (2021). Advances in revascularization for peripheral artery disease: Revascularization in PAD. *Circulation Research, 128*, 1885–1912. https://doi.org/10.1161/CIRCRESAHA.121.318261

Criqui, M. H., Matsushita, K., Aboyans, V., Hess, C. N., Hicks, C. W., Kwan, T. W., McDermott, M. M., Misra, S., Ujueta, F., American Heart Association Council on, E., et al. (2021). Lower extremity peripheral artery disease: Contemporary epidemiology, management gaps, and future directions: A scientific statement from the American heart association. *Circulation, 144*, e171–e191. https://doi.org/10.1161/CIR.0000000000001005

Gerhard-Herman, M. D., Gornik, H. L., Barrett, C., Barshes, N. R., Corriere, M. A., Drachman, D. E., Fleisher, L. A., Fowkes, F. G., Hamburg, N. M., Kinlay, S., et al. (2017). 2016 AHA/ACC guideline on the management of patients with lower extremity peripheral artery disease: Executive summary: A report of the American college of cardiology/American heart association task force on clinical practice guidelines. *Circulation, 135*, e686–e725. https://doi.org/10.1161/CIR.0000000000000470

Hirsch, A. T., Haskal, Z. J., Hertzer, N. R., Bakal, C. W., Creager, M. A., Halperin, J. L., Hiratzka, L. F., Murphy, W. R., Olin, J. W., Puschett, J. B., et al. (2006). ACC/AHA guidelines for the management of patients with peripheral arterial disease (lower extremity, renal, mesenteric, and abdominal aortic): A collaborative report from the American associations for vascular surgery/society for vascular surgery, society for cardiovascular angiography and Interventions, society for vascular medicine and biology, society of interventional radiology, and the ACC/AHA task force on practice guidelines (writing committee to develop guidelines for the management of patients with peripheral arterial disease)–summary of recommendations. *Journal of Vascular and Interventional Radiology, 17*, 1383–1397. https://doi.org/10.1097/01.RVI.0000240426.53079.46

Jelani, Q. U., Petrov, M., Martinez, S. C., Holmvang, L., Al-Shaibi, K., & Alasnag, M. (2018). Peripheral arterial disease in women: An overview of risk factor profile, clinical features, and outcomes. *Current Atherosclerosis Reports, 20*, 40. https://doi.org/10.1007/s11883-018-0742-x

Kim, E. S. H., Sharma, A. M., Scissons, R., et al. (2020). Interpretation of peripheral arterial and venous doppler waveforms: A consensus statement from the society for vascular medicine and society for vascular ultrasound. *Journal for Vascular Ultrasound, 44*(3), 118–143. https://doi.org/10.1177/1544316720943099

Krawisz, A. K., Raja, A., & Secemsky, E. A. (2021). Femoral-popliteal peripheral artery disease: From symptom presentation to management and treatment controversies. *Progress in Cardiovascular Diseases, 65*, 15–22. https://doi.org/10.1016/j.pcad.2021.02.004

Patel, M. R., Conte, M. S., Cutlip, D. E., Dib, N., Geraghty, P., Gray, W., Hiatt, W. R., Ho, M., Ikeda, K., Ikeno, F., et al. (2015). Evaluation and treatment of patients with lower extremity peripheral artery disease: Consensus definitions from peripheral academic research consortium (PARC). *Journal of the American College of Cardiology, 65*, 931–941. https://doi.org/10.1016/j.jacc.2014.12.036

Conte, M. S., Pomposelli, F. B., Clair, D. G., Geraghty, P. J., McKinsey, J. F., Mills, J. L., Moneta, G. L., Murad, M. H., Powell, R. J., et al., Society for Vascular Surgery Lower Extremity Guidelines Writing G. (2015). Society for vascular surgery practice guidelines for atherosclerotic occlusive disease of the lower extremities: Management of asymptomatic disease and claudication. *Journal of Vascular Surgery, 61*, 2S–41S. https://doi.org/10.1016/j.jvs.2014.12.009

8

Medical therapy of PAD

McCall Walker[1] and Joshua Beckman[2]

[1]University of Texas Southwestern, Dallas, TX, United States; [2]University of Texas Southwestern Medical Center, Dallas, TX, United States

Pathophysiology and Treatment of Atherosclerotic Disease in Peripheral Arteries. https://doi.org/10.1016/B978-0-443-13593-4.00008-1

The medical treatment of peripheral artery disease (PAD) is primarily focused on the reduction of major adverse cardiovascular and limb events (secondary prevention), as PAD greatly increases this risk regardless of the presence or absence of other cardiovascular disease (CVD) (Criqui et al., 1992; Gerhard-Herman et al., 2017). Prevention of incident PAD (primary prevention) is contingent solely on risk factor control (such as diabetes, hypertension, smoking cessation, and lipid management) (Table 8.1). Both pharmacological and nonpharmacological interventions are currently recommended for the treatment of PAD to reduce cardiovascular and limb events, increase walking distance, and improve health-related quality of life (Criqui et al., 2021). This chapter will discuss the current medical therapies for PAD from both a hard outcomes standpoint and symptomatic improvement in those with PAD.

Medical therapies that reduce major adverse cardiovascular and limb events in PAD

Therapies will be described by risk factor modification grouping.

Smoking cessation management

Smoking is likely the most important risk factor for PAD development and progression (Joosten et al., 2012). There is an 11-fold increased risk of disease progression in those who smoke tobacco products (Fowkes et al., 2017). Observational data have shown that smokers who underwent endovascular or open revascularization for intermittent claudication had a higher 30-day mortality (0.6% vs. 0.1%) and higher rate of postprocedural 30-day complications (12.6% vs. 8.9%) (Creager & Hamburg, 2022). Compared to active smokers, those who were never-smokers had a 65% lower risk of any complication and former smokers had a 29% lower risk. Smokers who continue smoking after lower extremity bypass have a threefold increase in risk of graft failure, but cessation of smoking at any point increases graft patency rates approaching the rates of never-smokers (Willigendael et al., 2005). As such, smoking abstinence (or cessation) is guideline recommended in all patients with PAD (Gerhard-Herman et al., 2017). Therapies to aid in smoking cessation have been described in detail and include nicotine replacement, non nicotine medications that reduce withdrawal symptoms, and counseling.

Table 8.1 Cardiovascular and limb outcome trials relevant to PAD risk factor modification.

Risk factor	Study (year)	Total N	Population	Intervention	Median follow-up	MACE/MALE endpoint (HR or RR [95% CI])	Interpretation
Glucose	EMPA-REG OUTCOME (2017),[a] Verma et al. (2018)	1461	Prior limb revascularization, amputation, or ABI <0.9 with DM2 and CVD	Empagliflozin versus placebo	3.1	MACE: 0.84 [0.62 –1.14]CV death: 0.57 [0.37–0.88] All-cause death: 0.62 [0.35–0.92]	Empagliflozin improved mortality in PAD patients
	CANVAS (2017). Perkovic et al. (2019)	10,142	PAD (not defined) with DM2 and CVD or at least 2 CVD risk factors	Canagliflozin versus placebo	2.4	MACE: 0.86 [0.75 –0.97]Amputation: 1.97 [1.41–2.75]	Canagliflozin decreased MACE in CVD patients with an increase in amputation risk
	DECLARE-TIMI 58 (2020),[a] Bonaca, Wiviott, et al. (2020)	1025	ABI <0.9 with claudication or prior revascularization or amputation with DM2 and CVD or multiple CVD risk factors	Dapagliflozin versus placebo	4.2	MACE: 1.05 [0.77 –1.42]Amputation: 1.09 [0.84–1.40]	Dapagliflozin did not decrease MACE or increase amputation risk
	Harmony outcomes (2018),[a] Hernandez et al. (2018)	2354	ABI <0.9 with claudication or prior revascularization or amputation with DM2, CVD, and age >40	Albiglutide versus placebo	1.6	MACE: 0.96 [0.73 –1.25]	Albiglutide decreased MACE in the primary study but not in the PAD subgroup
	EXCEL (2019),[a] Badjatiya et al. (2019)	2800	ABI <0.9 with claudication or prior revascularization or amputation with DM2	Exenatide versus placebo	3.2	MACE: 0.85 [0.69 –1.04]	Exenatide did not decrease MACE in PAD
	LEADER (2018),[a] Dhatariya et al. (2018)	367	Diabetic foot ulcer with DM2 and high risk of CV events	Liraglutide versus placebo	3.8	Amputation: 0.65 [0.45–0.95]	Liraglutide decreased diabetic-foot-ulcer-related amputations compared with placebo in those with DM2 and high risk of CV events

Continued

Table 8.1 Cardiovascular and limb outcome trials relevant to PAD risk factor modification.—*continued*

Risk factor	Study (year)	Total N	Population	Intervention	Median follow-up	MACE/MALE endpoint (HR or RR [95% CI])	Interpretation
Lipids	Heart protection study (2007),[a] Randomized Trial of the Effects of Cholesterol-Lowering with Simvastatin on Peripheral Vascular and Other Major Vascular Outcomes in 20,536 People with Peripheral Arterial Disease and Other High-Risk Conditions (2007)	6748	Claudication, prior revascularization, amputation, or aneurysm repair with history of CVD or DM2	Simvastatin versus placebo	5	MACE: 0.22 [0.15—0.29] noncoronary revascularizations: 0.16 [0.05—0.26]	Simvastatin reduced the risk of first major adverse cardiovascular event and reduced noncoronary revascularizations (including amputations) compared to placebo in PAD
	FOURIER (2017),[a] Bonaca et al. (2018)	3642	Symptomatic PAD (IC and ABI<0.85, prior revascularization or amputation) and CVD while on high-intensity statin	Evolocumab + statin versus placebo + statin	2.2	MACE: 0.73 [0.59 —0.91]MALE: 0.63 [0.39—1.03]MALE (no MI or stroke): 0.43 [0.19—0.99]	Evolocumab significantly decreased MACE in PAD patients and decreased MALE in PAD patients with no prior MI or stroke
	ODYSSEY OUTCOMES (2019),[a] Schwartz et al. (2020)	610	PAD (determined from medical history) and dyslipidemia with ACS in prior 12 months	Alirocumab versus placebo	2.8	MACE: 0.93 [0.76—1.30]	Alirocumab did not decrease MACE in PAD patients with recent ACS
	FIELD (2009),[a] Rajamani et al. (2009)	115	Age 50—75 with DM2 and non-traumatic amputation	Fenofibrate versus placebo	5	First amputation: 0.64 [0.44—0.94]Minor amputation: 0.53 [0.30—0.94]Major amputation: 0.93 [0.53—1.62]	Fenofibrate treatment was associated with a lower risk of amputations (particularly minor amputations) in DM2
Antiplatelets	AAA (2010), Fowkes et al. (2010)	3350	Asymptomatic PAD with ABI <0.95 and no clinical CVD	Aspirin versus placebo	8.2	MACE: 1.03 [0.84—1.27]	Aspirin did not decrease MACE in asymptomatic PAD

Trial	N	Population	Comparison	Duration	Outcome HR [CI]	Conclusion
POPADAD (2008), Belch et al. (2008)	1276	Asymptomatic PAD with ABI <0.99 and DM2	Aspirin versus placebo	6.7	MACE: 0.98 [0.76–1.26]	Aspirin did not decrease MACE in asymptomatic PAD and DM2
CLIPS (2007), Catalano et al. (2007)	366	Claudication, angiographic or ultrasound documented occlusion, ABI <0.85 or TBI <0.6	Aspirin versus placebo	1.7	MACE: 0.35 [0.15–0.82]	Aspirin decreased MACE in a heterogeneous PAD group
CAPRIE (1996),[a] A Randomised, Blinded, Trial of Clopidogrel vs. Aspirin in Patients at Risk of Ischaemic Events (CAPRIE) (1996)	6452	ABI <0.85 with claudication or prior revascularization or amputation for symptomatic PAD	Clopidogrel versus aspirin	1.9	MACE: 0.23 [0.089–0.362]	Clopidogrel decreased MACE compared to aspirin in symptomatic PAD
EUCLID (2017), Hiatt et al. (2017)	13,885	ABI <0.80 with claudication or prior revascularization for symptomatic PAD	Ticagrelor versus clopidogrel	2.5	MACE: 1.02 [0.92–1.13]	Ticagrelor was not superior to clopidogrel for MACE reduction in PAD
CHARISMA (2009),[a] Bhatt et al. (2006)	3096	Symptomatic PAD (ABI <0.08 with claudication or claudication with prior intervention) or asymptomatic PAD (ABI <0.90)	Clopidogrel + aspirin versus aspirin	2.3	MACE: 0.85 [0.66–1.08]	DAPT did not decrease MACE in stable PAD
PEGASUS-TIMI 54 (2016),[a] Bonaca et al (2016)	1143	ABI <0.90, prior revascularization, or intermittent claudication with prior MI and risk factors for atherosclerosis	Ticagrelor + aspirin versus placebo + aspirin	2.8	MACE: 0.69 [0.44–0.99]MALE: 0.65 [0.44–0.95]	DAPT reduced MACE and MALE in PAD patients with prior MI
TRA 2°P-TIMI 50 (2020),[a] Qamar et al. (2020)	6136	ABI <0.85 with claudication or prior revascularization in addition to prior MI or stroke	Vorapaxar versus placebo	2	MACE: 0.85 [0.73–0.99]MALE: 0.70 [0.53–0.92]	Vorapaxar reduced MACE and MALE in PAD patients with CVD at the expense of increased bleeding

Continued

Table 8.1 Cardiovascular and limb outcome trials relevant to PAD risk factor modification.—continued

Risk factor	Study (year)	Total N	Population	Intervention	Median follow-up	MACE/MALE endpoint (HR or RR [95% CI])	Interpretation
	MIRROR (2013), Strobl et al. (2013)	80	Chronic peripheral artery disease in the SFA and/or popliteal artery undergoing balloon angioplasty ± stenting	Aspirin + clopidogrel versus aspirin + placebo	0.5	TLR at 6 months: 5% DAPT versus 20% SAPT, $P = .04$ TLR at 12 months: 25% DAPT versus 32.4% SAPT, $P = .35$	DAPT decreased TLR at 6 months compared to placebo in postrevascularization PAD but this advantage does not persist after stopping clopidogrel
Antithrombotics	WAVE (2007), Anand et al. (2007)	2161	PAD (claudication with gangrene, prior revascularization, or amputation) or proven subclavian or carotid stenosis	Vitamin K antagonist + antiplatelet versus antiplatelet	2.9	MACE: 0.92 [0.73 –1.16]Bleeding: 3.41 [1.84–6.35]	Vitamin K antagonist + an antiplatelet was not more effective than antiplatelet alone for reducing MACE and increased bleeding
	COMPASS (2017),[a] Eikelboom et al. (2017)	5551	ABI <0.90, prior revascularization or amputation, or claudication with diagnostic confirmation on a background of CVD (subgroup included carotid disease)	Rivaroxaban + aspirin versus aspirin	1.8	MACE: 0.72 [0.57 –0.90]MALE: 0.54 [0.35–0.82] Bleeding: 1.75 [1.16 –2.65]	Low-dose twice-daily rivaroxaban + aspirin was superior to aspirin alone at reducing MACE and MALE in PAD at the expense of increased major bleeding
	VOYAGER PAD (2020), Bonaca, Bauersachs, et al. (2020)	6564	PAD and recent revascularization	Rivaroxaban + aspirin versus aspirin	3	MACE/MALE: 0.85 [0.76–0.96] Bleeding: 1.43 [0.97 –2.10]	Low-dose twice-daily rivaroxaban + aspirin was superior to aspirin alone at reducing a composite MACE/MALE endpoint in PAD with recent revascularization

Category	Trial	N	Inclusion criteria	Intervention	Follow-up	Results	Conclusion
Blood pressure	ABCD (2003),[a] Mehler et al. (2003)	53	ABI <0.90 with DM2	Enalapril or nisoldipine versus placebo	4	MACE: 13.6% intervention versus 38.7% placebo, P = .046	Intensive blood pressure control with enalapril or nisoldipine decreased MACE compared to placebo in PAD and DM2
	INVEST (2010),[a] Bavry et al. (2010)	2699	PAD based on questionnaire with concomitant CAD and HTN	Verapamil ± trandolapril versus atenolol ± hydrochlorothiazide	2.7	MACE: 1.69 for SBP ≤110 mmHg; 1.02 for SBP 135 mmHg; 1.01 for SBP 145 mmHg; 1.65 for SBP 170 mmHg	An SBP range of 135−145 mmHg is associated with lowest MACE in PAD
	ALLHAT (2018),[a] Itoga et al. (2018)	33,357	Baseline HTN and at least one other CAD risk factor with a PAD event (PAD hospitalization, procedure, medical treatment, or PAD-related death)	Treatment with chlorthalidone, amlodipine, lisinopril, or doxazosin	4.3	PAD event: 0.26 [0.05−0.52] for SBP <120 mmHg; 0.21 [0−0.48] for SBP ≥160 mmHg; 1.72 [1.38−2.16] for DBP <60 mmHg	Highest rates of PAD events were seen with SBP <120 mmHg and ≥160 mmHg and with DBP <60 mmHg
	HOPE (2004),[a] Östergren et al. (2004)	3099	ABI <0.90 without symptoms on a background of CVD without HFrEF	Ramipril versus placebo	4.5	MACE: 0.75 [0.61−0.92]	Ramipril decreased MACE in asymptomatic PAD compared to placebo

ABI, ankle-brachial index; ACS, acute coronary syndrome; CAD, coronary artery disease; CV, cardiovascular; CVD, cardiovascular disease; DAPT, dual-antiplatelet therapy; DBP, diastolic blood pressure; DM2, type 2 diabetes mellitus; HFrEF, heart failure with reduced ejection fraction; HR, hazard ratio; HTN, hypertension; MACE, major adverse cardiovascular event; MALE, major adverse limb event; MI, myocardial infarction; PAD, peripheral artery disease; RR, relative risk; SAPT, single-antiplatelet therapy; SBP, systolic blood pressure; SFA, superficial femoral artery; TBI, toe-brachial index; TLR, target-limb revascularization.

[a]Denotes a sub-group analysis of a randomized-controlled trial.

Nicotine replacement

In meta-analysis, nicotine replacement therapy of any type was superior to placebo for smoking cessation (Hartmann-Boyce et al., 2018). 133 studies including 64,6400 participants randomized to any type of nicotine replacement or placebo were analyzed. Overall, the relative risk of smoking abstinence for any nicotine replacement therapy compared to placebo was increased by 50%–60%. Individual nicotine replacement therapies all significantly improved abstinence compared to placebo and were similar in their effect size (this included nicotine gum, patches, tablets/lozenges, inhalators, and nasal sprays).

Non nicotine medications

Bupropion is an aminoketone atypical antidepressant that weakly inhibits neuronal norepinephrine and dopamine uptake. It was originally indicated for the treatment of major depressive disorder but more recently has been marketed as a non nicotine-based drug used for smoking cessation. Two seminal trials comparing bupropion to placebo form the basis for current use in smoking cessation. The first blinded, controlled trial randomized 615 participants to either placebo or bupropion at a dose of 100, 150, or 300 mg daily over a 7 week period (Hurt et al., 1997). Rates of smoking cessation were significantly higher in the groups receiving bupropion, and proportional to the dose allocated (19% in the placebo group, 28.8%, 38.6%, and 44.2% I the 100, 150, and 300 mg groups, respectively). At 1 year follow-up, the rates of abstinence were significantly higher in the 150 and 300 mg groups compared to placebo, but not the 100 mg group. The second large trial randomized participants to either 150 mg sustained-release bupropion (244 participants), a nicotine patch (244 participants), bupropion plus a nicotine patch (245 participants), or placebo (160 participants) (Jorenby et al., 1999). Bupropion was dosed at 150 mg daily for 3 days and then 150 mg twice daily for 9 wccks. At 12 months, there was a significantly higher abstinence rate in both the bupropion and bupropion/nicotine patch groups compared to either placebo or to nicotine patch alone. There was no significant difference between abstinence rates in the bupropion only or bupropion/nicotine patch groups, but combination therapy rates were numerically higher (30.3% compared to 35.5%). A later meta-analysis of 19 randomized trials showed double the rates of smoking cessation with bupropion compared to placebo (Hughes et al., 2004).

Varenicline is another non nicotine medication but as opposed to bupropion was designed specifically for the treatment of tobacco abuse disorder. It is a $\alpha4\beta2$ receptor partial agonist that stimulates dopamine release, mimicking the effects of nicotine and thus reducing withdrawal symptoms. Two randomized controlled trials compared varenicline 1 mg twice daily to both sustained-release bupropion 150 mg twice daily or to placebo over a 12-week period (Gonzales et al., 2006; Jorenby et al., 2006). Regarding abstinence from tobacco smoking, both studies showed superiority of varenicline compared to placebo up to and at 1 year and to bupropion up to 24 weeks in both studies and 1 year in one study. Notably both studies also included brief counseling on smoking cessation and abstinence for all groups.

Smoking cessation counseling

Counseling in the form of therapist-delivered interventions, group therapy, or individual counseling have all been shown to be efficacious in smoking cessation. Simple advice given to patients by medical practitioners, even if brief, can increase smoking cessation by 1%–3% (Stead et al., 2013). Individually delivered counseling for smoking cessation was assessed in a meta-analysis of 49 trials with ~19,000 participants in which face-to-face counseling sessions lasted for a minimum of 10 min (Lancaster & Stead, 2017). Individual therapy was compared with minimal behavioral intervention (brief advice, usually care, self-help materials) in 33 trials and was seen to increase the chances of quitting smoking by 40%–80%. Intensive counseling was more efficacious than brief counseling. Group therapy offers mutual support from group members in addition to the behavioral techniques delivered for smoking cessation. When compared to self-help, brief support from a healthcare provider, or usual care, a statistically significant increase in cessation was seen with group therapy (Stead et al., 2017). There was no evidence that group therapy was more effective than individual counseling in this review.

Smoking cessation is critical in decreasing progression of PAD and risk of major adverse events in this population. Of the methods discussed, bupropion, varenicline, and individual counseling seem to be the most efficacious in meta-analysis with varenicline having the strongest overall data for smoking cessation (Suissa et al., 2017). Moreover, all of the above therapies are considered safe in those with CVD. Combining behavioral support with pharmacotherapy can increase the success of smoking cessation by 10%–25% when compared to pharmacotherapy alone and should be considered for all patients with PAD (Stead & Lancaster, 2012a, 2012b).

Diabetes management

Sodium-glucose cotransporter 2 inhibitors (SGLT2i)

Empagliflozin, a SGLT2i, is currently the only glucose-mediating medication that has been shown to reduce mortality and cardiovascular outcomes in those with PAD. A subanalysis of the EMPA-REG OUTCOME trial (Empagliflozin, Cardiovascular Outcomes, and Mortality in Type 2 Diabetes) demonstrated that empagliflozin reduced cardiovascular death by 43% and all-cause mortality by 38% compared to placebo in patients with PAD with a number needed to treat of 29 to prevent 1 event (Verma et al., 2018). Moreover, there was no difference seen in overall adverse events between the two groups, including rates of lower extremity amputation.

Other in-class medications have not shown the same reduction in mortality and cardiovascular events as empagliflozin. Initially, a potential for harm was seen in the CANVAS trials (Canagliflozin Cardiovascular Assessment Study) with a twofold increase in rates of amputation for canagliflozin versus placebo in patients with type 2 diabetes mellitus (Neal et al., 2017). Later studies did not support this association (Perkovic et al., 2019). Another SGLT2i, dapagliflozin, compared to placebo in those with and without PAD was examined in an exploratory analysis of the DECLARE-TIMI 58 trail (Dapagliflozin and Cardiovascular Outcomes in Type 2 Diabetes). While there was no increased risk of amputation with dapagliflozin in those with or without PAD, there was also no decrease in major adverse cardiovascular events seen (Bonaca, Wiviott, et al., 2020).

Glucagon-like peptide 1 receptor agonists (GLP1RA)

Another class of glucose-regulating medications, GLP1RAs, have shown sustained decreases in major adverse cardiovascular events in the larger population of all CVD, but the benefits are controversial in the smaller PAD population. Albiglutide decreased major adverse cardiovascular events in those with type 2 diabetes and CVD, but did not show any additional benefit over that of the study population as a whole in a subset of participants with PAD (Hernandez et al., 2018). Another agent, exenatide, did not show benefit compared to placebo in regard to incidence of major cardiovascular events in those with or without PAD (Badjatiya et al., 2019). The most compelling data for benefit came from the LEADER trial (Liraglutide Effect and Action in Diabetes: Evaluation of Cardiovascular Outcomes Results) (Dhatariya et al., 2018). A retrospective analysis of this trial (with ~25% participants with PAD) showed that liraglutide use in patients with type 2 diabetes mellitus and at high risk for cardiovascular events had a significantly lower risk of amputations related to diabetic foot ulcers compared to placebo. Although this was not a primary foot ulcer trial, the presence of diabetic foot ulcers was a prespecified secondary endpoint in LEADER. Accordingly, this data should be viewed as exploratory and hypothesis generating only.

Lipid management

Lipid-lowering therapies are currently guideline recommended for all persons with PAD. The ACC/AHA multispecialty guidelines recommend those with symptomatic PAD and another major atherosclerotic cardiovascular event target an LDL-C of <70 mg/dL (Grundy et al., 2019); ESC guidelines recommend targeting an LDL-C <55 mg/dL in PAD (Mach et al., 2020). Dietary modification and lifestyle changes to reduce cholesterol levels should be considered as baseline therapy for all patients with vascular disease, including PAD (Grundy et al., 2019). In addition to this, two major classes of drugs, statins and proprotein convertase subtilisin/kexin type 9 inhibitors (PCSK9i), have been identified as beneficial in the treatment of PAD.

Statins

Statins lower cholesterol levels through LDL-C inhibition of 3-hydroxyl-3-methylglutaryl coenzyme A reductase (HMG-CoA reductase), a critical step in cholesterol biosynthesis. They have shown significant benefit in hard outcomes reduction in PAD. A prespecified PAD subgroup of the Heart Protection Study showed that simvastatin reduced risk of first major adverse cardiovascular event by 20%–25% compared to placebo regardless of presenting cholesterol levels (Randomized Trial of the Effects of Cholesterol-Lowering with Simvastatin on Peripheral Vascular and Other Major Vascular Outcomes in 20,536 People with Peripheral Arterial Disease and Other High-Risk Conditions, 2007). The relative reduction was 16% for incidence of first peripheral vascular event specifically. Simvastatin was also associated with a 38% reduction in new or worsening claudication in patients with coronary disease in the Scandinavian Simvastatin Survival Study (Pedersen et al., 1998). A meta-analysis including 14 studies with 19,368 patients showed that statin therapy in PAD was associated with a significant reduction in all-cause mortality (HR 0.77 [0.68–0.86]) (Antoniou et al., 2014). There was also a reduction seen in the incidence of cerebrovascular events (specifically, nonfatal stroke).

While there are no trials specifically addressing risk of major adverse limb events with statin therapy, a meta-analysis of 51 studies (mostly observational) demonstrated a 30% reduction in major adverse limb events and a 35% reduction in amputations with statin therapy in patients with PAD (Pastori et al., 2020). Accordingly, it is recommended by ACC/AHA guidelines that all patients with symptomatic PAD be on a high-intensity statin with a target LDL-C of <70 in those with PAD and another major ASCVD event (Gerhard-Herman et al., 2017; Grundy et al., 2019).

PCSK9i

Proprotein convertase subtilisin−kexin type 9 inhibitors (PCSK9i) are monoclonal antibodies that lower cholesterol levels, specifically LDL-C and lipoprotein(a), and have primarily been used in those who have not met a prespecified LDL goal or who are intolerant to statins. In an extension of the FOURIER trial (Further Cardiovascular Outcomes Research With PCSK9 Inhibition in Subjects With Elevated Risk), the PCSK9i evolocumab significantly reduced the rate of cardiovascular death, myocardial infarction, stroke, or hospital admission (a composite endpoint) compared to placebo in patients with PAD (Bonaca et al., 2018). A secondary endpoint removing hospital admission from the composite still demonstrated superiority of evolocumab. Even in those PAD patients without a history of myocardial infarction or stroke, a similar reduction in major adverse cardiovascular events was seen. Regarding limb events, evolocumab reduced the risk of acute limb ischemia, major amputation, or urgent revascularization by 42% in those with and without PAD.

Similarly, a prespecified analysis of the ODYSSEY OUTCOMES trial demonstrated that alirocumab, another PCSK9i, reduced limb events (including amputation for ischemia, limb revascularization, and critical limb-threatening ischemia) compared to placebo in statin-treated individuals with a recent myocardial infarction (Schwartz et al., 2020).

There is debate as to whether steep reductions in LDL-C levels or, alternatively, lipoprotein(a) levels are mechanistic for reductions in adverse limb outcomes in these trials. FOURIER achieved not-before-seen LDL-C reductions to a nadir of 10 mg/dL, however PAD event reduction in ODYSSEY OUTCOMES was associated with the lowest quartile of lipoprotein(a) levels and not LDL-C (Bonaca et al., 2018; Schwartz et al., 2020).

Overall, PCSK9i therapy in patients with PAD and poorly controlled lipids is likely beneficial from an event reduction standpoint, even in those without concomitant coronary or cerebrovascular disease to reduce major adverse cardiovascular and limb events.

Fibrates

Until recently, there were no known medical therapies that decreased amputation risk in PAD. As described in this chapter, several newer therapies including GLP1 agonists, PCSK9-i, and direct-acting oral anticoagulants have changed this landscape. Prior to this, fibrates were the only medication with signal for amputation reduction in this population. Fenofibrate is a peroxisome proliferator-activated receptor alpha activator, which in turn reduces levels of apoprotein C-III, altering lipid and glucose homeostasis. A prespecified analysis from the FIELD study (Fenofibrate Intervention and Event Lowering in Diabetes) in 9795 patients with type 2 diabetes demonstrated a significant reduction in below-the-knee amputations with fenofibrate as compared to placebo over 5 years duration (Rajamani et al., 2009). This was seen specifically in those without known large-vessel peripheral disease and despite similar mean lipid concentrations in the two groups. The authors postulate that this reduction in amputations was likely through nonlipid mechanisms and microvascular benefits provided by fibrates (reduction in proinflammatory markers and markers of endothelial dysfunction), but the mechanism of action still requires substantiation.

Antiplatelet management

Contemporary use of antiplatelet agents in PAD was first introduced by the Antithrombotic Trialists' Collaboration meta-analysis in 1994 and was later updated in 2002 (Collaboration, 2002; Collaborative Overview of Randomised Trials of Antiplatelet Therapy Prevention of Death, Myocardial Infarction, and Stroke by Prolonged Antiplatelet Therapy in Various Categories of Patients, 1994). Approximately 20% of the trials in the original and in the updated meta-analysis involved PAD. A 23% proportional reduction in vascular events was seen in patients with intermittent claudication or revascularization including both grafting and angioplasty in the update. Unfortunately, this outcome included several different antiplatelet agents, some of which are no-longer in use. This makes statements regarding the benefit of specific antiplatelet agents in PAD difficult. More recent comparisons of specific antiplatelet agents to placebo have shed some light on this problem.

Aspirin

Despite strong guideline recommendations for daily aspirin in those with symptomatic PAD (I, LOE: A) or asymptomatic PAD (IIa, LOE: C), little randomized data exists to support this endorsement (Gerhard-Herman et al., 2017).

Stand-alone trials of aspirin compared to placebo in asymptomatic patients with PAD have not shown benefit in reduction of major adverse cardiovascular events. The AAA trial (Aspirin for Asymptomatic Atherosclerosis) randomized 3350 participants with an ABI ≤ 0.95 but no clinical CVD to 100 mg aspirin or placebo daily and found no difference in composite of nonfatal coronary events, strokes, or revascularization at a mean follow-up of approximately 8 years (Fowkes et al., 2010). Similarly, The POPADAD trial (Prevention of Progression of Arterial Disease and Diabetes) found no difference in major adverse cardiovascular events (cardiovascular death, nonfatal myocardial infarction or stroke, or above the ankle amputation) in 1276 asymptomatic participants with diabetes and ABI ≤ 0.99 assigned to daily 100 mg aspirin compared to no aspirin (other options included antioxidant or placebo capsule; there was no interaction seen between aspirin and antioxidant) (Belch et al., 2008). Neither of these trials enrolled only patients now considered to have PAD and add only a modest amount to the evidence for aspirin.

The CLIPS trial (Critical Leg Ischemia Prevention Study) included participants with both symptomatic and asymptomatic PAD, although only a minority (22%) were asymptomatic (Catalano et al., 2007). Low-dose daily aspirin (100 mg) reduced the risk of major vascular events (including cardiovascular death, myocardial infarction, or stroke) and critical limb ischemia when compared to either placebo or antioxidants. This trial unfortunately had a small number of total participants (366) and a large portion of participants who dropped out (31%) of the study for nonvascular-related issues. This resulted in outcome comparisons including very small numbers of total events and renders comparisons between symptomatic and asymptomatic patients impossible.

A 2009 meta-analysis including 18 trials and 5269 participants with PAD compared to those taking aspirin alone or with dipyridamole to those in control groups (approximately half) (Berger et al., 2009). Therapy with daily midrange aspirin dosing was shown to reduce the incidence of nonfatal stroke but did not show reductions in mortality (both all-cause and cardiovascular) or myocardial infarction.

Although aspirin is effective for secondary prevention in the larger population of patients with CVD, the available randomized data suggest its role in PAD is likely of most benefit in those with symptomatic features of their disease and is of limited and questionable utility in those who are asymptomatic. While additional data exist that question this position, the observational nature of the studies make it difficult to interpret (McDermott et al., 2008).

P2Y12-i

The role of the non-aspirin P2Y12-i antiplatelet agents in PAD is better defined that of aspirin. The CAPRIE trial (Clopidogrel vs. Aspirin in Patients at Erisk of Ischemic Events) was the first antiplatelet study that included patients with CVD from noncardiac subgroups, including PAD, under a common protocol comparing daily aspirin to clopidogrel (A Randomised, Blinded, Trial of Clopidogrel vs. Aspirin in Patients at Risk of Ischaemic Events (CAPRIE), 1996). There was a modest benefit with clopidogrel in the composite primary outcome of ischemic stroke, myocardial infarction, or vascular death, but the relative risk reduction for the PAD subgroup was 23.8%; this was significantly higher than that for ischemic stroke or myocardial infarction. Whether there is a differential benefit of clopidogrel versus aspirin in PAD as compared to other vascular beds is not clear, but the idea that the two are of equal benefit only in patients with myocardial infarction cannot be ruled out. It should also be noted that bleeding was lower with clopidogrel monotherapy compared to aspirin monotherapy.

Ticagrelor, a more potent P2Y12-i than clopidogrel, reduces major adverse cardiovascular events and all-cause death in patients with acute coronary syndromes as compared to clopidogrel, but at the expense of increased bleeding and dyspnea (Wallentin et al., 2009). The EUCLID trial (Examining the Use of Ticagrelor in Peripheral Artery Disease) examined if ticagrelor was superior to clopidogrel for reduction of major adverse cardiovascular events in the symptomatic PAD population without clopidogrel resistance (Hiatt et al., 2017). In 13,885 patients randomized to either drug over a median of 30 months, there was no difference seen in the composite outcome of cardiovascular death, myocardial infarction, or stroke. Secondary exploratory endpoint analysis did however show a 0.5% absolute risk reduction in ischemic stroke with ticagrelor. Major bleeding profiles were similar between the two groups, but approximately 5% of those receiving ticagrelor discontinued the drug secondary to dyspnea. Accordingly, current data suggest that while ticagrelor monotherapy may not be inappropriate for secondary prevention in symptomatic PAD, the twice daily dosing and risk of dyspnea as a side effect make it less attractive than daily clopidogrel.

Dual antiplatelet therapy (DAPT)

DAPT has a proven role in acute coronary syndromes and after coronary revascularization. DAPT in the peripheral space, even after peripheral revascularization, is less studied and has unclear benefit (Aboyans et al., 2018; Gerhard-Herman et al., 2017). DAPT for secondary prevention in PAD has never been studied as a primary outcome in a dedicated trial, but several important secondary analyses of high-priority trials in mixed vascular disease have been performed. The CHARISMA trial (Clopidogrel for High Atherothrombotic Risk and Ischemic Stabilization, Management, and Avoidance) comparing clopidogrel and aspirin to aspirin and placebo in those at high risk of atherothrombotic events did not meet its primary endpoint for reduction in major adverse cardiovascular events with DAPT, and increased bleeding (Bhatt et al., 2006). A subgroup analysis of 3096 patients with PAD also failed to show a difference in the primary endpoint of cardiovascular death, myocardial infarction, or stroke, but showed a signal for reduction in the secondary endpoint of myocardial infarction and hospitalization for ischemic events, again with the caveat of increased bleeding (Cacoub et al., 2009). Similarly, a PEGASUS-TIMI 54 trial (Prevention of Cardiovascular Events in Patients With Prior Heart Attack Using Ticagrelor Compared to Placebo on a Background of Aspirin—Thrombolysis in Myocardial Infarction 54) substudy compared DAPT, this time with ticagrelor, to aspirin monotherapy in 1143 patients with PAD and prior myocardial infarction (Bonaca et al., 2016). The benefit in reduction of major adverse cardiovascular events with DAPT was consistent regardless of presence of PAD, however a significant reduction in major adverse limb events (35%) was observed. These data suggest that patients with polyvascular disease (CAD and PAD) may have a different risk profile and medication response; a hypothesis that has not been tested prospectively.

A novel antiplatelet agent, vorapaxar, is a PAR-1 platelet antagonist that has shown some benefit in reduction of cardiovascular and limb events when added to baseline therapy in patients with CVD (Qamar et al., 2020). A subgroup analysis of the TRA 2°P—TIMI 50 trial examined vorapaxar in 6136 patients with PAD and demonstrated a relative risk reduction of 15% for major cardiovascular events and 30% for major adverse limb events but with an increase in major bleeding. The benefit observed was most pronounced in patients with concomitant PAD and CAD as well as in those with prior extremity revascularization. Despite the increase in major bleeding, the net clinical benefit was in favor of vorapaxar.

Regarding DAPT for PAD after endovascular revascularization, only one randomized, placebo-controlled study has been performed to date. The MIRROR (Management of Peripheral Arterial Interventions with Mono or Dual Antiplatelet Therapy) 12-month follow-up study randomized 80 patients to receive pre- and post-femoropopliteal angioplasty therapy with aspirin and clopidogrel or aspirin and placebo (Strobl et al., 2013). At 6-months follow-up, those receiving DAPT had lower rates of repeat target-limb revascularization compared to the aspirin only group. This difference was not appreciated at 12 month follow up, however notably patients stopped clopidogrel/placebo at 6 months.

The potential harm of DAPT as medical therapy for secondary prevention of PAD alone probably outweighs the benefit based on current data. In those with concomitant CAD and especially in those with a prior myocardial infarction, there is a greater signal for long-term benefit with DAPT. For the subset of patients with PAD, who have undergone endovascular revascularization, a predetermined course of DAPT seems to be beneficial in terms of decreasing repeat revascularization. Currently, no strong postrevascularization guideline recommendations exist, and antithrombotic therapy choice is largely up to the proceduralist postintervention.

Antithrombotic management

Vitamin K antagonists

The first study addressing anticoagulation as a potential therapy for the medical treatment of PAD was the WAVE (Warfarin Antiplatelet Vascular Evaluation) trial in 2007. Warfarin (targeting an INR of 2—3) was added onto a background of aspirin therapy and was compared to aspirin monotherapy in 2161 patients with primarily symptomatic PAD (Anand et al., 2007). No difference was seen between groups for the coprimary endpoints of cardiovascular death, myocardial infarction, or stroke and myocardial infarction, stoke, severe ischemia requiring revascularization, or cardiovascular death. However, there was a significant signal for harm, with 4% life-threatening bleeds in the warfarin/aspirin arm compared to 1.2% in the aspirin arm. As a result of this work, the addition of warfarin anticoagulation to aspirin therapy for PAD, per se, receives a Class III Harm recommendation in the multispecialty guidelines. Warfarin anticoagulation should be reserved for patients with other indications for therapy (i.e., atrial fibrillation).

Direct-acting oral anticoagulants (DOACs)

Two trials have assessed the addition of low or arterial dose DOACs, namely rivaroxaban, to a baseline of aspirin therapy in patients with PAD. The COMPASS trial (Cardiovascular Outcomes for People Using Anticoagulation Strategies) randomized 27,395 participants with CAD and/or PAD to low-dose rivaroxaban with or without aspirin compared to aspirin alone over median 21 months (Eikelboom et al., 2017). The primary outcome of cardiovascular death, myocardial infarction, or stroke occurred in significantly fewer patients in the rivaroxaban plus aspirin arm than did in the aspirin alone group (relative risk reduction of 24%) or rivaroxaban alone group. Combination therapy and rivaroxaban alone therapy increased bleeding events as compared to aspirin alone, however risk of intracranial and fatal bleeds was not different between the rivaroxaban/aspirin group and the aspirin alone group. A substudy of COMPASS evaluating only patients with objective evidence of PAD (including carotid disease) showed that rivaroxaban/aspirin combination significantly reduced major adverse cardiovascular (relative risk reduction of 24%) and limb events (relative risk reduction of 45%) when compared to aspirin therapy alone over a mean of 23 months (Anand et al., 2018). Rivaroxaban therapy alone (5 mg twice daily) also reduced major adverse limb events (relative risk reduction of 33%) but did not decrease major adverse cardiovascular events when compared to aspirin alone. Both outcomes came at the expense of increased major bleeding (although no fatal or critical organ bleeding) when compared to the aspirin monotherapy group.

The VOYAGER PAD study (Vascular Outcomes Study of ASA Along with Rivaroxaban in Endovascular or Surgical Limb Revascularization for PAD) assessed similar outcomes as COMPASS but in a PAD population who had undergone extremity revascularization (endovascular or surgical) in the previous 10 days (Bonaca, Bauersachs, et al., 2020). This primary study randomized 6564 participants to 2.5 mg rivaroxaban twice daily plus aspirin versus aspirin and placebo over 3 years. There was a significant reduction (relative risk reduction of 15%, absolute risk reduction of 2.6%) in the composite of acute limb ischemia, major amputation, myocardial infarction, ischemic stroke, or cardiovascular death in the combination therapy arm compared to the aspirin therapy arm. Major bleeding as defined by Thrombolysis in Myocardial Infarction classification was not different between the groups, however, it was higher in the combination therapy arm when defined by the International Society on Thrombosis and Hemostasis classification.

Alone, the utility of anticoagulant therapy for medical treatment of PAD is minimal. 5 mg twice daily rivaroxaban is no better (and likely worse) at reducing major adverse cardiovascular and limb events than vascular dose (2.5 mg twice daily) rivaroxaban plus aspirin and increases major bleeding risk. Therapeutic anticoagulation with warfarin is overall harmful in this population. When compared to low-dose antiplatelet monotherapy with aspirin, vascular dose rivaroxaban plus aspirin is superior. While there are no direct comparisons of vascular dose rivaroxaban plus aspirin to DAPT, the overall data for the former are more compelling with two large positive randomized clinical trials than the latter's failed randomized controlled trial, even in those with recent extremity revascularization. When a P2Y12i (specifically, clopidogrel) is added on top of therapy with low-dose aspirin and vascular dose rivaroxaban in patients postrevascularization, outcomes are similar regardless of clopidogrel use, but bleeding may be higher with >30 days of use (Hiatt et al., 2020). Future studies comparing rivaroxaban/aspirin with DAPT, as well as comparisons between rivaroxaban/aspirin and single antiplatelet therapy with clopidogrel may better define benefit and bleeding risk with these agents.

Blood pressure management

In general, antihypertensive therapy is recommended in patients with elevated blood pressure and PAD to reduce the risk of major adverse cardiovascular events (Gerhard-Herman et al., 2017). Currently, patients with PAD are not treated differently than those with other CVD and guidelines recommend a target of <130/80 mmHg for all patients at high cardiovascular risk (which includes PAD) (Whelton et al., 2018). The support for this recommendation comes from several antihypertensive trials that included patients with PAD.

A subset analysis of the ABCD trial (Appropriate Blood Pressure Control in Diabetes) demonstrated that in patients diagnosed with type 2 diabetes and PAD at baseline visit (ABI <0.9), cardiovascular events were significantly less frequent with intensive blood pressure treatment (with enalapril or nisoldipine to a mean of 128/75 mmHg) compared to moderate blood pressure control (Mehler et al., 2003). Unfortunately, the absolute number of events in this analysis was small (3 events in the intensive treatment arm and 12 events in the moderate treatment arm) but consistent with other contemporary studies regarding event reduction in CAD and cerebrovascular disease. A posthoc analysis of the INVEST trial (International Verapamil-SR/Trandolapril Study) including 2699 patients with PAD followed over a mean of 2.7 years found that the primary composite outcome of all-cause death, nonfatal myocardial infarction, or nonfatal stroke occurred least frequently with blood pressure treated to a mean of 135–145 mmHg/60–90 mmHg (Bavry et al., 2010). Interestingly, those with PAD demonstrated a J-shaped relationship with systolic blood pressure and the primary outcome, with harm at lower systolic blood pressures as well (most robust at ≤110 mmHg), whereas those without PAD did not.

Recently, a reanalysis ALLHAT (Antihypertensive and Lipid-Lowering Treatment to Prevent Heart Attack Trial) has further brought into question intensive blood pressure control in PAD (Itoga et al., 2018). Time to first lower extremity PAD event (PAD-related hospitalization, procedure, medical treatment, or PAD-related death) in 33,357 patients over medial 4.3 years was evaluated. There was a significantly higher percent of PAD events in those with systolic blood pressure <120 mmHg (26%) and >160 mmHg (21%) when compared to a systolic blood pressure of 120–129 mmHg. Those with lower, but not higher, diastolic blood pressures (<60 mmHg) also demonstrated a higher hazard of PAD-related events.

Only one study to date has provided evidence of benefit with a specific antihypertensive medication in PAD. The HOPE trial (Heart Outcomes Prevention Evaluation) subgroup analysis included 3099 patients with PAD (ABI ≤0.9) followed for 4.5 years (Östergren et al., 2004). Therapy with ramipril compared to placebo significantly reduced cardiovascular events in those with both clinical and subclinical PAD. Of note, patients were not hypertensive at baseline.

Overall, blood pressure control reduces major adverse cardiovascular events in PAD. As described, intensive blood pressure control to <120 mmHg systolic and <70 mmHg diastolic may increase PAD events. This data are seemingly conflicting with that of the SPRINT trial in which a targeted blood pressure <120 mmHg in patients at high risk of cardiovascular events significantly reduced future cardiovascular events and mortality (Wright et al., 2015). While patients with PAD were included in this study, the numbers were overall small and events in this group were lacking. Given this, the ideal blood pressure goal in PAD remains unknown, but based on extrapolated data a goal of 120−130/70−80 mmHg may be reasonable once PAD is objectively diagnosed. Otherwise, those at risk of developing PAD or who have other CVD should continue to target recommended comorbidity-specific goals.

Multimodality drug therapy

Guideline-based optimal medical therapy for patients with PAD consists of an antiplatelet agent (namely, aspirin or clopidogrel), a statin medication, and antihypertensive medications in those patients who have hypertension and PAD (all class I LOE:A recommendations). Individually, these interventions have been shown to reduce major adverse cardiovascular and limb events in this population as previously discussed. Collectively, observational data points toward an additive effect on major adverse outcomes. Data from the National Health and Nutrition Examination Survey of patients with PAD (ABI ≤0.90) identified a 65% lower all-cause mortality in those on multiple preventive therapies (aspirin, statin, and ACEi/ARB) (Pande et al., 2011). Similarly, a retrospective cohort of patient who underwent elective surgical lower extremity bypass for claudication found that those on optimal medical therapy (antiplatelet agent, statin, and ACEi/ARB) before surgery had 55% lower odds of mortality and 54% lower odds of myocardial infarction at 30 days compared to those not on optimal therapy. At 1 year, odds of mortality were 43% lower and myocardial infarction 52% lower in those on optimal therapy than those not (Howard et al., 2022). Despite no randomized data to show the magnitude of event reduction in those on multidrug therapy for PAD compared to single drug therapy or placebo, at minimum practitioners should consider antiplatelet and statin therapy in this population. Additionally, treatment of other comorbid conditions such as hypertension, diabetes, and tobacco use disorders likely further decreases overall risk in PAD and should be implemented for secondary prevention.

Noninvasive therapies that improve symptoms in PAD

Much of the data regarding benefit in PAD has been centered on reduction of mortality and secondary adverse cardiovascular and limb events. While this is critically important, interventions focused on symptom improvement and quality of life may be just as important to patients as intermittent claudication and inability to perform activities of daily living can be devastating. Several medical therapies previously discussed may impact symptomatology in PAD in addition to hard outcomes, but with limited, observational evidence and rarely as a primary trial outcome. For example, lipid-lowering therapy may improve local symptoms in those with PAD, including total walking distance and pain-free walking (Aung et al., 2007). Unfortunately, many studies addressing outcomes such as improvement in claudication or quality of life measures are by nature subjective and difficult to interpret. In this section, we will discuss the noninvasive therapies with the strongest evidence for symptom improvement in PAD.

Cilostazol

Cilostazol is a phosphodiesterase III inhibitor that increases circulating levels of cyclic AMP thus promoting vasodilation as well as some degree of antiplatelet activity. The basis of cilostazol use stemmed from a randomized, controlled trial of cilostazol versus pentoxifylline versus placebo (Dawson et al., 2000). Prior to this, pentoxifylline was the only United States Food and Drug Administration approved medication for treatment of claudication. 698 patients with objective evidence of PAD (ABI ≤ 0.9 or predetermined drop in postexercise ankle pressure in the affected limb) were randomized to one of the three therapies. After 24 weeks of treatment, mean max walking distance increased by 54% (mean of 107 m increase) in the cilostazol treated group compared to $\sim 30\%$ in both the pentoxifylline and placebo groups. Notably, there was a greater frequency of minor side effects such as headache, palpitations, and diarrhea in the cilostazol group compared to the other two groups. A more recent meta-analysis of 15 double-blind, randomized, controlled trials comparing cilostazol to either placebo or pentoxifylline determined that cilostazol does, indeed, improve walking distance in those with PAD and intermittent claudication (Bedenis et al., 2014). The authors note that available data does not make clear whether cilostazol significantly improves quality of life.

Exercise therapy

Supervised exercise therapy

As a lone therapy, supervised treadmill exercise training in those with PAD is supported by multiple randomized clinical trials and a Class I LOE: A recommendation in multiple PAD guidelines and scientific statements (Gerhard-Herman et al., 2017; Treat-Jacobson et al., 2019). Claudication onset time, peak walking distance, and 6-minute walk test distance are all improved with supervised treadmill exercise training in those with and without classic symptoms of claudication (Treat-Jacobson et al., 2019). Conversely, symptomatic improvement of intermittent claudication with extremity revascularization is excellent in observational studies but controversial as there is cost of procedural risk to the patient and questionable long-term benefit (Ahimastos et al., 2011; Frans et al., 2012). Several trials have evaluated the effectiveness of exercise therapy compared to medical or procedural treatments for PAD with favorable outcomes. The CLEVER trial (Claudication: Exercise vs. Endoluminal Revascularization) demonstrated comparable benefits for supervised exercise as compared to stent revascularization. The study randomized 111 patients with aortoiliac disease to optimal medical care alone or with the addition of either supervised exercise or stent revascularization (Murphy et al., 2015). At 6 months, the change in peak walking time (the primary outcome) in the medical therapy plus supervised exercise group was significantly higher than in the medical therapy alone or the medical therapy plus stent revascularization groups. At 18 months, the supervised exercise and the stent revascularization groups had similar improvement in peak walking time but were both significantly better than medical therapy alone.

When combining both therapies (supervised exercise and revascularization), outcomes may be better than with individual therapy alone. The ERASE (Endovascular Revascularization and Supervised Exercise) trial randomized 212 participants with PAD to endovascular revascularization plus supervised exercise therapy to supervised exercise therapy alone (Fakhry et al., 2015). At 12 months, combination therapy significantly improved both maximum walking distance (mean difference of 282 m) and pain-free walking distance (mean difference of 408 m) as well as several quality-of-life metrics compared to supervised exercise therapy alone.

Home-based exercise therapy

Despite the proven benefit of supervised exercise therapy, it can unfortunately be costly, is time-intensive, and requires significant effort on the part of the patient. The majority of these supervised exercise programs include three 30-to-60-minute sessions weekly over a minimum of 12 weeks that occur in a hospital outpatient setting or a physician office. A proposed solution to this problem is home-based exercise therapy. Several randomized trials over the last decade have addressed this. A meta-analysis including 11 of these trials involving 807 patients published in 2019 showed significant improvements in maximum walking distance, onset of intermittent claudication, and distance achieved during 6-minute walk test as compared to controls not enrolled in a supervised exercise program (Golledge et al., 2019). Unfortunately, adherence to home walking programs is poor and this has affected community deliverance. More recently, the LITE trial (Low Intensity Exercise Intervention in PAD) examined if a low-intensity home walking program (aimed at improving adherence to exercise) compared to a standard, high-intensity program and to a nonexercise control group improved walking distance in those with PAD (McDermott et al., 2021). Despite not being numerically worse than the nonexercise control group, no statistical difference was seen between low-intensity exercise and the control group in terms of walking distance (both groups actually had a decrease in 6-minute walk distance over 12 months) and low-intensity exercise was significantly less effective than high-intensity exercise.

Interestingly, quality of life changes and changes in walking distance do not always correlate. In the secondary outcome analysis of the LITE trial, although there was no difference seen in 6-minute walk distance between the low-intensity and non-exercise control groups, self-reported walking limitations assessed by the walking impairment questionnaire were significantly lower in both distance and speed outcomes (i.e., a positive outcome) at 6 and 12 months in the low-intensity walking group (McDermott et al., 2021). Additionally, at 6 months, quality of life as measured by the Short Form 36 questionnaire was significantly higher in the low-intensity exercise group as compared to the nonexercise control group. Surprisingly, low-intensity exercise walking impairment questionnaire distance scores at 6 months were also better than those in the high-intensity exercise group. Despite no evidence that low-intensity exercise improves objective walking outcomes in PAD, an improvement in these patient-reported outcomes may have a significant impact on quality of life. This discordant observation was also seen in a trilogy of similar randomized trials. In total, 404 people were randomized to either an exercise or control group and all completed 6-minute walk tests and the Walking Impairment Questionnaire. There was a significant improvement and a significant decline in 6-minute walk distance in the exercise and control arms, respectively, among those who reported no change in their ability to walk on the Walking Impairment Questionnaire. Similarly, in those who reported worsening in their ability to walk, 6-minute walk distance in the exercise group significantly improved and in the control group significantly declined.

Physical activity is recommended for all patients with PAD in both the American and European guidelines and supervised exercise is recommended for those with intermittent claudication with a high class of recommendation and level of evidence (Aboyans et al., 2018; Gerhard-Herman et al., 2017). Extremity revascularization can provide immediate symptom relief in those with claudication and can be used as a complementary treatment to exercise therapy with the potential for additive benefits (Sobieszczyk & Beckman, 2015). Home-based exercise is a potential answer for those who either cannot travel to a center providing supervised exercise or in those in which this is cost prohibitive. Unfortunately, at this time the Centers for Medicare and Medicaid Services do not reimburse for home-based exercise, limiting generalizability of this important and less-burdensome therapy. Finally, patient-centered and reported outcomes regarding symptom improvement in PAD does not always correlate with objective changes in walking distance and should be taken into greater consideration in future research on this topic.

Conclusions

Smoking, hypertension, hypercholesterolemia, and type 2 diabetes mellitus account for the majority of the risk of developing and of progression of PAD. These risk factors are seemingly additive with a progressive increase in risk in those with multiple risk factors and is highest in those with all four risk factors (186 cases/100,000 person-years) (Joosten et al., 2012). At least one of these risk factors is present in 80% of individuals with CAD, but as high as 95% of cases of severe PAD (Joosten et al., 2012). As such, therapies aimed at treatment of these comorbid conditions is paramount in PAD. Noninvasive therapies such as smoking cessation and exercise, whether supervised or at home, should be recommended for all given the favorable risk/benefit profile.

Statin therapy aimed at reduction of LDL-C and addition of medications such as PCSK9i contingent upon patient risk profile have shown significant reduction in cardiovascular and limb events. Similarly, antithrombotic therapy with either aspirin or clopidogrel—and now vascular dose rivaroxaban—reduces hard outcomes in patients with PAD, especially in those who are symptomatic. Comorbid conditions such as diabetes mellitus and hypertension increase major adverse cardiovascular events in PAD and accordingly need to be treated. Addition of empagliflozin in those with type 2 diabetes mellitus and CVD reduced death and all-cause mortality in a trial substudy, but this does not seem to be an SGLT2i class effect and needs to be prospectively analyzed as a primary outcome. ACEi and ARBs may be more effective that other agents for treatment of hypertension in PAD. Overall, multi-modal treatment of PAD that incorporates therapies to reduce both patient symptoms and important cardiovascular and limb outcomes should be standard for all patients.

References

Aboyans, V., Ricco, J. B., Bartelink, M. L. E. L., Björck, M., Brodmann, M., Cohnert, T., Collet, J. P., Czerny, M., De Carlo, M., Debus, S., Espinola-Klein, C., Kahan, T., Kownator, S., Mazzolai, L., Naylor, A. R., Roffi, M., Röther, J., Sprynger, M., Tendera, M., … Obiekezie, A. (2018). 2017 ESC guidelines on the diagnosis and treatment of peripheral arterial diseases, in collaboration with the European society for vascular surgery (ESVS). *European Heart Journal, 39*(9), 763–816. https://doi.org/10.1093/eurheartj/ehx095

Ahimastos, A. A., Pappas, E. P., Buttner, P. G., Walker, P. J., Kingwell, B. A., & Golledge, J. (2011). A meta-analysis of the outcome of endovascular and noninvasive therapies in the treatment of intermittent claudication. *Journal of Vascular Surgery, 54*(5), 1511–1521. https://doi.org/10.1016/j.jvs.2011.06.106

Anand, S. S., Bosch, J., Eikelboom, J. W., Connolly, S. J., Diaz, R., Widimsky, P., Aboyans, V., Alings, M., Kakkar, A. K., Keltai, K., Maggioni, A. P., Lewis, B. S., Störk, S., Zhu, J., Lopez-Jaramillo, P., O'Donnell, M., Commerford, P. J., Vinereanu, D., Pogosova, N., … Chioncel, Ovidiu (2018). Rivaroxaban with or without aspirin in patients with stable peripheral or carotid artery disease: An international, randomised, double-blind, placebo-controlled trial. *The Lancet, 391*(10117), 219–229. https://doi.org/10.1016/s0140-6736(17)32409-1

Anand, S., Yusuf, S., Xie, C., Pogue, J., Eikelboom, J., Budaj, A., Sussex, B., Liu, L., Guzman, R., Cina, C., Crowell, R., Keltai, M., & Gosselin, G. (2007). Oral anticoagulant and antiplatelet therapy and peripheral arterial disease. *New England Journal of Medicine, 357*(3), 217–227. https://doi.org/10.1056/NEJMoa065959

Antoniou, G. A., Fisher, R. K., Georgiadis, G. S., Antoniou, S. A., & Torella, F. (2014). Statin therapy in lower limb peripheral arterial disease: Systematic review and meta-analysis. *Vascular Pharmacology, 63*(2), 79–87. https://doi.org/10.1016/j.vph.2014.09.001

A randomised, blinded, trial of clopidogrel versus aspirin in patients at risk of ischaemic events (CAPRIE). *The Lancet, 348*(9038), (1996), 1329–1339. https://doi.org/10.1016/s0140-6736(96)09457-3

Aung, P. P., Maxwell, H. G., Jepson, R. G., Price, J. F., & Leng, G. C. (2007). Lipid-lowering for peripheral arterial disease of the lower limb. *Cochrane Database of Systematic Reviews*, (4) https://doi.org/10.1002/14651858.CD000123.pub2

Badjatiya, A., Merrill, P., Buse, J. B., Goodman, S. G., Katona, B., Iqbal, N., Pagidipati, N. J., Sattar, N., Holman, R. R., Hernandez, A. F., Mentz, R. J., Patel, M. R., & Jones, W. S. (2019). Clinical outcomes in patients with type 2 diabetes mellitus and peripheral artery disease. *Circulation: Cardiovascular Interventions, 12*(12). https://doi.org/10.1161/circinterventions.119.008018

Bavry, A. A., Anderson, R. D., Gong, Y., Denardo, S. J., Cooper-DeHoff, R. M., Handberg, E. M., & Pepine, C. J. (2010). Outcomes among hypertensive patients with concomitant peripheral and coronary artery disease. *Hypertension, 55*(1), 48–53. https://doi.org/10.1161/hypertensionaha.109.142240

Bedenis, R., Stewart, M., Cleanthis, M., Robless, P., Mikhailidis, D. P., & Stansby, G. (2014). Cilostazol for intermittent claudication. *Cochrane Database of Systematic Reviews, 2014*(10). https://doi.org/10.1002/14651858.CD003748.pub4

Belch, J., MacCuish, A., Campbell, I., Cobbe, S., Taylor, R., Prescott, R., Lee, R., Bancroft, J., MacEwan, S., Shepherd, J., Macfarlane, P., Morris, A., Jung, R., Kelly, C., Connacher, A., Peden, N., Jamieson, A., Matthews, D., Leese, G., ... MacWalter, R. (2008). The prevention of progression of arterial disease and diabetes (POPADAD) trial: Factorial randomised placebo controlled trial of aspirin and antioxidants in patients with diabetes and asymptomatic peripheral arterial disease. *BMJ, 337*, a1840. https://doi.org/10.1136/bmj.a1840

Berger, J. S., Krantz, M. J., Kittelson, J. M., & Hiatt, W. R. (2009). Aspirin for the prevention of cardiovascular events in patients with peripheral artery disease: A meta-analysis of randomized trials. *JAMA, 301*(18), 1909–1919. https://doi.org/10.1001/jama.2009.623

Bhatt, D. L., Fox, K. A. A., Hacke, W., Berger, P. B., Black, H. R., Boden, W. E., Cacoub, P., Cohen, E. A., Creager, M. A., Easton, J. D., Flather, M. D., Haffner, S. M., Hamm, C. W., Hankey, G. J., Johnston, S. C., Mak, K.-H., Mas, J.-L., Montalescot, G., Pearson, T. A., ... Topol, E. J. (2006). Clopidogrel and aspirin versus aspirin alone for the prevention of atherothrombotic events. *New England Journal of Medicine, 354*(16), 1706–1717. https://doi.org/10.1056/NEJMoa060989

Bonaca, M. P., Nault, P., Giugliano, R. P., Keech, A. C., Pineda, A. L., Kanevsky, E., Kuder, J., Murphy, S. A., Jukema, J. W., Lewis, B. S., Tokgozoglu, L., Somaratne, R., Sever, P. S., Pedersen, T. R., & Sabatine, M. S. (2018). Low-density lipoprotein cholesterol lowering with evolocumab and outcomes in patients with peripheral artery disease. *Circulation, 137*(4), 338–350. https://doi.org/10.1161/circulationaha.117.032235

Bonaca, M. P., Bauersachs, R. M., Anand, S. S., Debus, E. S., Nehler, M. R., Patel, M. R., Fanelli, F., Capell, W. H., Diao, L., Jaeger, N., Hess, C. N., Pap, A. F., Kittelson, J. M., Gudz, I., Mátyás, L., Krievins, D. K., Diaz, R., Brodmann, M., Muehlhofer, E., ... Hiatt, W. R. (2020). Rivaroxaban in peripheral artery disease after revascularization. *New England Journal of Medicine, 382*(21), 1994–2004. https://doi.org/10.1056/NEJMoa2000052

Bonaca, M. P., Bhatt, D. L., Storey, R. F., Steg, P. G., Cohen, M., Kuder, J., Goodrich, E., Nicolau, J. C., Parkhomenko, A., López-Sendón, J., Dellborg, M., Dalby, A., Špinar, J., Aylward, P., Corbalán, R., Abola, M. T. B., Jensen, E. C., Held, P., Braunwald, E., & Sabatine, M. S. (2016). Ticagrelor for prevention of ischemic events after myocardial infarction in patients with peripheral artery disease. *Journal of the American College of Cardiology, 67*(23), 2719–2728. https://doi.org/10.1016/j.jacc.2016.03.524

Bonaca, M. P., Wiviott, S. D., Zelniker, T. A., Mosenzon, O., Bhatt, D. L., Leiter, L. A., Mcguire, D. K., Goodrich, E. L., De Mendonca Furtado, R. H., Wilding, J. P. H., Cahn, A., Gause-Nilsson, I. A. M., Johanson, P., Fredriksson, M., Johansson, P. A., Langkilde, A. M., Raz, I., & Sabatine, M. S. (2020). Dapagliflozin and cardiac, kidney, and limb outcomes in patients with and without peripheral artery disease in DECLARE-TIMI 58. *Circulation, 142*(8), 734–747. https://doi.org/10.1161/CIRCULATIONAHA.119.044775

Cacoub, P. P., Bhatt, D. L., Steg, P. G., Topol, E. J., & Creager, M. A. (2009). Patients with peripheral arterial disease in the CHARISMA trial. *European Heart Journal, 30*(2), 192–201. https://doi.org/10.1093/eurheartj/ehn534

Catalano, M., Pilger, E., Pabst, E., Kostner, G., Wautrecht, J. C., Baitsch, G., Breddin, K., Diehm, C., Podhaisky, H., Taute, B. M., Diamantoupolos, E. J., Aimar, T., Alari, G., Albano, S., Altamura, N., Arosio, E., Bortolon, M., Caccia, R., Carotta, M., ... Mahler, F. (2007). Prevention of serious vascular events by aspirin amongst patients with peripheral arterial disease: Randomized, double-blind trial. *Journal of Internal Medicine, 261*(3), 276–284. https://doi.org/10.1111/j.1365-2796.2006.01763.x

Collaboration, A. T. (2002). Collaborative meta-analysis of randomised trials of antiplatelet therapy for prevention of death, myocardial infarction, and stroke in high risk patients. *BMJ, 324*(7329), 71–86. https://doi.org/10.1136/bmj.324.7329.71

Collaborative overview of randomised trials of antiplatelet therapy Prevention of death, myocardial infarction, and stroke by prolonged antiplatelet therapy in various categories of patients. *BMJ, 308*(6921), (1994), 81–106. https://doi.org/10.1136/bmj.308.6921.81

Creager, M. A., & Hamburg, N. M. (2022). Smoking cessation improves outcomes in patients with peripheral artery disease. *JAMA Cardiology, 7*(1), 15–16. https://doi.org/10.1001/jamacardio.2021.3987

Criqui, M. H., Langer, R. D., Feigelson, H. S., Klauber, M. R., Mccann, T. J., Browner, D., Criqui, M. H., & Fronek, A. (1992). Mortality over a period of 10 years in patients with peripheral arterial disease. *New England Journal of Medicine, 326*(6), 381–386. https://doi.org/10.1056/NEJM199202063260605

Criqui, M. H., Matsushita, K., Aboyans, V., Hess, C. N., Hicks, C. W., Kwan, T. W., McDermott, M. M., Misra, S., & Ujueta, F. (2021). Lower extremity peripheral artery disease: Contemporary epidemiology, management gaps, and future directions: A scientific statement from the American heart association. *Circulation*, E171–E191. https://doi.org/10.1161/CIR.0000000000001005

Dawson, D. L., Cutler, B. S., Hiatt, W. R., Hobson, R. W., Martin, J. D., Bortey, E. B., Forbes, W. P., & Strongness, D. E. (2000). A comparison of cilostazol and pentoxifylline for treating intermittent claudication. *The American Journal of Medicine, 109*(7), 523–530. https://doi.org/10.1016/S0002-9343(00)00569-6

Dhatariya, K., Bain, S. C., Buse, J. B., Simpson, R., Tarnow, L., Kaltoft, M. S., Stellfeld, M., Tornøe, K., & Pratley, R. E. (2018). The impact of liraglutide on diabetes-related foot ulceration and associated complications in patients with type 2 diabetes at high risk for cardiovascular events: Results from the LEADER trial. *Diabetes Care, 41*(10), 2229–2235. https://doi.org/10.2337/dc18-1094

Eikelboom, J. W., Connolly, S. J., Bosch, J., Dagenais, G. R., Hart, R. G., Shestakovska, O., Diaz, R., Alings, M., Lonn, E. M., Anand, S. S., Widimsky, P., Hori, M., Avezum, A., Piegas, L. S., Branch, K. R. H., Probstfield, J., Bhatt, D. L., Zhu, J., Liang, Y., … Yusuf, S. (2017). Rivaroxaban with or without aspirin in stable cardiovascular disease. *New England Journal of Medicine, 377*(14), 1319−1330. https://doi.org/10.1056/NEJMoa1709118

Fakhry, F., Spronk, S., Van Der Laan, L., Wever, J. J., Teijink, J. A. W., Hoffmann, W. H., Smits, T. M., Van Brussel, J. P., Stultiens, G. N. M., Derom, A., Den Hoed, P. T., Ho, G. H., Van Dijk, L. C., Verhofstad, N., Orsini, M., Van Petersen, A., Woltman, K., Hulst, I., Van Sambeek, M. R. H. M., … Hunink, M. G. M. (2015). Endovascular revascularization and supervised exercise for peripheral artery disease and intermittent claudication: A randomized clinical trial. *JAMA, the Journal of the American Medical Association, 314*(18), 1936−1944. https://doi.org/10.1001/jama.2015.14851

Fowkes, F. G. R., Aboyans, V., Fowkes, F. J. I., McDermott, M. M., Sampson, U. K. A., & Criqui, M. H. (2017). Peripheral artery disease: Epidemiology and global perspectives. *Nature Reviews Cardiology, 14*(3), 156−170. https://doi.org/10.1038/nrcardio.2016.179

Fowkes, F. G. R., Price, J. F., Stewart, M. C. W., Butcher, I., Leng, G. C., Pell, A. C. H., Sandercock, P. A. G., Fox, K. A. A., Lowe, G. D. O., & Murray, G. D. (2010). Aspirin for prevention of cardiovascular events in a general population screened for a low ankle brachial index: A randomized controlled trial. *JAMA, 303*(9), 841−848. https://doi.org/10.1001/jama.2010.221

Frans, F. A., Bipat, S., Reekers, J. A., Legemate, D. A., & Koelemay, M. J. W. (2012). Systematic review of exercise training or percutaneous transluminal angioplasty for intermittent claudication. *British Journal of Surgery, 99*(1), 16−28. https://doi.org/10.1002/bjs.7656

Gerhard-Herman, M. D., Gornik, H. L., Barrett, C., Barshes, N. R., Corriere, M. A., Drachman, D. E., Fleisher, L. A., Fowkes, F. G. R., Hamburg, N. M., Kinlay, S., Lookstein, R., Misra, S., Mureebe, L., Olin, J. W., Patel, R. A. G., Regensteiner, J. G., Schanzer, A., Shishehbor, M. H., Stewart, K. J., Treat-Jacobson, D., & Walsh, M. E. (2017). 2016 AHA/ACC guideline on the management of patients with lower extremity peripheral artery disease: Executive summary: A report of the American college of cardiology/American heart association task force on clinical practice guidelines. *Circulation, 135*(12), e686−e725. https://doi.org/10.1161/CIR.0000000000000470

Golledge, J., Singh, T. P., Alahakoon, C., Pinchbeck, J., Yip, L., Moxon, J. V., & Morris, D. R. (2019). Meta-analysis of clinical trials examining the benefit of structured home exercise in patients with peripheral artery disease. *British Journal of Surgery, 106*(4), 319−331. https://doi.org/10.1002/bjs.11101

Gonzales, D., Rennard, S. I., Nides, M., Oncken, C., Azoulay, S., Billing, C. B., Watsky, E. J., Gong, J., Williams, K. E., & Reeves, K. R. (2006). Varenicline, an α4β2 nicotinic acetylcholine receptor partial agonist, vs sustained-release bupropion and placebo for smoking cessation: A randomized controlled trial. *JAMA, 296*(1), 47−55. https://doi.org/10.1001/jama.296.1.47

Grundy, S. M., Stone, N. J., Bailey, A. L., Beam, C., Birtcher, K. K., Blumenthal, R. S., Braun, L. T., De Ferranti, S., Faiella-Tommasino, J., Forman, D. E., Goldberg, R., Heidenreich, P. A., Hlatky, M. A., Jones, D. W., Lloyd-Jones, D., Lopez-Pajares, N., Ndumele, C. E., Orringer, C. E., Peralta, C. A., … Yeboah, J. (2019). 2018 AHA/ACC/AACVPR/AAPA/ABC/ACPM/ADA/AGS/APhA/ASPC/NLA/PCNA guideline on the management of blood cholesterol: A report of the American college of cardiology/American heart association task force on clinical practice guidelines. *Circulation, 139*(25), E1082–E1143. https://doi.org/10.1161/CIR.0000000000000625

Hartmann-Boyce, J., Chepkin, S. C., Ye, W., Bullen, C., & Lancaster, T. (2018). Nicotine replacement therapy versus control for smoking cessation. *Cochrane Database of Systematic Reviews, 2018*(5). https://doi.org/10.1002/14651858.CD000146.pub5

Hernandez, A. F., Green, J. B., Janmohamed, S., D'Agostino, R. B., Granger, C. B., Jones, N. P., Leiter, L. A., Rosenberg, A. E., Sigmon, K. N., Somerville, M. C., Thorpe, K. M., McMurray, J. J. V., Del Prato, S., Del Prato, S., McMurray, J. J. V., D'Agostino, R. B., Granger, C. B., Hernandez, A. F., Janmohamed, S., … Mandal, T. (2018). Albiglutide and cardiovascular outcomes in patients with type 2 diabetes and cardiovascular disease (harmony outcomes): A double-blind, randomised placebo-controlled trial. *The Lancet, 392*(10157), 1519–1529. https://doi.org/10.1016/s0140-6736(18)32261-x

Hiatt, W. R., Bonaca, M. P., Patel, M. R., Nehler, M. R., Debus, E. S., Anand, S. S., Capell, W. H., Brackin, T., Jaeger, N., Hess, C. N., Pap, A. F., Berkowitz, S. D., Muehlhofer, E., Haskell, L., Brasil, D., Madaric, J., Sillesen, H., Szalay, D., & Bauersachs, R. (2020). Rivaroxaban and aspirin in peripheral artery disease lower extremity revascularization impact of concomitant clopidogrel on efficacy and safety. *Circulation, 142*(23), 2219–2230. https://doi.org/10.1161/CIRCULATIONAHA.120.050465

Hiatt, W. R., Fowkes, F. G. R., Heizer, G., Berger, J. S., Baumgartner, I., Held, P., Katona, B. G., Mahaffey, K. W., Norgren, L., Jones, W. S., Blomster, J., Millegård, M., Reist, C., & Patel, M. R. (2017). Ticagrelor versus clopidogrel in symptomatic peripheral artery disease. *New England Journal of Medicine, 376*(1), 32–40. https://doi.org/10.1056/NEJMoa1611688

Howard, R., Albright, J., Powell, C., Osborne, N., Corriere, M., Laveroni, E., Sukul, D., Goodney, P., & Henke, P. (2022). Underutilization of medical management of peripheral artery disease among patients with claudication undergoing lower extremity bypass. *Journal of Vascular Surgery, 76*(4), 1037–1044.e2. https://doi.org/10.1016/j.jvs.2022.05.016

Hughes, J., Stead, L., & Lancaster, T. (2004). Antidepressants for smoking cessation. *Cochrane Database of Systematic Reviews.* https://doi.org/10.1002/14651858.CD000031.pub2

Hurt, R. D., Sachs, D. P. L., Glover, E. D., Offord, K. P., Johnston, J. A., Dale, L. C., Khayrallah, M. A., Schroeder, D. R., Glover, P. N., Sullivan, C. R., Croghan, I. T., & Sullivan, P. M. (1997). A comparison of sustained-release bupropion and placebo for smoking cessation. *New England Journal of Medicine, 337*(17), 1195–1202. https://doi.org/10.1056/NEJM199710233371703

Itoga, N. K., Tawfik, D. S., Lee, C. K., Maruyama, S., Leeper, N. J., & Chang, T. I. (2018). Association of blood pressure measurements with peripheral artery disease events. *Circulation, 138*(17), 1805–1814. https://doi.org/10.1161/circulationaha.118.033348

Joosten, M. M., Pai, J. K., Bertoia, M. L., Rimm, E. B., Spiegelman, D., Mittleman, M. A., & Mukamal, K. J. (2012). Associations between conventional cardiovascular risk factors and risk of peripheral artery disease in men. *JAMA, 308*(16), 1660–1667. https://doi.org/10.1001/jama.2012.13415

Jorenby, D. E., Hays, J. T., Rigotti, N. A., Azoulay, S., Watsky, E. J., Williams, K. E., Billing, C. B., Gong, J., & Reeves, K. R. (2006). Efficacy of varenicline, an α4β2 nicotinic acetylcholine receptor partial agonist, vs placebo or sustained-release bupropion for smoking cessation: A randomized controlled trial. *JAMA, 296*(1), 56–63. https://doi.org/10.1001/jama.296.1.56

Jorenby, D. E., Leischow, S. J., Nides, M. A., Rennard, S. I., Johnston, J. A., Hughes, A. R., Smith, S. S., Muramoto, M. L., Daughton, D. M., Doan, K., Fiore, M. C., & Baker, T. B. (1999). A controlled trial of sustained-release bupropion, a nicotine patch, or both for smoking cessation. *New England Journal of Medicine, 340*(9), 685–691. https://doi.org/10.1056/NEJM199903043400903

Lancaster, T., & Stead, L. F. (2017). Individual behavioural counselling for smoking cessation. *Cochrane Database of Systematic Reviews, 2017*(3). https://doi.org/10.1002/14651858.CD001292.pub3

Mach, F., Baigent, C., Catapano, A. L., Koskinas, K. C., Casula, M., Badimon, L., Chapman, M. J., De Backer, G. G., Delgado, V., Ference, B. A., Graham, I. M., Halliday, A., Landmesser, U., Mihaylova, B., Pedersen, T. R., Riccardi, G., Richter, D. J., Sabatine, M. S., Taskinen, M. R., ... Patel, R. S. (2020). 2019 ESC/EAS guidelines for the management of dyslipidaemias: Lipid modification to reduce cardiovascular risk. *European Heart Journal, 41*(1), 111–188. https://doi.org/10.1093/eurheartj/ehz455

McDermott, M. M., Guralnik, J. M., Ferrucci, L., Tian, L., Liu, K., Liao, Y., Green, D., Sufit, R., Hoff, F., Nishida, T., Sharma, L., Pearce, W. H., Schneider, J. R., & Criqui, M. H. (2008). Asymptomatic peripheral arterial disease is associated with more adverse lower extremity characteristics than intermittent claudication. *Circulation, 117*(19), 2484–2491. https://doi.org/10.1161/CIRCULATIONAHA.107.736108

McDermott, M. M., Spring, B., Tian, L., Treat-Jacobson, D., Ferrucci, L., Lloyd-Jones, D., Zhao, L., Polonsky, T., Kibbe, M. R., Bazzano, L., Guralnik, J. M., Forman, D. E., Rego, A., Zhang, D., Domanchuk, K., Leeuwenburgh, C., Sufit, R., Smith, B., Manini, T., Criqui, M. H., & Rejeski, W. J. (2021). Effect of low-intensity vs high-intensity home-based walking exercise on walk distance in patients with peripheral artery disease: The LITE randomized clinical trial. *JAMA, the Journal of the American Medical Association, 325*(13), 1266–1276. https://doi.org/10.1001/jama.2021.2536

Mehler, P. S., Coll, J. R., Estacio, R., Esler, A., Schrier, R. W., & Hiatt, W. R. (2003). Intensive blood pressure control reduces the risk of cardiovascular events in patients with peripheral arterial disease and type 2 diabetes. *Circulation, 107*(5), 753–756. https://doi.org/10.1161/01.CIR.0000049640.46039.52

Murphy, T. P., Cutlip, D. E., Regensteiner, J. G., Mohler, E. R., Cohen, D. J., Reynolds, M. R., Massaro, J. M., Lewis, B. A., Cerezo, J., Oldenburg, N. C., Thum, C. C., Jaff, M. R., Comerota, A. J., Steffes, M. W., Abrahamsen, I. H., Goldberg, S., & Hirsch, A. T. (2015). Supervised exercise, stent revascularization, or medical therapy for claudication due to aortoiliac peripheral artery disease. *Journal of the American College of Cardiology, 65*(10), 999–1009. https://doi.org/10.1016/j.jacc.2014.12.043

Neal, B., Perkovic, V., Mahaffey, K. W., de Zeeuw, D., Fulcher, G., Erondu, N., Shaw, W., Law, G., Desai, M., & Matthews, D. R. (2017). Canagliflozin and cardiovascular and renal events in type 2 diabetes. *New England Journal of Medicine, 377*(7), 644–657. https://doi.org/10.1056/nejmoa1611925

Östergren, J., Sleight, P., Dagenais, G., Danisa, K., Bosch, J., Qilong, Y., & Yusuf, S. (2004). Impact of ramipril in patients with evidence of clinical or subclinical peripheral arterial disease. *European Heart Journal, 25*(1), 17–24. https://doi.org/10.1016/j.ehj.2003.10.033

Pande, R. L., Perlstein, T. S., Beckman, J. A., & Creager, M. A. (2011). Secondary prevention and mortality in peripheral artery disease: National health and nutrition examination study, 1999 to 2004. *Circulation, 124*(1), 17–23. https://doi.org/10.1161/CIRCULATIONAHA.110.003954

Pastori, D., Farcomeni, A., Milanese, A., Del Sole, F., Menichelli, D., Hiatt, W. R., & Violi, F. (2020). Statins and major adverse limb events in patients with peripheral artery disease: A systematic review and meta-analysis. *Thrombosis and Haemostasis, 120*(05), 866–875. https://doi.org/10.1055/s-0040-1709711

Pedersen, T. R., Kjekshus, J., Pyörälä, K., Olsson, A. G., Cook, T. J., Musliner, T. A., Tobert, J. A., & Haghfelt, T. (1998). Effect of simvastatin on ischemic signs and symptoms in the scandinavian simvastatin survival study (4S). *The American Journal of Cardiology, 81*(3), 333–335. https://doi.org/10.1016/S0002-9149(97)00904-1

Perkovic, V., Jardine, M. J., Neal, B., Bompoint, S., Heerspink, H. J. L., Charytan, D. M., Edwards, R., Agarwal, R., Bakris, G., Bull, S., Cannon, C. P., Capuano, G., Chu, P. L., De Zeeuw, D., Greene, T., Levin, A., Pollock, C., Wheeler, D. C., Yavin, Y., … Mahaffey, K. W. (2019). Canagliflozin and renal outcomes in type 2 diabetes and nephropathy. *New England Journal of Medicine, 380*(24), 2295–2306. https://doi.org/10.1056/NEJMoa1811744

Qamar, A., Morrow, D. A., Creager, M. A., Scirica, B. M., Olin, J. W., Beckman, J. A., Murphy, S. A., & Bonaca, M. P. (2020). Effect of vorapaxar on cardiovascular and limb outcomes in patients with peripheral artery disease with and without coronary artery disease: Analysis from the TRA 2°P-TIMI 50 trial. *Vascular Medicine, 25*(2), 124–132. https://doi.org/10.1177/1358863X19892690

Rajamani, K., Colman, P. G., Li, L. P., Best, J. D., Voysey, M., D'Emden, M. C., Laakso, M., Baker, J. R., & Keech, A. C. (2009). Effect of fenofibrate on amputation events in people with type 2 diabetes mellitus (FIELD study): A prespecified analysis of a randomised controlled trial. *The Lancet, 373*(9677), 1780–1788. https://doi.org/10.1016/s0140-6736(09)60698-x

Randomized trial of the effects of cholesterol-lowering with simvastatin on peripheral vascular and other major vascular outcomes in 20,536 people with peripheral arterial disease and other high-risk conditions. *Journal of Vascular Surgery, 45*(4), (2007), 645. https://doi.org/10.1016/j.jvs.2006.12.054

Schwartz, G. G., Steg, P. G., Szarek, M., Bittner, V. A., Diaz, R., Goodman, S. G., Kim, Y.-U., Jukema, J. W., Pordy, R., Roe, M. T., White, H. D., & Bhatt, D. L. (2020). Peripheral artery disease and venous thromboembolic events after acute coronary syndrome. *Circulation, 141*(20), 1608–1617. https://doi.org/10.1161/circulationaha.120.046524

Sobieszczyk, P. S., & Beckman, J. A. (2015). Intervention or exercise? *Journal of the American College of Cardiology, 65*(10), 1010–1012. https://doi.org/10.1016/j.jacc.2015.01.006

Stead, L. F., Buitrago, D., Preciado, N., Sanchez, G., Hartmann-Boyce, J., & Lancaster, T. (2013). Physician advice for smoking cessation. *Cochrane Database of Systematic Reviews, 2017*(12). https://doi.org/10.1002/14651858.CD000165.pub4

Stead, L. F., Carroll, A. J., & Lancaster, T. (2017). Group behaviour therapy programmes for smoking cessation. *Cochrane Database of Systematic Reviews, 2017*(3). https://doi.org/10.1002/14651858.CD001007.pub3

Stead, L. F., & Lancaster, T. (2012a). Behavioural interventions as adjuncts to pharmacotherapy for smoking cessation. *Cochrane Database of Systematic Reviews, 2012*(12). https://doi.org/10.1002/14651858.CD009670.pub2

Stead, L. F., & Lancaster, T. (2012b). Combined pharmacotherapy and behavioural interventions for smoking cessation. *Cochrane Database of Systematic Reviews, 10*, CD008286.

Strobl, F. F., Brechtel, K., Schmehl, J., Zeller, T., Reiser, M. F., Claussen, C. D., & Tepe, G. (2013). Twelve-month results of a randomized trial comparing mono with dual antiplatelet therapy in endovascularly treated patients with peripheral artery disease. *Journal of Endovascular Therapy, 20*(5), 699–706. https://doi.org/10.1583/13-4275MR.1

Suissa, K., Larivière, J., Eisenberg, M. J., Eberg, M., Gore, G. C., Grad, R., Joseph, L., Reynier, P. M., & Filion, K. B. (2017). Efficacy and safety of smoking cessation interventions in patients with cardiovascular disease: A network meta-analysis of randomized controlled trials. *Circulation: Cardiovascular Quality and Outcomes, 10*(1). https://doi.org/10.1161/CIRCOUTCOMES.115.002458

Treat-Jacobson, D., McDermott, M. M., Bronas, U. G., Campia, U., Collins, T. C., Criqui, M. H., Gardner, A. W., Hiatt, W. R., Regensteiner, J. G., & Rich, K. (2019). Optimal exercise programs for patients with peripheral artery disease: A scientific statement from the American heart association. *Circulation, 139*(4), E10–E33. https://doi.org/10.1161/CIR.0000000000000623

Verma, S., Mazer, C. D., Al-Omran, M., Inzucchi, S. E., Fitchett, D., Hehnke, U., George, J. T., & Zinman, B. (2018). Cardiovascular outcomes and safety of empagliflozin in patients with type 2 diabetes mellitus and peripheral artery disease. *Circulation, 137*(4), 405–407. https://doi.org/10.1161/circulationaha.117.032031

Wallentin, L., Becker, R. C., Budaj, A., Cannon, C. P., Emanuelsson, H., Held, C., Horrow, J., Husted, S., James, S., Katus, H., Mahaffey, K. W., Scirica, B. M., Skene, A., Steg, P. G., Storey, R. F., & Harrington, R. A. (2009). Ticagrelor versus clopidogrel in patients with acute coronary syndromes. *New England Journal of Medicine, 361*(11), 1045–1057. https://doi.org/10.1056/NEJMoa0904327

Whelton, P. K., Carey, R. M., Aronow, W. S., Casey, D. E., Collins, K. J., Himmelfarb, C. D., DePalma, S. M., Gidding, S., Jamerson, K. A., Jones, D. W., MacLaughlin, E. J., Muntner, P., Ovbiagele, B., Smith, S. C., Spencer, C. C., Stafford, R. S., Taler, S. J., Thomas, R. J., Williams, K. A., Williamson, J. D., & Wright, J. T. (2018). 2017 ACC/AHA/AAPA/ABC/ACPM/AGS/APhA/ASH/ASPC/NMA/PCNA guideline for the prevention, detection, evaluation, and management of high blood pressure in adults: Executive summary: A report of the American college of cardiology/American heart association task force on clinical practice guidelines. *Hypertension, 71*(6), 1269–1324. https://doi.org/10.1161/HYP.0000000000000066

Willigendael, E. M., Teijink, J. A. W., Bartelink, M. L., Peters, R. J. G., Büller, H. R., & Prins, M. H. (2005). Smoking and the patency of lower extremity bypass grafts: A meta-analysis. *Journal of Vascular Surgery, 42*(1), 67–74. https://doi.org/10.1016/j.jvs.2005.03.024

Wright, J. T., Williamson, J. D., Whelton, P. K., Snyder, J. K., Sink, K. M., Rocco, M. V., Reboussin, D. M., Rahman, M., Oparil, S., Lewis, C. E., Kimmel, P. L., Johnson, K. C., Goff, D. C., Fine, L. J., Cutler, J. A., Cushman, W. C., Cheung, A. K., & Ambrosius, W. T. (2015). A randomized trial of intensive versus standard blood-pressure control. *New England Journal of Medicine, 373*(22), 2103–2116. https://doi.org/10.1056/NEJMoa1511939

9

Intravascular ultrasound: Role in PAD

Ramya Mosarla[1] and Eric Secemsky[2]

[1]NYU Langone Health, New York, NY, United States; [2]Beth Israel Medical Center, Harvard University, Boston, MA, United States

Introduction

Intravascular ultrasound (IVUS) is a novel technology that relies on piezoelectric transducers to generate high-resolution, cross-sectional imaging of blood vessels and provides real-time procedural guidance. IVUS overcomes the limitations of contrast angiography and venography, which produce two-dimensional representations of three-dimensional vessels and are susceptible to inaccuracies related to differences in projection, vascular tortuosity, and eccentric remodeling. The use of IVUS in percutaneous coronary intervention (PCI) is associated with reductions in repeat target lesion interventions, major adverse cardiovascular events, and mortality (Choi et al., 2021; Hong et al., 2020; Lee et al., 2022; Mentias et al., 2020; Zhang et al., 2018). There has been a rapid uptake of IVUS to guide both peripheral arterial and venous interventions with emerging data suggesting a benefit similar to that seen in PCI (Divakaran, Parikh, et al., 2022, Divakaran, Meissner, et al., 2022). Here we will cover the basics of IVUS, its application in arterial and venous peripheral interventions, its impact on clinical outcomes, current indications for use, and several ongoing areas of debate.

The basics of IVUS in peripheral vascular interventions

Image generation with IVUS relies on transmission of electrical energy through piezoelectric crystals. These crystals convert electrical energy into sound waves, which then propagate through adjacent tissues (Mintz et al., 2001). The sound waves are differentially reflected back to the transducer by the tissues due to their specific acoustic properties (e.g., calcium is echogenic, fat is echolucent) (Mintz et al., 2001). The duration it takes for a sound wave to be reflected back is determined by the depth of a structure relative to the transducer (Mintz et al., 2001). Contemporary IVUS catheters come in two different transducer configurations: (1) Rotational, which has a single spinning transducer and (2) solid state, which has multiple circumferentially arrayed transducers (Mintz et al., 2001). This allows IVUS to generate circumferential tomographic images from within the vascular lumen.

Traditionally, IVUS catheters used transducers with frequencies ranging from 20 to 40 Megahertz (MHz) with an axial resolution of roughly 100 μm (Xu & Lo, 2020). However, newer generation devices provide a broader range of frequencies that include both higher for increased resolution and lower for increased depth penetration (Secemsky, Parikh, et al., 2022). The highest frequency probe is 60 MHz, which allows a remarkable axial resolution of <40 μm, providing high-definition images of smaller vessels, but with a decreased depth of penetration (Secemsky, Parikh, et al., 2022). The lower frequency probes (10−15 MHz) are useful in imaging large central veins and the aorta and have a role in virtual histology, which can provide a histological classification of adjacent plaque (Secemsky, Parikh, et al., 2022). Peripheral IVUS catheters currently on the market also come in a variety of guidewire and sheath size

Table 9.1 Peripheral IVUS catheters.

Transducer Configuration	Catheter	Manufacturer	Frequency (MHz)	Guidewire	Sheath	Penetration depth (mm)
Rotational	OptiCross/OptiCross	Boston Scientific	40	0.014″	5–6 Fr	6
	OptiCross HD	Boston Scientific	60	0.014″	5 Fr	6
	OptiCross 18	Boston Scientific	30	≤0.018″	6 Fr	12
	OptiCross 35	Boston Scientific	15	≤0.035″	8 Fr	70
Solid state	Visions PV 0.014/ 0.014P RX	Boston Scientific	20	0.014″	5 Fr	20
	Visions PV 0.018	Boston Scientific	20	≤0.018″	6 Fr	24
	Visions PV 0.035	Boston Scientific	10	≤0.038″	8.5 Fr	60
	Eagle eye platinum/ platinum ST	Boston Scientific	20	0.014″	5 Fr	20
	Pioneer plus reentry system	Boston Scientific	20	0.014″	6 Fr	20

compatibilities to accommodate a broad range of vessel sizes encountered in PVI (Table 9.1). Either mechanical or manual pull-back can be done and produce a stack of cross-sectional images to generate a longitudinal representation of the vessel (Secemsky, Parikh, et al., 2022). Postacquisition processing software can be used to determine cross-sectional area (CSA); measure vessel diameter; identify branching vessels; highlight plaque composition, intraluminal thrombus, and degree of vascular calcification; investigate for vascular complications including dissections; and evaluate stents for adequate expansion and apposition.

IVUS in peripheral arterial interventions

IVUS use in peripheral arterial interventions has steadily grown. A recent analysis of a contemporary nationwide database saw a 23.6% increase in IVUS use from quarter one of 2016 to quarter four of 2019, driven by rapid uptake in office-based labs (OBLs) and ambulatory surgery centers (Divakaran, Parikh, et al., 2022). This enthusiasm is likely driven by several advantages that IVUS offers compared to angiographic guidance alone (Table 9.2). The utility of IVUS in peripheral arterial interventions may be described by its application to three distinct phases: preinterventional, intraprocedural, and postprocedural optimization.

Table 9.2 Intravascular ultrasound (IVUS) versus angiography and venography to evaluate vascular characteristics.

Characteristics	IVUS	Angiography
Stenosis	+++	++
Plaque morphology	+++	−
Adherent thrombus	+++	+
Dissection	+++	++
Flow	−	+++
Extrinsic compression	+++	++
Stent apposition	+++	++
Minimizing contrast	+++	−

+, Fair; ++, Good; +++, Excellent; -, Not applicable.
Adapted from Mosarla, RC., Secemsky E.A. (2020). Peripheral matters, IVUS-guided peripheral vascular intervention.

The preinterventional utility of IVUS is related to its ability to clearly delineate plaque morphology and characterize filling defects, which can have important implications for vessel preparation (Fig. 9.1). IVUS can subclassify plaque into four major categories including fibrous, fibro-fatty, necrotic-lipidic, and calcific (Suh et al., 2011). In particular, IVUS is more sensitive than angiography at identifying and classifying both superficial and deep calcium. In a study conducted to validate peripheral artery calcification scoring systems with IVUS, IVUS detected

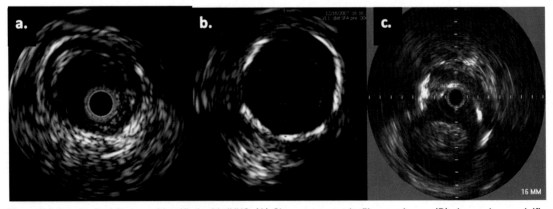

Figure 9.1 Intraluminal features identified with IVUS: (A) Shows concentric fibrous plaque; (B) shows deep calcific plaque with shadowing; (C) shows a mural thrombus.

calcium in 44/47 (93.6%) of lesions compared to angiography, which detected calcium in 26/47 (55.3%) (Yin et al., 2017). Further, the extent of plaque can be better characterized in the face of eccentric remodeling, which may not be appreciated on luminal angiography. IVUS can also more accurately delineate vascular dimensions including CSA, vessel diameter, and lesion length compared to angiography, which can aid in proper device selection and sizing. A histological study of popliteal and tibial vessels taken after amputation noted that histological arterial diameter was routinely greater than angiographic diameter determination (Kashyap et al., 2008). IVUS offers increased accuracy in assessing vascular dimensions and has an improved ability detecting true vessel diameter, assessing degree of vascular stenosis, and identifying concentric plaques, which may be missed on angiography (Arthurs et al., 2010; Pliagas et al., 2020) (Fig. 9.2).

Intraprocedural use of IVUS can be helpful in determining the next therapeutic step by providing real-time feedback during interventions. For instance, IVUS is helpful in navigating chronic total occlusions (CTOs). IVUS reliably demonstrates luminal wire passing in the management of CTOs, and a study of 82 de novo femoropopliteal CTOs showed higher rates of true lumen angioplasty compared to non-IVUS-guided intervention (91.1% vs. 51.3; $P < .001$), which was associated with lower target vessel revascularization at 12-months (83.9% vs. 62.8%; $P = .036$) (Tsubakimoto et al., 2021) (Fig. 9.3). Real-world data also suggest

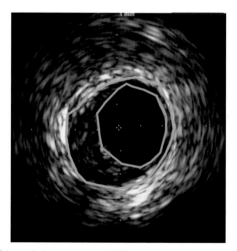

Figure 9.2 IVUS-based device sizing. IVUS is used to accurately size the native vessel area (green circle) and remaining luminal area (blue circle) in light of stenosis caused by concentric atherosclerotic plaque.

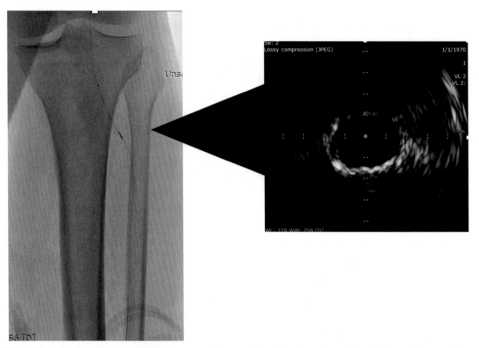

Figure 9.3 IVUS use to confirm intraluminal passage in crossing of a chronic total occlusion wire passing seen on angiography confirmed to be within the lumen on adjacent IVUS.

that the use of IVUS can systematize procedure and device selection, which is critical given an emerging and already vast array of peripheral devices. A retrospective study of 970 patients undergoing interventions between January 2016 and December 2018 was able to derive a decision tree based on the use of IVUS and angiography-based parameters and subsequent device election. Notably, they demonstrated that when the most popular endovascular device for a particular IVUS-based subtype was utilized, the restenosis rate was similarly low across subtypes, suggesting IVUS helps tailor interventions (Yazu et al., 2022).

Postinterventional optimization with IVUS includes improved sensitivity at detecting suboptimal implant placement (malapposition and underexpansion) as well as vascular complications, such as dissections. Notably, dissections are grossly underappreciated with angiography alone, yet their presence contributes substantially to risk of restenosis. A meta-analysis of 11 observational studies including 1521 patients found that increased minimum stent area was positively associated with patency (standardized mean difference [SMD] = -0.30; 95% CI: 0.46 to -0.15), while the presence of dissections was negatively associated with

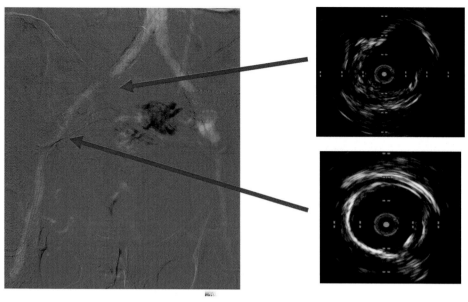

Figure 9.4 Carbon dioxide angiography combined with IVUS. IVUS use in conjunction with CO_2 angiography to perform a contrast-sparing peripheral intervention.

midterm patency (odds ratio 1.58; 95% CI: 1.01–2.49, $P = .047$) (Jiang & Xu, 2022).

Another benefit of IVUS that applies to all procedural phases is minimizing the total volume of contrast administered. A randomized trial of 83 patients undergoing PCIs studied angiography-guided versus IVUS-guided approaches and found significantly less contrast was used in the IVUS-guided arm (64.5 mL interquartile range [IQR] 42.8–97.0 mL in vs. 20.0 mL IQR 12.5–30.0 mL $P < .001$) (Mariani et al., 2014). While such randomized comparisons are not available for PVI, given the larger caliber of proximal peripheral vessels and comorbid renal dysfunction present in many patients undergoing PVI, this benefit is likely maintained, if not enhanced, during PVI, especially in conjunction with contrast-sparing imaging like carbon dioxide angiography (Fig. 9.4).

Outcomes in peripheral arterial interventions

To date, randomized data with angiography alone versus angiography with IVUS guidance in peripheral arterial interventions remain limited. A recent prospective trial by Allan et al. randomized 150 patients undergoing femoropopliteal interventions to angiography alone versus angiography with IVUS. At 12-month, the IVUS arm had lower binary restenosis compared to angiography alone (72.5% vs. 55.4%; $P = .008$) (Allan et al., 2022). While there was no significant difference in clinically driven target lesion revascularization, the study was not powered for clinical outcomes. A large meta-analysis of observational studies including 93,551 patients showed no difference in rates of reintervention but noted lower rates of adverse periprocedural events and vascular complications with IVUS use (Sheikh et al., 2020). A recent claim-based study of 543,488 PVIs performed from 2016 to 2019 similarly found an association with a lower risk of major adverse limb events at a median of 514 days (Divakaran, Parikh, et al., 2022). Large, sufficiently powered randomized data and analyses of accumulating real-world data are still warranted to adjudicate the full impact of IVUS on longer term patency outcomes beyond 12 month, major adverse limb events, mortality, and quality of life.

Indications for IVUS in peripheral arterial interventions

Given limited randomized data yet expanding clinical use, the guidance for indications for IVUS in peripheral arterial interventions is presently based on consensus opinion. A recent global consensus document involving more than 40 international vascular experts evaluated the appropriate use criteria (AUC) of peripheral IVUS. The survey tool used for evaluation was organized based on the aforementioned procedural phases, including preinterventional, intraprocedural, and postinterventional optimization, as well as arterial segment (Fitch et al., 2001; Secemsky et al., 2022).

In iliac artery interventions, the use of IVUS was considered "appropriate" in the preinterventional phase to evaluate ambiguous lesions, assess severity, size vessels, and minimize contrast (Secemsky et al., 2022). It was rated as "may be appropriate" assessing the etiology of vessel occlusion, plaque morphology, and filling defects (Secemsky et al., 2022). It was considered "appropriate" for intraprocedural optimization to determine the location of the wire crossing track and for determining the next therapeutic step (Secemsky et al., 2022). In postprocedural optimization of iliac interventions, it was rated as "appropriate" in identifying dissections and residual stenosis and as "may be appropriate" in determining the need for stent postdilation.

In femoropopliteal interventions, IVUS use was considered "appropriate" in preinterventional scenarios of evaluating lesion severity, filling defects, vessel sizing, and minimizing contrast and "may be appropriate" for determining the etiology of vessel occlusion and evaluating plaque morphology (Secemsky et al., 2022). It was rated "appropriate" in all intraprocedural and post-procedural phases of femoropopliteal interventions. IVUS was also rated "appropriate" for all phases of tibial artery interventions (Secemsky et al., 2022). Overall, IVUS use was felt to be widely indicated in optimizing peripheral arterial interventions.

IVUS in peripheral venous interventions

IVUS is frequently utilized in iliofemoral venous interventions and is increasingly considered the standard of care (Lau et al., 2019). It has several advantages when compared to venography alone in accurately characterizing intraluminal anatomy. Venous architecture is complex and can include features such as native valves, webs, and trabeculations that can be noted after recanalization of deep vein thromboses (DVT) (Neglén & Raju, 2002) (Fig. 9.5). These features can be more accurately assessed with intraluminal imaging compared to contrast venography, which obscures luminal architecture. In the treatment of DVT, IVUS can distinguish acute from chronic DVT due to increased fibrin deposition and the echogenicity of chronic clots (McLafferty, 2012). It can also more reliably determine the burden of preprocedural and residual thrombus burden (McLafferty, 2012).

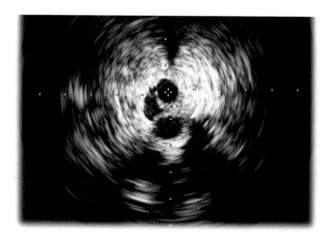

Figure 9.5 Venous web on IVUS shows complex venous architecture with venous trabeculations.

Identification of these features has pronounced utility in selecting specific devices aimed at reducing venous congestion and in the case of trabeculated chronic DVTs, provides an improved ability to navigate the true lumen when compared with venography alone (Gagne et al., 2018). Further, phlebitis and postthrombotic states can result in important anatomic changes to vein walls, including mural edema and scarring (Secemsky, Parikh, et al., 2022), which are only able to be detailed with intraluminal imaging.

IVUS is especially advantageous when evaluating phenomenon related to extrinsic compression and phasic collapse. Pathologies of extrinsic compression, such as May–Thurner syndrome, are important mediators of venous luminal stenosis (Fig. 9.6). While extrinsic compression may be identified with venography based on features, including pancaking, contrast thinning, and collaterals, IVUS has superior sensitivity at demonstrating ovoid deformation and can accurately define location, contour, and extent of compression. As an example, in a study of 107 patients

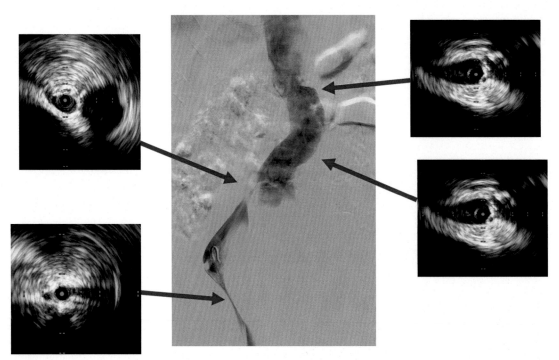

Figure 9.6 External compression of iliac vein venogram demonstrating contrast thinning and narrowing of common femoral vein. IVUS assessment demonstrating discrete external compression with variable deformation along the length of the vein.

who underwent venous stenting guided by venography and IVUS, the use of IVUS revealed obstruction in a 48% of patients undergoing common femoral vein interventions, which were not seen on venography, resulting in a change in treatment plan (Lau et al., 2019). Improved accuracy in sizing of vessels for implants also has the potential to minimize complications related to undersizing, such as stent migration, and oversizing, which may result in chronic pelvic pain, vessel damage, and progression of disease at stent margins. IVUS also allows improved identification of healthy proximal and distal landing zones, which improves stent patency by facilitating complete coverage of diseased segments (Montminy et al., 2019). Due to lower venous pressures, veins also exhibit dynamic collapse related to loading conditions. This is impacted by volume status and respirophasic flux and can be demonstrated with maneuvers such as Valsalva (Villalba & Tosenovsky, 2018). IVUS is more readily able to detect this compared to venography, which can then minimize unnecessary stenting.

Outcomes in peripheral venous interventions

At present, there are no randomized data regarding the impact of IVUS on patency or clinical outcomes in iliofemoral venous disease. Nonrandomized prospective data suggest IVUS-based measurements of stenosis and stenotic change are more predictive of clinical improvement after stenting and use may be associated with clinical benefits. In a prospective study of 68 patients undergoing treatment of iliofemoral venous outflow disease, IVUS baseline measurement of area stenosis with >54% estimated an optimal threshold for intervention. Postprocedure IVUS-derived measurements of area stenosis were most predictive (area under the curve, 0.70; $P = .004$) of subsequent clinical improvement. In a subset of 48 patients being treated for nonthrombotic obstruction, a higher threshold of stenosis of >61% was determined to be necessary (Gagne et al., 2018). While determination of hemodynamically significant venous lesions is complex and may not be determined by a set threshold of diameter stenosis, the information may provide important actionable information for interpretation depending on clinical context. Observational studies have supported improved clinical outcomes with IVUS-guided stenting, as well as decreased complications. In a recent analysis of claims-based data, 20,984 deep venous interventions with stenting were studied, among which 15,184 (72.4%) utilized IVUS. In this study, IVUS use was associated with reduced hospitalization and reintervention.

Importantly, IVUS-guided stent placement lowered the incidence of venous stent thrombosis and stent migration (Divakaran, Meissner, et al., 2022). Additional studies on the impact of IVUS use during peripheral venous interventions on clinical outcomes and quality of life need to be performed.

Indications for IVUS in peripheral venous interventions

In a global consensus opinion on the use of IVUS in peripheral venous interventions, the application of IVUS to iliofemoral venous interventions received the AUC grading of "appropriate," in all three procedural phases, including preintervention, intraprocedure, and postprocedure (Secemsky et al., 2022). The preintervention criterion pertained to characterizing lesions and filling defects, assessing lesion severity, appropriately sizing vessels, and minimizing use of contrast in select scenarios. The intraprocedure criterion pertained to utility in determination of next therapeutic step and vessel sizing for devices. The postprocedure criterion was based on utility of IVUS in stent optimization and postdilation. These resoundingly high marks speak to the indispensable nature of IVUS in iliofemoral venous interventions.

Controversies and concerns

Practice patterns and cost effectiveness

Despite growing IVUS use in PVI, the uptake has not been homogenous across operators and care settings. In a large claims-based analysis of 58,522 femoropopliteal interventions in Medicare beneficiaries, IVUS was used in 11,394 (19%) and was associated with higher-volume providers and those with higher rates of service provided in office-based labs (OBLs). In this analysis, it was also more commonly used in procedures done for claudication compared to those done for critical limb ischemia and was associated with atherectomy use. The growing use of IVUS in ambulatory surgical centers and OBLs, where it is more heavily reimbursed and use in conjunction with other highly reimbursed treatments, raises concerns about cost-effectiveness. A claims-based analysis of 543,488 PVIs in Medicare beneficiaries by Divakaran et al. similarly replicated that IVUS growth was most prominent in OBLs and ambulatory surgical centers and showed evidence of significant heterogeneity in operator use. This study however noted a reassuring association with the use of IVUS correlating with lower risk of short- and long-term major adverse limb events (Divakaran, Meissner, et al., 2022). A cost-effectiveness analysis from the Nationwide Inpatient Sample including 92,714 patients noted that while the use of IVUS resulted in a nonsignificant increases in hospital costs, these were offset by a significant reduction in postprocedural complications and lower amputation rates (Panaich et al., 2016). Further cost-effectiveness analyses, particularly those evaluating cost-effectiveness in IVUS-guided PVI in the ambulatory settings, are warranted; however, the association with improved outcomes in studies to date is positive.

Safety

To date there is only one study that suggests a potential safety concern with IVUS. A posthoc analysis of the CAPSICUM (Contemporary Outcomes achieved with Paclitaxel-Eluting Peripheral Stents to Treat Symptomatic Lower Limb Ischemia and Lesions in the Superficial Femoral Artery or Proximal Popliteal Artery) studying the impact of IVUS on 1-year clinical outcomes raised concerns about increased frequency of aneurysmal degeneration in those treated with IVUS (Tsujimura et al., 2022). This may be related to more aggressive device sizing to match the larger IVUS measured vessel diameter and CSA. However, this was a post-hoc analysis and it should be noted that the primary trial suggested that newer generation fluoropolymer stents themselves may be associated with an increased risk of aneurysmal degeneration, the clinical significance of which is not yet determined (Iida et al., 2022). Furthermore, the majority of procedures in this study utilized IVUS, and thus treatment selection bias likely influenced the comparator group of procedures performed without IVUS. That said, IVUS is commonly associated with increased angioplasty balloon and implant sizing (Allan et al., 2022), and in general, a judicious approach is warranted to avoid significant oversizing, which can cause late complications such as edge restenosis.

Workflow

A growing concern with rapid adoption of IVUS is adequate training of operators to acquire and accurately interpret image as well as streamlining workflows to allow ease of use. Among potential concerns include inefficiencies leading to lengthening of procedures as well as inappropriate application of devices or treatments based on incorrect image interpretation. In fact, some of these challenges may explain the present heterogeneity in national use. However, as IVUS use grows and gains greater acceptance in consensus and guideline recommendations, these implementation barriers will need to be addressed.

Conclusion

IVUS has a growing and important role in guiding both peripheral arterial and venous interventions. It has demonstrated superiority in identifying luminal features, assessing vessel dimensions, and identifying postprocedural complications compared to angiographic or venographic guidance alone. While the evidence to date suggests that it can have an important role in optimizing procedural and patient outcomes, the full impact on prospective long-term clinical outcomes, quality of life metrics, and cost-effectiveness profile remain to be fully elucidated. Further, as trends in use suggest accelerating adoption, provider education to facilitate accurate use, and interpretation as well as implementation of streamlined work-flow to minimize procedural delays remain major goals.

References

Allan, R. B., Puckridge, P. J., Spark, J. I., & Delaney, C. L. (2022). The impact of intravascular ultrasound on femoropopliteal artery endovascular interventions: A randomized controlled trial. *JACC: Cardiovascular Interventions, 15*, 536−546.

Arthurs, Z. M., Bishop, P. D., Feiten, L. E., Eagleton, M. J., Clair, D. G., & Kashyap, V. S. (2010). Evaluation of peripheral atherosclerosis: A comparative analysis of angiography and intravascular ultrasound imaging. *Journal of Vascular Surgery, 51*, 933−938. discussion 939.

Choi, I. J., Lim, S., Choo, E. H., Hwang, B. H., Kim, C. J., Park, M. W., Lee, J. M., Park, C. S., Kim, H. Y., Yoo, K. D., Jeon, D. S., Youn, H. J., Chung, W. S., Kim, M. C., Jeong, M. H., Ahn, Y., & Chang, K. (2021). Impact of intravascular ultrasound on long-term clinical outcomes in patients with acute myocardial infarction. *JACC: Cardiovascular Interventions, 14*, 2431−2443.

Divakaran, S., Meissner, M. H., Kohi, M. P., Chen, S., Song, Y., Hawkins, B. M., Rosenfield, K., Parikh, S. A., & Secemsky, E. A. (2022). Utilization of and outcomes associated with intravascular ultrasound during deep venous stent placement among Medicare beneficiaries. *Journal of Vascular and Interventional Radiology, 33*, 1476−1484.e2.

Divakaran, S., Parikh, S. A., Hawkins, B. M., Chen, S., Song, Y., Banerjee, S., Rosenfield, K., & Secemsky, E. A. (2022). Temporal trends, practice variation, and associated outcomes with IVUS use during peripheral arterial intervention. *JACC: Cardiovascular Interventions, 15*, 2080−2090.

Fitch, K., Bernstein, S. J., Aguilar, M. D., Burnand, B., LaCalle, J. R., Lazaro, P., van het Loo, M., McDonnell, J., Vader, J., & Kahan, J. P. (2001). *The RAND/ UCLA appropriateness method user's manual.* Santa Monica, CA: RAND Corporation.

Gagne, P. J., Tahara, R. W., Fastabend, C. P., Dzieciuchowicz, L., Marston, W., Vedantham, S., Ting, W., & Iafrati, M. D. (2017). Venography versus intravascular ultrasound for diagnosing and treating iliofemoral vein obstruction. *Journal of Vascular Surgery Venous Lymphatic Disorder, 5,* 678−687.

Gagne, P. J., Gasparis, A., Black, S., Thorpe, P., Passman, M., Vedantham, S., Marston, W., & Iafrati, M. (2018). Analysis of threshold stenosis by multiplanar venogram and intravascular ultrasound examination for predicting clinical improvement after iliofemoral vein stenting in the VIDIO trial. *Journal of Vascular Surgery Venous Lymphatic Disorder, 6,* 48−56.e1.

Hong, S. J., Mintz, G. S., Ahn, C. M., Kim, J. S., Kim, B. K., Ko, Y. G., Kang, T. S., Kang, W. C., Kim, Y. H., Hur, S. H., Hong, B. K., Choi, D., Kwon, H., Jang, Y., & Hong, M. K. (2020). Effect of intravascular ultrasound-guided drug-eluting stent implantation: 5-Year follow-up of the IVUS-XPL randomized trial. *JACC: Cardiovascular Interventions, 13,* 62−71.

Iida, O., Takahara, M., Soga, Y., Yamaoka, T., Fujihara, M., Kawasaki, D., Ichihashi, S., Kozuki, A., Nanto, S., Sakata, Y., & Mano, T. (2022). 1-Year outcomes of fluoropolymer-based drug-eluting stent in femoropopliteal practice: Predictors of restenosis and aneurysmal degeneration. *JACC: Cardiovascular Interventions, 15,* 630−638.

Jiang, J., & Xu, W. (2022). Predictability and usefulness of intravascular ultrasound-guided angioplsaty in patients with femoropopliteal lesions. *International Journal of Angiology, 41,* 74−81. https://doi.org/10.23736/ S0392-9590.21.04769-6

Kashyap, V. S., Pavkov, M. L., Bishop, P. D., Nassoiy, S. P., Eagleton, M. J., Clair, D. G., & Ouriel, K. (2008). Angiography underestimates peripheral atherosclerosis: Lumenography revisited. *Journal of Endovascular Therapy, 15,* 117−125.

Lau, I., Png, C. Y. M., Eswarappa, M., Miller, M., Kumar, S., Tadros, R., Vouyouka, A., Marin, M., Faries, P., & Ting, W. (2019). Defining the utility of anteroposterior venography in the diagnosis of venous iliofemoral obstruction. *Journal of Vascular Surgery Venous Lymphatic Disorder, 7,* 514−521.

Lee, S. Y., Zhang, J. J., Mintz, G. S., Hong, S. J., Ahn, C. M., Kim, J. S., Kim, B. K., Ko, Y. G., Choi, D., Jang, Y., Kan, J., Pan, T., Gao, X., Ge, Z., Chen, S. L., & Hong, M. K. (2022). Procedural Characteristics of intravascular ultrasound-guided percutaneous coronary intervention and their clinical implications. *Journal of the American Heart Association, 11,* e025258.

Mariani, J., Jr., Guedes, C., Soares, P., Zalc, S., Campos, C. M., Lopes, A. C., Spadaro, A. G., Perin, M. A., Filho, A. E., Takimura, C. K., Ribeiro, E., Kalil-Filho, R., Edelman, E. R., Serruys, P. W., & Lemos, P. A. (2014). Intravascular ultrasound guidance to minimize the use of iodine contrast in percutaneous coronary intervention: The MOZART (minimizing contrast utilization with IVUS guidance in coronary angioplasty) randomized controlled trial. *JACC: Cardiovascular Interventions, 7,* 1287−1293.

McLafferty, R. B. (2012). The role of intravascular ultrasound in venous thromboembolism. *Seminars in Interventional Radiology, 29,* 10−15.

Mentias, A., Sarrazin, M. V., Saad, M., Panaich, S., Kapadia, S., Horwitz, P. A., & Girotra, S. (2020). Long-term outcomes of coronary stenting with and without use of intravascular ultrasound. *JACC: Cardiovascular Interventions, 13*, 1880–1890.

Mintz, G. S., Nissen, S. E., Anderson, W. D., Bailey, S. R., Erbel, R., Fitzgerald, P. J., Pinto, F. J., Rosenfield, K., Siegel, R. J., Tuzcu, E. M., & Yock, P. G. (2001). American College of Cardiology clinical expert consensus document on standards for acquisition, measurement and reporting of intravascular ultrasound studies (IVUS). A report of the American College of Cardiology Task Force on clinical expert consensus documents. *Journal of the American College of Cardiology, 37*, 1478–1492.

Montminy, M. L., Thomasson, J. D., Tanaka, G. J., Lamanilao, L. M., Crim, W., & Raju, S. (2019). A comparison between intravascular ultrasound and venography in identifying key parameters essential for iliac vein stenting. *Journal of Vascular Surgery Venous Lymphatic Disorder, 7*, 801–807.

Mosarla, R. C., & Secemsky, E. A. (2020). *Peripheral matters, IVUS-guided peripheral vascular intervention.*

Neglén, P., & Raju, S. (2002). Intravascular ultrasound scan evaluation of the obstructed vein. *Journal of Vascular Surgery, 35*, 694–700.

Panaich, S. S., Arora, S., Patel, N., Patel, N. J., Savani, C., Patel, A., Thakkar, B., Singh, V., Patel, S., Patel, N., Agnihotri, K., Bhatt, P., Deshmukh, A., Gupta, V., Attaran, R. R., Mena, C. I., Grines, C. L., Cleman, M., Forrest, J. K., & Badheka, A. O. (2016). Intravascular ultrasound in lower extremity peripheral vascular interventions: Variation in utilization and impact on in-hospital outcomes from the nationwide inpatient Sample (2006-2011). *Journal of Endovascular Therapy, 23*, 65–75.

Pliagas, G., Saab, F., Stavroulakis, K., Bisdas, T., Finton, S., Heaney, C., McGoff, T., Hardy, K., Adams, G., & Mustapha, J. A. (2020). Intravascular ultrasound imaging versus digital subtraction angiography in patients with peripheral vascular disease. *Journal of Invasive Cardiology, 32*, 99–103.

Secemsky, E. A., Mosarla, R. C., Rosenfield, K., Kohi, M., Lichtenberg, M., Meissner, M., Varcoe, R., Holden, A., Jaff, M. R., Chalyan, D., Clair, D., Hawkins, B. M., & Parikh, S. A. (2022). Appropriate use of intravascular ultrasound during arterial and venous lower extremity interventions. *JACC: Cardiovascular Interventions, 15*, 1558–1568.

Secemsky, E. A., Parikh, S. A., Kohi, M., Lichtenberg, M., Meissner, M., Varcoe, R., Holden, A., Jaff, M., Chalyan, D., Clair, D., Hawkins, B., & Rosenfield, K. (2022). Intravascular ultrasound guidance for lower extremity arterial and venous interventions. *EuroIntervention, 18*, 598–608.

Sheikh, A. B., Anantha-Narayanan, M., Smolderen, K. G., Jelani, Q. U., Nagpal, S., Schneider, M., Llanos, F., Ionescu, C., Regan, C., Attaran, R., Altin, S. E., & Mena-Hurtado, C. (2020). Utility of intravascular ultrasound in peripheral vascular interventions: Systematic review and meta-analysis. *Vascular and Endovascular Surgery, 54*, 413–422.

Suh, W. M., Seto, A. H., Margey, R. J. P., Cruz-Gonzalez, I., & Jang, I.-K. (2011). Intravascular detection of the vulnerable plaque. *Circulation: Cardiovascular Imaging, 4*, 169–178.

Tsubakimoto, Y., Isodono, K., Fujimoto, T., Kirii, Y., Shiraga, A., Kasahara, T., Ariyoshi, M., Irie, D., Sakatani, T., Matsuo, A., Inoue, K., & Fujita, H. (2021). IVUS-guided wiring improves the clinical outcomes of angioplasty for long femoropopliteal CTO compared with the conventional intraluminal approach. *Journal of Atherosclerosis and Thrombosis, 28*, 365–374.

Tsujimura, T., Iida, O., Takahara, M., Soga, Y., Yamaoka, T., Fujihara, M., Kawasaki, D., Ichihashi, S., Kozuki, A., Nanto, S., Sakata, Y., & Mano, T. (2022). Clinical impact of intravascular ultrasound-guided fluoropolymer-based drug-eluting stent implantation for femoropopliteal lesions. *JACC: Cardiovascular Interventions, 15*, 1569–1578.

Villalba, L. M., & Tosenovsky, P. J. (2018). *Tips and tricks for venous IVUS success.*

Xu, J., & Lo, S. (2020). Fundamentals and role of intravascular ultrasound in percutaneous coronary intervention. *Cardiovascular Diagnosis and Therapy, 10*, 1358–1370.

Yazu, Y., Fujihara, M., Takahara, M., Kurata, N., Nakata, A., Yoshimura, H., Ito, T., Fukunaga, M., Kozuki, A., & Tomoi, Y. (2022). Intravascular ultrasound-based decision tree model for the optimal endovascular treatment strategy selection of femoropopliteal artery disease-results from the ONION Study. *CVIR Endovascular, 5*, 52.

Yin, D., Maehara, A., Shimshak, T. M., Ricotta, J. J., 2nd, Ramaiah, V., Foster, M. T., 3rd, Davis, T. P., Matsumura, M., Mintz, G. S., & Gray, W. A. (2017). Intravascular ultrasound validation of contemporary angiographic scores evaluating the severity of calcification in peripheral arteries. *Journal of Endovascular Therapy, 24*, 478–487.

Zhang, J., Gao, X., Kan, J., Ge, Z., Han, L., Lu, S., Tian, N., Lin, S., Lu, Q., Wu, X., Li, Q., Liu, Z., Chen, Y., Qian, X., Wang, J., Chai, D., Chen, C., Li, X., Gogas, B. D., ... Chen, S. L. (2018). Intravascular ultrasound versus angiography-guided drug-eluting stent implantation: The ultimate trial. *Journal of the American College of Cardiology, 72*, 3126–3137.

10

Atherectomy in endovascular procedures

Craig Walker, McCall Walker and Matthew T. Finn

Cardiovascular Institute of the South, Gray, LA, United States

Introduction

Endovascular atherectomy employs a variety of mechanisms to "modify" the vessel wall to improve device passage, increase luminal gain with angioplasty balloons/stents, and prevent stent underexpansion. In this chapter, we examine the evidence base and clinical guidelines for atherectomy in peripheral arterial disease (PAD) with specific discussions of device application in various encountered pathologies; i.e., calcific atherosclerosis, noncalcific atherosclerosis, thrombus, and in-stent restenosis (ISR). We will also highlight remaining areas of clinical need and ongoing research.

Pathophysiology and Treatment of Atherosclerotic Disease in Peripheral Arteries. https://doi.org/10.1016/B978-0-443-13593-4.00010-X

Atherectomy device utilization

Atherectomy device utilization has expanded in recent years, growing from approximately 10% of cases in 2010 to 20% in 2019 (Nfor et al., 2022). This increase has occurred based on primarily nonrandomized clinical registry data. Due to a paucity of randomized controlled trials (RCT) and longer-term outcomes to determine guidelines and differential payor reimbursement, significant treatment variability has developed in the United States ranging from 0% to 32% utilization across US geographic regions with similar variabilities of use occurring between inpatient and outpatient settings (Haqqani et al., 2023; Mohan et al., 2018). An important significant exception to the lack of RCTs was the EXCImer Laser Randomized Controlled Study for Treatment of FemoropopliTEal In-Stent Restenosis (EXCITE) trial discussed further, which was a powered comparison of laser and plain old balloon angioplasty (POBA) versus POBA alone for ISR, and demonstrated superiority of laser plus POBA over POBA alone (Dippel et al., 2015).

Scientific statements on atherectomy

There is currently an absence of strong recommendations regarding atherectomy device use across professional societies in the United States and Europe. The Society of Vascular Surgery guidelines on PAD/critical limb threatening ischemia, American College of Cardiology guidelines, and the Trans-Atlantic Inter-Society Consensus Document (TASC) II guidelines mention atherectomy as an important adjuvant for successful endovascular treatment but do not offer additional specific guidance for use (Conte et al., 2015, 2019; Hirsch et al., 2006; Norgren et al., 2007).

The 2018 Appropriate Use Criteria for Peripheral Artery Intervention label atherectomy as "may be appropriate" in femoropopliteal and below the knee (BTK) lesions and "rarely appropriate" in suprainguinal lesions (due to a lack of study of lesions in this location).

The Society for Cardiac Angiography and Interventions (SCAI) statement on device selection in femoropopliteal disease asserts that atherectomy treatment is adjunctive before definitive balloon/stent treatment (Bailey et al., 2019; Feldman et al., 2018). The statement also underscores that atherectomy is helpful for severely calcified vessels, but does not define how to classify calcium severity.

Evidence base supporting atherectomy

A multitude of atherectomy/plaque modification options exist, including those employing laser, directional, rotational, orbital, and lithotripsy treatments. Further, we review the mechanisms, technical specification, and standards of use for the currently available devices in the United States. Furthermore, we describe the published major safety and efficacy data for these technologies (Tables 10.1 and 10.2).

Laser

Laser-guided atherectomy (Excimer 308 nm Laser, *Philips*, Amsterdam, Netherlands, Fig. 10.1 **panel A** and Auryon 355 nm Laser, Angiodynamics, Latham, NY) utilizes high-frequency pulses of monochromatic light to create photochemical, -mechanical and -thermal effects on the treated vascular segment. Laser has been extensively studied and has been deployed in the coronary arteries, as well as in the periphery. Its use in the coronaries actually predates the use of stents, as it was initially utilized as an adjuvant to improve luminal gain and patency with angioplasty. Laser has broad applications for use: calcific de novo lesions, ISR, and acute limb ischemia.

The single-arm CliRpath Excimer Laser System to Enlarge Lumen Openings (CELLO) study (Dave et al., 2009) examined 65 patients with moderate-to-severely calcified femoropopliteal disease. The study demonstrated a patency rate of 76.9% at 1 year. The 2014 EXCImer Laser Randomized Controlled Study for Treatment of FemoropopliTEal In-Stent Restenosis (EXCITE) study (Dippel et al., 2015) randomized 250 patients with femoropopliteal in-stent restenosis (ISR) to excimer laser plus plain old balloon angioplasty (POBA) versus POBA alone. Freedom from target lesion (TLR) revascularization at 6 months was: 73.5% versus 51.8% in favor of laser + POBA ($P = .05$). This trial demonstrated superiority of laser atherectomy for treatment of ISR and supported this additional FDA indication and remains one of the most cited trials when discussing atherectomy as it was a powered RCT. The ongoing ELABORATE study will evaluate the efficacy of laser plus drug coated balloons (DCB) versus DCB alone and will further clarify the role of laser in treatment of de novo lesions (Jiang et al., 2022).

Table 10.1 Summary major of studies examining atherectomy technologies by year.

Study reverse chronologic order	Year	Trial design/device/n	Pathologic subset	Primary patency at 1 year (unless noted otherwise)	Other major outcomes	Conclusion/Major limitations
DISRUPT PAD III	2022	Shockwave lithotripsy + DCB versus POBA alone	Femoropopliteal calcific disease	Primary patency at 1 year was significantly greater in the Shock Wave + DCB arm (80.5% vs. 68.0%, $P = .017$)	2 year TLR 70.3% with Shockwave + DCB compared to 51.3% with POBA alone, $P = .003$	Shockwave is safe and efficacious. Trial somewhat unbalance as DCB used in experimental arm and POBA only in controls.
JET-ISR	2022	Jet Stream multicenter registry, single arm N = 60	Femoropopliteal ISR		Freedom from TLR at 6 months and 1 year were 79.3% and 60.7%	JetSteam for ISR is a treatment option with adequate success. Note, drug eluting devices were not used in this study.
Rotarex for atherectomy and thrombectomy (BD's Rotarex Atherectomy and Thrombectomy Catheter System Assessed at 12, 2022)	2022	Rotarex multicenter registry, single arm N = 220		Primary patency at 1, 6, and 12 months was 87.2%, 68.1%, and 57.8%, respectively.		Prelim presentation final publication pending

Study	Year	Design	Lesion characteristics	Patency	Findings
J-SUPREME II	2021	Prospective multicenter registry in Japan Jet stream + DCB N = 31	Femoropopliteal disease severe calcification required	6 month patency 96.7%	Jet stream safe and efficacious in patients with de novo lesions with severe calcification
VIVA REALITY (Rocha-Singh et al., 2021)	2021	Multicenter single arm registry Hawk directional atherectomy systems N = 102	Complex femoropopliteal 86.2% mod to severe calcium 39.0% CTO	12 month patency was 76.7%	Directional atherectomy was safe and effective in complex lesion subsets with low rate of provisional stenting.
Disrupt PAD II (Brodmann et al., 2019)	2019	Multicenter, single arm Shock wave Lithotripsy N = 60	Femoropopliteal Mod -Sev calcification 93.3% CTO 16.7%	12 months patency was 54.5%	30-day MAE rate was 1.7% with one grade D dissection. Clinically driven TLR at 12 months was 20.7%
Liberty 360 (LIBERTY 360° Two-Year Data Show High Freedom from Major Amputation, 2018)	2019	Prospective, multicenter registry divided by rutherford class Diamond back 360 N = 1204	Femoropopliteal and BTK lesions 58.5% with calcification CTO in ~⅓ of pts	1 year freedom from MAE: 82.6% in RC 2, 3, 73.2% in RC 4, 5%, and 59.3% in RC 6 patients.	Endovascular treatment had high success and low MAE across all rutherford groups. Rutherford class 6: unplanned amputation is frequently not necessary with 91% amputation free at 1 year.
Rotarex	2019	Single center registry Rotarex N = 74	Femoropopliteal and/or iliac arteries 100% ISR 100% CTO	12 month the restenosis rate 20.5%. TLR 5.5%	Rotarex may efficacious in ISR CTO lesions

Continued

Table 10.1 Summary major of studies examining atherectomy technologies by year.—*continued*

Study reverse chronologic order	Year	Trial design/device/n	Pathologic subset	Primary patency at 1 year (unless noted otherwise)	Other major outcomes	Conclusion/Major limitations
JET-SCE (Shammas et al., 2018)	2018	Single center Jet stream N = 75	Femoropopliteal de novo or ISR (18%) 80% significant calcium CTO 30%	12 month TLR free survival: Jetstream + DCB versus Jetstream with POBA (94.7% vs. 68.0%, *P* = .002)	Distal embolization requiring treatment occurred in 1.2% of patients	Jetstream + DCB had superior 1 year TLR rates compared to Jet stream + POBA alone.
JET (Gray et al., 2018)	2018	Prospective, multicenter registry Jet stream atherectomy N = 241	Femoropopliteal de novo and ISR lesions	12 months patency was 77.2% based on duplex ultrasound		In patients with complex, long lesions, jet stream based intervention had a high primary patency at 1 year and low complication rate
EASE (Davis et al., 2017)	2017	Single arm, registry, multicenter The Phoenix system N = 128	Infrainguinal de novo and ISR lesions	6 month TLR freedom: 88%	Device success was 99%	Adequate safety and efficacy per authors.
VISION (Schwindt et al., 2017)	2017	Single arm Registry Pantheris-Directional (OCT guided) N = 158	Infrainguinal vessels Mod-Sev calcium excluded 20% CTOs	Procedural success (stenosis <30% after pantheris + adjunctive treatment): 97%	MAEs after 6 months: 4% TLR: 16.6% device related events Quality of life metrics improved at 6 months compared to baseline	High rate of procedural success with low rate of TLR

Study	Year	Design	Vessel/Lesion	Clinical outcomes	Procedural outcomes	Summary
Freitas et al.	2017	Single center Registry Rotarex N = 525	Femoropopliteal and iliac vessels	TLR 12 months 10.1% major amputation 2.3%	Procedural technical success rate was 97.7% Mortality 12 months 8%	Atherectomy and mechanical thrombectomy with the rotarex device demonstrated efficacy in a large single center
DEFINITIVE-AR (Zeller et al., 2017)	2017	Multicenter RCT Pilot Silver Hawk or Turbo Hawk + DCB versus DCB alone N = 102	Femoropopliteal 84% severe calcification CTOs ≥5 mm excluded	DA + DCB - 84.6% DCB - 81.3% $P = .88$	Flow limiting dissection 2% versus 19% in favor of DA + DCB	DA + DCB safe and effective but there was no significant difference in 1 year outcomes (underpowered)
DEFINITIVE-LE (McKinsey et al., 2014)	2014	Single arm Registry Silver Hawk Directional N = 797 (596 claudicants, 201 CLI)	Infrainguinal vessels 37% calcified 17% CTO	78% in the claudicant group, 71% in patients with CLI	Perforation: 5.3% Stent rate: 3.2% target vessel femoropopliteal: 81.6% infrapopliteal: 18.5% limb salvage 95% in CLI population	Acute safety and 12 month durability in claudicants and CLI
CONFIRM Series (I, II, & III) (Lee et al., 2015)	2014	Prospective registry single arm Diamond back 360, Predator 360, and Stealth 360 N = 3135	"All comers" 81.1% mod-sev calcium CTO percentage not defined			Variety of subanalyses regarding orbital atherectomy on outcomes.
COMPLIANCE 360 (Dattilo et al., 2014)	2014	Multicenter RCT Pilot Diamond back 360 + balloon angioplasty versus BA alone N = 50	Femoropopliteal Sig calcium	Freedom from TLR in 77.1% of lesions in the atherectomy group versus 11.5% in the POBA group ($P < .001$) at 6 month. 12 months no significant difference remained	Lower max ATM for balloon inflations in the atherectomy group (4 atm vs 9.1 atm) $P < .001$ Lower rate of bail-out stenting in the orbital atherectomy arm	At 12 months, TLR or restenosis was similar in both groups despite the large difference in stent use at the time of initial treatment.

Continued

Table 10.1 Summary major of studies examining atherectomy technologies by year.—*continued*

Study reverse chronologic order	Year	Trial design/device/n	Pathologic subset	Primary patency at 1 year (unless noted otherwise)	Other major outcomes	Conclusion/Major limitations
EXCITE (Dippel et al., 2015)	2014	Multicenter RCT excimer laser atherectomy + POBA versus POBA alone for ISR N = 250	Femoropopliteal bare metal stent ISR CTO 30.5% in laser arm and 36.8 in POBA arm	6 month primary patency 71.1% versus 56.4%, in favor of laser P = .004. Freedom TLR 6 months: 73.5% versus 51.8% in favor of laser (P < .005) (P = .37)	30-day MAE ates were 5.8% versus 20.5% (P < .001 in favor of laser + POBA)	Superiority of laser + POBA over POBA alone in ISR.
PATENT (Schmidt et al., 2014)	2014	Single Arm laser for ISR N = 90	Femoropopliteal bare metal stent ISR Mod-Sev calcification 76% CTO 34.1%	37.8% duplex patency at 12 months	9 (10.0%) patients experienced distal embolization. Freedom from TLR at 6 and 12 months were 87.8% and 64.4%.	High procedural success rate but low primary patency rate at 1 year suggest laser alone does not sufficiently treat ISR.
CALCIUM 360 (Shammas et al., 2012)	2012	Multicenter, multiarm registry Diamond back 360 + balloon angioplasty versus POBA alone N = 50	CLI patients infrapopliteal	Freedom from mortality at 1 year 100% in diamondback + POBA versus 68.4% in POBA alone (P = .01)	No difference in procedural success rate or bailout stenting	No difference in freedom from target lesion revascularization but lower mortality in orbital atherectomy + POBA versus POBA alone. Authors encourage larger confirmatory studies

Study	Year	Design	Lesion characteristics	Outcome	Additional findings	Comments
Pathway PVD (Zeller et al., 2009)	2009	Single arm, Registry, Pathway PV system followed by POBA N = 172	Mostly SFA/Pop Few BTK (9%) Mod Sev calcium 51% CTO 31%	61.8% patency at 12 months by duplex	99% technical success	Adequate safety and efficacy per authors. Single arm study.
CELLO (Dave et al., 2009)	2009	Single arm, registry turbo-booster/Turbo-elite laser catheters N = 65	Femoropopliteal 61.5% mod-sev calcium CTO 20%	76.9% at 1 year	23% had stenting though not clearly due to dissection/ recoil etc	Adequate safety and efficacy per authors. Single arm study.
LACI (Laird et al., 2006)	2006	Single arm, multicenter registry Laser N = 145	Infra-inguinal CTO 92%	Limb salvage 92% of limbs at 6 months		Laser-assisted angioplasty for CLTI - high technical success and high limb salvage rates
Henry et al. (1995)	1995	Single arm, registry rotablator N = 150	Femoropopliteal 50% and BTK 50%	After an avg of 14 mo follow up 76% patent	Broadly defined complication rate was high at 25%, 97% reported technical success	High rates of success with good patency result however with high complication rates although broadly defined

Atherectomy, Atherectomy; BTK, below the knee; CLTI, critical threatening limb ischemia; CTO, chronic total occlusion; DA, directional atherectomy; DCB, drug coated balloon; ISR, in-stent restenosis; MAE, major adverse events per trial design; Mod -Sev, moderate-severe; N, number; OCT, optical coherence tomography; POBA, plain old balloon angioplasty; RC, Rutherford class; RCT, randomized controlled trial; TLR, target lesion revascularization.
Table modified with permission. Anarow, H.A. (2020). Updates in Peripheral Vascular Intervention, An Issue of Interventional Cardiology Clinics, first Edition. Elsevier.

Table 10.2 Major atherectomy/atherectomy devices, specifications, and utilization for peripheral arterial disease.

Device	Mechanism	Rail guidewire size (inches)	Sheath size	Eccentric calcium	CTO lesion with sub intimal segment	Thrombotic lesions efficacy	ISR lesions	BTK lesions
Excimer laser	Monochromatic light to dissolve/soften plaque	0.014 (nonhydrophilic)	6 Fr	Yes	Yes	Yes	Yes	Yes
Auryon laser	Monochromatic light to dissolve/soften plaque	0.014 (nonhydrophilic)	4 Fr–6 Fr	Yes	Yes	Yes	Yes	Yes
Rotablator	Rotational	Specialty wire: tapered wire with 0.014 spring tip	Depends on burr size. 6 Fr sheath generally acceptable					Yes
Jetstream	Rotational	0.014	7 Fr	Yes		Yes	Yes	
Phoenix	Rotational	Specialty wire: 0.014	5–7 Fr depending on device size	Yes				
Rotarex	Rotational	0.014	6 Fr/8 Fr	Yes	Yes	Yes	Yes	Large BTK vessels only for 6 Fr (at least 4 mm in diameter)
Ocelot	Rotational - OCT image guid	0.014	6 Fr	Yes	Yes			

Device	Type	Wire		Size		
Pantheris	Directional-OCT image guided	0.014	Yes	7 or 8 Fr	Yes	Yes
Hawk	Directional	0.014	Yes	6 or 7 Fr	Yes	Yes (M or S devices)
Diamondback 360	Orbital	0.014; 0.14 with 0.18 tip (for use with removable embolic protection device)	Yes	4 Fr 1.25 mm crown 5 Fr 1.50–1.75 mm crown 6 Fr 2.0 mm crown	Yes	Yes
Shockwave	Lithotripsy	0.014	Yes	M5 device 3.5–6.0 6 Fr; 6.5–7.0 7 Fr S5 device 3.0–4.0 5 Fr	Yes	Yes (S4 device)

BTK, below the knee; CTO, chronic total occlusions; Fr, French; ISR, in-stent restenosis; OCT, optical coherence tomography.
Table modified with permission. Anarow, H.A. (2020). Updates in Peripheral Vascular Intervention, An Issue of Interventional Cardiology Clinics, first Edition. Elsevier.

Figure 10.1 Commonly utilized devices for atherectomy clockwise from top left: (A) Excimer laser (B) Rotablator (C) Jetstream (D) Phoenix (E) Hawk (F) Diamond back 360 (G) Shockwave. Images compliments of their respective device companies. Table modified with permission. Anarow, H.A. (2020). Updates in Peripheral Vascular Intervention, An Issue of Interventional Cardiology Clinics, first Edition. Elsevier.

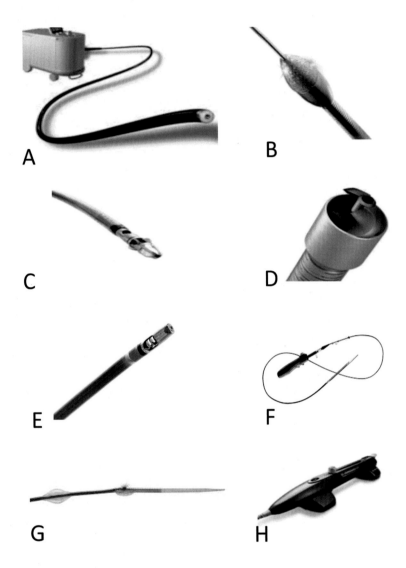

Rotational

There are multiple atherectomy devices on the market in the United States, which utilize a rotational burr or head to modify lesions. The rotablator system (**panel B**) is available for use in infrainguinal (particularly BTK) disease. Limited contemporary studies of rotablator exist in the peripheral vasculature. A 1995 single center study of 150 patients reported a complication rate of 25%, but complications were broadly defined in the study

(Henry et al., 1995). Primary patency after rotablator plus POBA at 14-month was 76%.

JetStream (Boston Scientific, Marlborough, MA, **panel C**), which uses rotational atherectomy with aspiration of debris, was examined with two registries: JET and JET Single Center Experience (JET-SCE) (Gray et al., 2018; Shammas et al., 2018). In the multicenter JET prospective registry, 241 patients with de novo or restenotic (non-ISR) femoropopliteal lesions received atherectomy with the device. At 12 month follow up, primary patency was 77.2%. JET-SCE examined Jetstream atherectomy plus DCB versus Jetstream atherectomy plus POBA. The 12-month incidence of TLR free survival was 94.7% for Jetstream + DCB versus 68.0% for Jetstream plus POBA ($P = .002$). Based on these studies, many operators now utilize the Jetstream device for the treatment of ISR in addition to de novo calcific femoropopliteal disease. More recently, the JetStream Atherectomy for the Treatment of In-Stent Restenosis (JET-ISR) study was published examining 60 patients with femoropopliteal ISR. Freedom from TLR at 6 months and 1 year was 79.3% and 60.7%, respectively (Shammas et al., 2021).

Additional rotational atherectomy options include the Phoenix system (Philips, **panel D**) and the Rotarex atherectomy (B-D, Franklin Lakes, NJ). Phoenix, which combines front-end cutting atherectomy with debris clearance, was studied in the 2014 multicenter Endovascular Atherectomy Safety and Effectiveness (EASE) registry. (Davis et al., 2017) demonstrated an 88% 6 month freedom from TLR and a <1% rate of procedural embolization.

Rotarex was evaluated in a single-center prospective registry in 74 high-risk patients with chronic total occlusions (CTOs) and ISR. Patients were treated with Rotarex atherectomy followed by DCB. At 12 months, the restenosis rate determined by duplex ultrasonography was 20.5%. Rotarex also has active aspiration capabilities and has a long history of use in acute and subacute arterial thrombotic lesions in Europe where it was initially approved. A 2017 single-center study examined Rotarex in 525 patients with acute or subacute arterial thrombosis. The study demonstrated a procedural technical success rate of 97.7% with a 12-month TLR rate of 10.1% and a major amputation rate of 2.3%. This was followed by the recent clinical report of procedural success in 220 patients at 14 centers in Europe treated with the device. Primary patency at 1, 6, and 12 months was 87.2%, 68.1%, and 57.8%, respectively (BD's Rotarex Atherectomy and Thrombectomy Catheter System Assessed at 12, 2022).

Directional

The "Hawk" systems (Medtronic, Minneapolis, MN, **panel E**) and Pantheris (Avinger, Redwood City, CA) are examples of directional atherectomy devices, which use rotating cutting discs to resect and then remove the atherosclerotic plaque.

In a single arm registry called Determination of EFfectiveness of the SilverHawk PerIpheral Plaque ExcisioN System (SIlver-Hawk Device) for the Treatment of Infrainguinal VEssels/Lower Extremities (DEFINITIVE-LE) (McKinsey et al., 2014) trial, 797 patients with claudication or critical limb threatening limb ischemia (CTLI) underwent directional atherectomy. At 1 year, the primary patency rate was 78% in claudicants and 71% in patients with CTLI. The subsequent DEFINITIVE-AR (Zeller et al., 2017) was a small multicenter randomized controlled trial compared treatment with Hawk atherectomy + DCB versus DCB alone in 102 patients with calcified femoropopliteal lesions. The study showed no difference between treatment arms but was underpowered. Nevertheless, on subanalysis, DEFINITIVE-AR did show that directional atherectomy plus DCB had a lower frequency of flow limiting dissection compared with DCB alone (19% vs. 2%, $P = .01$). Distal embolization in the study was very rare, although embolic protection devices were deployed in most cases. The more recent multicenter, single arm study of Hawk in complex femoropopliteal disease called the DiRectional AthErectomy + Drug CoAted BaLloon to Treat Long, CalcifIed FemoropopliTeal ArterY Lesions VIVA REALITY study showed a 1 year primary patency and freedom from major adverse events among patients treated with Hawk directional atherectomy plus DCB of 76.7% with a freedom from TLR of 92.6% (Rocha-Singh et al., 2021). Importantly, only 8.8% of treated lesions required bailout stenting.

The Avinger (Redwood City, CA) Pantheris directional atherectomy system combines optical coherence tomography (OCT) with directional atherectomy. The OCT imaging component is designed to allow for targeted atherectomy of diseased vessel segments. The Pantheris device was studied in the 2017 EValuatIon of the PantheriS OptIcal COherence Tomography ImagiNg Atherectomy System for Use in the Peripheral Vasculature (VISION) Study. The VISION study showed a 97% procedural success rate with only a 4% rate of target lesion revascularization at 6 months (lesions with moderate-to-severe calcification were excluded) (Schwindt et al., 2017).

Orbital

The Diamondback360 orbital atherectomy system (Cardiovascular Systems Inc., St. Paul, MN, **panel F**) has a diamond coated crown, which orbits inside the vessel through a 360-degree arc allowing for differential atherectomy for varying vessel sizes. Diamondback 360 atherectomy is available in multiple crown sizes, shapes, and lengths to treat different vessel segments and sizes. Long-shaft-length devices are available to allow for treatment of femoropopliteal and tibial lesions from radial artery access sites.

Compliance 360 was a randomized, multicenter pilot study of 50 patients with calcified femoropopliteal disease comparing Diamondback360 orbital atherectomy plus POBA versus POBA alone (Dattilo et al., 2014). The primary endpoint, freedom from TLR or restenosis, was observed at 12 months in 81.2% in the orbital atherectomy plus POBA arm versus 78.3% in the POBA arm, $P > .99$. Despite the lack of a difference in the primary outcome, there was less need for stenting in the orbital plus POBA arm when compared with POBA alone (5.3% vs. 77.8%, $P < .001$).

Endovascular lithotripsy

ShockWave (Fig. 10.2) lithotripsy balloons (ShockWave Medical, Santa Clara, Ca, **panel G**) use pulsatile sound ultrasound energy to modify calcific plaque in and beyond intimal layer. DISRUPT PAD II (Brodmann et al., 2019), a nonrandomized, multicenter single arm trial, assessed intravascular lithotripsy in 60 patients with moderate-to-severe femoropopliteal calcific stenosis. The frequency of the study's primary safety endpoint, 30-day major adverse events was 1.7% with only one serious dissection and no distal embolization. The study's primary effectiveness endpoint, patency at 12 months, was 54.5%; and clinically driven TLR was 20.7% at that time point. This was followed by DISRUPT PAD III examining lithotripsy in patients with femoropopliteal calcified lesions followed by treatment with DCB. The 2-year follow-up data are currently published and demonstrated a freedom from TLR rate after ShockWave treatment of 70.3% compared with 51.3% with POBA alone, $P = .003$ (Tepe et al., 2022).

Knowledge gaps and future directions

With only three randomized control trials as described earlier (with only EXCITE being fully powered), future research in this

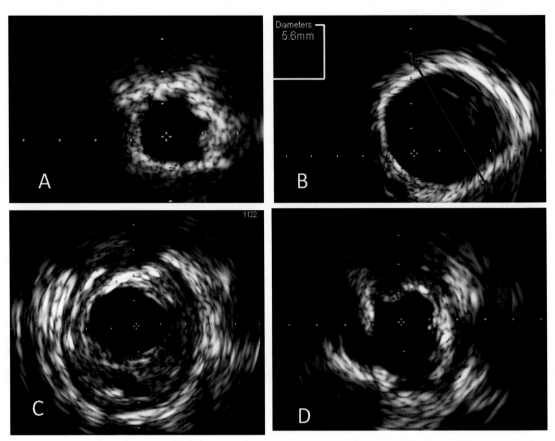

Figure 10.2 Intravascular ultrasound examples. (A and B) Demonstrate a 360 circumferentially calcified lesion in the popliteal and accompanying distal reference measurement. (C) Represents neointimal hyperplasia that may occur with stenting. (D) represents a severely calcified lesion with calcium fractions after treatment with an intravascular lithotripsy balloon.

space needs randomized data to enable guideline changing indications. The majority of atherectomy studies in PAD have been conducted below the femoropopliteal and BTK vessels. Evaluating these devices in alternative vascular beds is an exciting area of potential study (i.e., intravascular lithotripsy in calcified carotid lesions prior to stenting). Studies of these devices in isolated patient, anatomic and lesion subsets (i.e., claudicants, CLTI, BTK disease, ISR, etc.) will be forthcoming (and many have recently been published) generating "niches" for certain device types. Additionally, the comparative efficacy of novel technologies, when used alone or in combination with DCB, remains to be determined and is unlikely to be closely evaluated given current marketplace dynamics and an overall lack of impetus from device manufactures. Lastly, longer-term data regarding the effects of these devices would be useful and are currently lacking.

Conclusion

Atherectomy is an important adjuvant therapy in the treatment of complex peripheral lesions and may be utilized in a variety of pathologic subsets (i.e., calcium, ISR, etc.). The recent significant increase in use of these devices has driven device proliferation and iteration. Additional head-to-head randomized data and longer-term studies would be useful to further guide device selection in the treatment peripheral artery disease.

Disclosures

Dr. Finn receives speaker Honorarium from Janssen. Dr. Walker
All other authors have no disclosures.

References

Bailey, S. R., Beckman, J. A., Dao, T. D., Misra, S., Sobieszczyk, P. S., White, C. J., Wann, L. S., Bailey, S. R., Dao, T., Aronow, H. D., Fazel, R., Gornik, H. L., Gray, B. H., Halperin, J. L., Hirsch, A. T., Jaff, M. R., Krishnamurthy, V., Parikh, S. A., Reed, A. B., … Yucel, E. K. (2019). ACC/AHA/SCAI/SIR/SVM 2018 appropriate use Criteria for peripheral artery intervention. *Journal of the American College of Cardiology, 73*(2), 214−237. https://doi.org/10.1016/j.jacc.2018.10.002

BD's Rotarex Atherectomy and Thrombectomy Catheter System Assessed at 12 Months. (November 4, 2022). https://evtoday.com/news/bds-rotarex-atherectomy-and-thrombectomy-catheter-system-assessed-at-12-months.

Brodmann, M., Werner, M., Holden, A., Tepe, G., Scheinert, D., Schwindt, A., Wolf, F., Jaff, M., Lansky, A., & Zeller, T. (2019). Primary outcomes and mechanism of action of intravascular lithotripsy in. *Catheterization and Cardiovascular Interventions, 93*(2), 335−342. https://doi.org/10.1002/ccd.27943

Conte, M. S., Bradbury, A. W., Kolh, P., White, J. V., Dick, F., Fitridge, R., Mills, J. L., Ricco, J.-B., Suresh, K. R., Murad, M. H., Aboyans, V., Aksoy, M., Alexandrescu, V.-A., Armstrong, D., Azuma, N., Belch, J., Bergoeing, M., Bjorck, M., Chakfé, N., , … Wang, S., & GVG Writing Group for the Joint Guidelines of the Society for Vascular Surgery (SVS), European Society for Vascular Surgery (ESVS)and World Federation of Vascular Societies (WFVS). (2019). Global vascular guidelines on the management of chronic limb-threatening. *European Journal of Vascular and Endovascular Surgery, 58*(1S), S1−S109.e33. https://doi.org/10.1016/j.ejvs.2019.05.006

Conte, M. S., Pomposelli, F. B., Clair, D. G., Geraghty, P. J., McKinsey, J. F., Mills, J. L., Moneta, G. L., Murad, M. H., Powell, R. J., Reed, A. B., Schanzer, A., & Sidawy, A. N. (2015). Society for Vascular Surgery practice guidelines for atherosclerotic occlusive disease of the lower extremities: Management of asymptomatic disease and claudication. *Journal of Vascular Surgery, 61*(3), 2–41. https://doi.org/10.1016/j.jvs.2014.12.009

Dattilo, R., Himmelstein, S. I., & Cuff, R. F. (2014). The compliance 360° trial: A randomized, prospective, multicenter, pilot study comparing acute and long-term results of orbital atherectomy to balloon angioplasty for calcified femoropopliteal disease. *Journal of Invasive Cardiology, 26*(8), 355–360. http://www.invasivecardiology.com/archive.

Dave, R. M., Patlola, R., Kollmeyer, K., Bunch, F., Weinstock, B. S., Dippel, E., Jaff, M. R., Popma, J., Weissman, N., & CELLO Investigators. (2009). Excimer laser recanalization of femoropopliteal lesions and 1-year. *Journal of Endovascular Therapy, 16*(6), 665–675. https://doi.org/10.1583/09-2781.1

Davis, T., Ramaiah, V., Niazi, K., Martin Gissler, H., & Crabtree, T. (2017). Safety and effectiveness of the phoenix atherectomy system in lower extremity arteries: Early and midterm outcomes from the prospective multicenter EASE study. *Vascular, 25*(6), 563–575. https://doi.org/10.1177/1708538117712383

Dippel, E. J., Makam, P., Kovach, R., George, J. C., Patlola, R., Metzger, D. C., Mena-Hurtado, C., Beasley, R., Soukas, P., Colon-Hernandez, P. J., Stark, M. A., & Walker, C. (2015). Randomized controlled study of excimer laser atherectomy for treatment of femoropopliteal in-stent restenosis: Initial results from the EXCITE ISR Trial (EXCImer laser randomized controlled study for treatment of FemoropopliTEal in-stent restenosis). *JACC: Cardiovascular Interventions, 8*(1), 92–101. https://doi.org/10.1016/j.jcin.2014.09.009

Feldman, D. N., Armstrong, E. J., Aronow, H. D., Gigliotti, O. S., Jaff, M. R., Klein, A. J., Parikh, S. A., Prasad, A., Rosenfield, K., Shishehbor, M. H., Swaminathan, R. V., & White, C. J. (2018). SCAI consensus guidelines for device selection in femoral-popliteal arterial interventions. *Catheterization and Cardiovascular Interventions, 92*(1), 124–140. https://doi.org/10.1002/ccd.27635

Gray, W. A., Garcia, L. A., Amin, A., & Shammas, N. W. (2018). Jetstream atherectomy system treatment of femoropopliteal arteries: Results of the post-market JET registry. *Cardiovascular Revascularization Medicine, 19*(5), 506–511. https://doi.org/10.1016/j.carrev.2017.12.015

Haqqani, M. H., Alonso, A., Kobzeva-Herzog, A., Farber, A., King, E. G., Meltzer, A. J., Eslami, M. H., Garg, K., Rybin, D., & Siracuse, J. J. (2023). Variations in practice patterns for peripheral vascular interventions across clinical settings. *Annals of Vascular Surgery, 92*, 24–32. https://doi.org/10.1016/j.avsg.2023.01.010

Henry, M., Amor, M., Ethevenot, G., Henry, I., & Allaoui, M. (1995). Percutaneous peripheral atherectomy using the rotablator: A single-center experience. *Journal of Endovascular Surgery: The Official Journal of the International Society for Endovascular Surgery, 2*(1), 51–66. https://doi.org/10.1583/1074-6218(1995)002<0051:PPAUTR>2.0.CO;2

Hirsch, A. T., Haskal, Z. J., Hertzer, N. R., Bakal, C. W., & others. (2006). *ACC/AHA task force on practice guidelines (writing committee).* http://www.onlinejacc.org/content/accj/47/6/e1.full.pdf.

Jiang, X., Fan, L., Chen, B., Jiang, J., Liu, J., Qiao, G., Ju, S., Shi, Y., Ma, T., Lin, C., Fang, G., Guo, D., Xu, X., Dong, Z., & Fu, W. (2022). Excimer laser ablation combined with drug-coated balloon versus drug-coated balloon in the treatment of de novo atherosclerotic lesions in lower extremities (ELABORATE): study protocol for a real-world clinical trial. *BMC Cardiovascular Disorders, 22*(1). https://doi.org/10.1186/s12872-022-02751-1

Laird, J. R., Zeller, T., Gray, B. H., Scheinert, D., Vranic, M., Reiser, C., Biamino, G., & LACI Investigators. (2006). Limb salvage following laser-assisted angioplasty for critical limb. *Journal of Endovascular Therapy, 13*(1), 1−11. https://doi.org/10.1583/05-1674.1

Lee, M.S., Canan, T., Rha, S.W., Mustapha, J., Adams, G.L., 2015. Share pooled analysis of the CONFIRM registries: impact of gender on procedure and angiographic outcomes in patients undergoing orbital atherectomy for peripheral artery disease. Journal of Endovascular Therapy 22 (1), 57-62. https://doi.org/10.1177/1526602814564367. PMID: 25775681.

Liberty 360° two-year data show high freedom from major amputation. (August 15, 2018). Vascular News. https://vascularnews.com/liberty-360-two-year-data/.

McKinsey, J. F., Zeller, T., Rocha-Singh, K. J., Jaff, M. R., & Garcia, L. A. (2014). Lower extremity revascularization using directional atherectomy: 12-month prospective results of the definitive le study. *JACC: Cardiovascular Interventions, 7*(8), 923−933. https://doi.org/10.1016/j.jcin.2014.05.006

Mohan, S., Flahive, J. M., Arous, E. J., Judelson, D. R., Aiello, F. A., Schanzer, A., & Simons, J. P. (2018). Peripheral atherectomy practice patterns in the United States from the vascular quality initiative. *Journal of Vascular Surgery, 68*(6), 1806−1816. https://doi.org/10.1016/j.jvs.2018.03.417

Nfor, T., Dababneh, E., Jan, M. F., Khitha, J., Allaqaband, S. Q., Bajwa, T., & Mewissen, M. W. (2022). National trends and variability of atherectomy use for peripheral vascular interventions from 2010 to 2019. *Journal of Vascular Surgery, 76*(3), 778−785. https://doi.org/10.1016/j.jvs.2022.03.864

Norgren, L., Hiatt, W. R., Dormandy, J. A., Nehler, M. R., Harris, K. A., & Fowkes, F. G. R. (2007). Inter-society consensus for the management of peripheral arterial disease (TASC II). *European Journal of Vascular and Endovascular Surgery, 33*(1), S1−S75. https://doi.org/10.1016/j.ejvs.2006.09.024

Rocha-Singh, K. J., Sachar, R., DeRubertis, B. G., Nolte-Ernsting, C. C. A., Winscott, J. G., Krishnan, P., Scott, E. C., Garcia, L. A., Baeriswyl, J. L., Ansel, G., Rosenfield, K., & Zeller, T. (2021). Directional atherectomy before paclitaxel coated balloon angioplasty in complex femoropopliteal disease: The VIVA REALITY study. *Catheterization and Cardiovascular Interventions, 98*(3), 549−558. https://doi.org/10.1002/ccd.29777

Schmidt, A., Zeller, T., Sievert, H., Krankenberg, H., Torsello, G., Stark, M. A., & Scheinert, D. (2014). P hoto a blation Using the T urbo-Booster and E xcimer Laser for In-Stent. *Journal of Endovascular Therapy, 21*(1), 52−60. https://journals.sagepub.com/doi/full/10.1583/13-4538R.1?casa_token=yuvwEdZQNIYAAAAA:Z9xEJXsuzr7d3lIKHAB7jVbCVcPG4N1_A80iCVdPVM-Q3XzRIfmWFBisqKpQ4TJM_sVTpBkm0BY.

Schwindt, A. G., Bennett, J. G., Crowder, W. H., Dohad, S., Janzer, S. F., George, J. C., Tedder, B., Davis, T. P., Cawich, I. M., Gammon, R. S., Muck, P. E., Pigott, J. P., Dishmon, D. A., Lopez, L. A., Golzar, J. A., Chamberlin, J. R., Moulton, M. J., Zakir, R. M., Kaki, A. K., ... Desai, A. (2017).

Lower extremity revascularization using optical coherence tomography-guided directional atherectomy: Final results of the e valuation of the pantheris optical coherence tomography imaging atherectomy system for use in the peripheral vasculature (VISION) study. *Journal of Endovascular Therapy, 24*(3), 355–366. https://doi.org/10.1177/1526602817701720

Shammas, N. W., Lam, R., Mustapha, J., Ellichman, J., Aggarwala, G., Rivera, E., Niazi, K., & Balar, N. (2012). Comparison of orbital atherectomy plus balloon angioplasty vs. balloon angioplasty alone in patients with critical limb ischemia: Results of the CALCIUM 360 randomized pilot trial. *Journal of Endovascular Therapy: An Official Journal of the International Society of Endovascular Specialists, 19*(4), 480–488.

Shammas, N. W., Petruzzi, N., Henao, S., Armstrong, E. J., Shimshak, T., Banerjee, S., Latif, F., Eaves, B., Brothers, T., Golzar, J., Shammas, G. A., Jones-Miller, S., Christensen, L., & Shammas, W. J. (2021). Jetstream atherectomy for the treatment of in-stent restenosis of the femoropopliteal segment: One-year results of the JET-ISR study. *Journal of Endovascular Therapy, 28*(1), 107–116. https://doi.org/10.1177/1526602820951916

Shammas, N. W., Shammas, G. A., Jones-Miller, S., Shammas, W. J., Bou-Dargham, B., Shammas, A. N., Banerjee, S., Rachwan, R. J., & Daher, G. E. (2018). Long-term outcomes with Jetstream atherectomy with or without drug coated balloons in treating femoropopliteal arteries: A single center experience (JET-SCE). *Cardiovascular Revascularization Medicine, 19*(7), 771–777. https://doi.org/10.1016/j.carrev.2018.02.003

Tepe, G., Brodmann, M., Bachinsky, W., Holden, A., Zeller, T., Mangalmurti, S., Nolte-Ernsting, C., Virmani, R., Parikh, S. A., & Gray, W. A. (2022). *Intravascular lithotripsy for peripheral artery calcification: Mid-term.* Universität. https://books.google.com/books/about/Intravascular_Lithotripsy_for_Peripheral.html?hl=&id=Qs60zwEACAAJ.

Zeller, T., Krankenberg, H., Steinkamp, H., Rastan, A., Sixt, S., Schmidt, A., Sievert, H., Minar, E., Bosiers, M., Peeters, P., Balzer, J. O., Gray, W., Tübler, T., Wissgott, C., Schwarzwälder, U., & Scheinert, D. (2009). One-year outcome of percutaneous rotational atherectomy with aspiration in infrainguinal peripheral arterial occlusive disease: The multicenter pathway PVD trial. *Journal of Endovascular Therapy: An Official Journal of the International Society of Endovascular Specialists, 16*(6), 653–662.

Zeller, T., Langhoff, R., Rocha-Singh, K. J., Jaff, M. R., Blessing, E., Amann-Vesti, B., Krzanowski, M., Peeters, P., Scheinert, D., Torsello, G., Sixt, S., Tepe, G., & DEFINITIVE AR Investigators. (2017). Directional atherectomy followed by a paclitaxel-coated balloon to inhibit restenosis and maintain vessel patency: Twelve-month results of the DEFINITIVE AR study. *Circulation Cardiovascular Interventions, 10*(9). https://doi.org/10.1161/CIRCINTERVENTIONS.116.004848

Zeller, T., Langhoff, R., Rocha-Singh, K. J., Jaff, M. R., Blessing, E., Amann-Vesti, B., Krzanowski, M., Peeters, P., Scheinert, D., Torsello, G., Sixt, S., & Tepe, G. (2017). Directional atherectomy followed by a paclitaxel-coated balloon to inhibit restenosis and maintain vessel patency twelve-month results of the DEFINITIVE AR study. *Circulation: Cardiovascular Interventions, 10*(8). https://doi.org/10.1161/CIRCINTERVENTIONS.116.004848

Further reading

Michael, S. L., Yang, T., & Adams, G. (2014). Pooled analysis of the CONFIRM registries: Safety outcomes in diabetic. *Journal of Endovascular Therapy, 21*(2), 258–265. https://doi.org/10.1583/13-4449MR.1. https://journals.sagepub.com/doi/pdf/10.1583/13-4449MR.1?casa_token=dDwht9a1xGsAAA AA:R1nXOYYA-6zgV1_8TRnJts_DfQe9oSX4aSv1Y3N_eMEwTr96cIoN3IkG_2x_ 5xKLNiNWsLZXx50

11

Interventional treatment of PAD: Drug-coated balloons and stents

Gary M. Ansel

Department of Medicine, University of Toledo, Toledo, OH, United States

Introduction

Atherosclerotic peripheral artery disease (PAD) leading to claudication commonly involves the femoropopliteal arteries (fempop), while limb-threatening CLI is more commonly associated with multilevel PAD including the infrapopliteal or tibial arteries. Historically, percutaneous transluminal angioplasty (PTA) has been the cornerstone of the less invasive, endovascular approach; however, suboptimally high rates of restenosis have now limited its usefulness except for very focal lesions (Rocha-Singh et al., 2007). Bare metal stents (BMSs) for the fempop were originally stainless steel in makeup and included both balloon-expandable and self-expanding designs. However,

Pathophysiology and Treatment of Atherosclerotic Disease in Peripheral Arteries. https://doi.org/10.1016/B978-0-443-13593-4.00011-1

balloon-expandable stents were associated with bending, twisting, and crushing pressures (commonly referred to as "crush"), while the self-expanding variety of these stents have been replaced primarily by self-expanding stents manufactured from straight tubular nitinol, as well as by stent grafts covered in polytetrafluoroethylene (Lammer et al., 2013; Rosenfield et al., 1997; Zollikofer et al., 1991).

The current designs of peripheral stents have demonstrated superior results in randomized trials compared with PTA (Krankenberg et al., 2007; Schillinger et al., 2006). Though an improvement, most stent/stent graft technology is still associated with clinically significant restenosis, which often proves more difficult to treat than the original lesion (Ho & Owens, 2017). Improved results have been noted, however, with nitinol mesh stents and more recently, angulated swirling flow stents (Garcia et al., 2017; Zeller et al., 2016). Though drug-coated balloon angioplasty (DCB) preceded any drug-eluting stent (DES) in Europe, in the United States (US), paclitaxel-based DCB approval followed DES into the treatment paradigm. DCBs all utilize a varying excipient or carrier for drug delivery, so a class effect cannot be assumed (Laird et al., 2015). There has been limited advancement of drug-based devices designed for the tibial vascular bed. The quest for a successful drug-based platform for the tibial vasculature continues. It must be recognized that the fempop and tibial disease processes are not the same. Fempop blockage is typically of atherosclerotic makeup with thrombus and atherosclerotic heterogeneous calcification being mixed in. In the tibial vessels, it appears that less than 50% of the lesions are primarily of atherosclerotic etiology. Medial arterial calcification is more widely spread and uniform in variety. Both acute and chronic thrombus are present in over 50% of the tibial blockages (Narula et al., 2018).

Current chemotherapy medications

The two chemotherapeutic agents approved to date for prevention of restenosis are paclitaxel and sirolimus, or in the "-limus" category of drugs. Paclitaxel, primarily thought of as a cytotoxic agent, is readily absorbed into the vascular tissue and was the initial agent utilized in the cardiovascular space. Paclitaxel has a somewhat narrow safety window and, in the cardiovascular space, has largely been supplanted by "-limus"-based technology due to superior antirestenotic results. Limus compounds have a much larger safety margin but, due to poor uptake in the tissues, is much more dependent on a carrier or polymer. The importance of dose and tissue retention of the drug is reflected in rates of restenosis. In the peripheral vascular space where stents had been demonstrated to have a patency benefit compared with balloon angioplasty (PTA), drug-coated stents were the first devices evaluated. Due to the success in the coronary vascular bed, limus-based agents were placed on polymerically coated stents. The success in the cardiovascular space was not transferred to the PAD space (Duda et al., 2005; Lammer et al., 2011). Utilization of a paclitaxel/excipient drug-coated *balloon* technology first demonstrated significant benefit in the fempop space and utilized successfully in Europe to improve patency and reduce the need for repeat procedures. However, a drug-coated *stent* was the first device approved in the United States, and drug-coated balloon technology was delayed due to concerns of bench-top particulate embolization associated with the early European-approved DCB (Tepe, Schnorr, et al., 2015).

Safety concerns, similar to those voiced with the use of paclitaxel coatings in coronary devices, were heavily publicized before being subsequently dismissed (Nordmann et al., 2006; Stone et al., 2007). This safety of paclitaxel-based peripheral devices was called into question after a decade of successful fempop usage (Katsanos et al., 2018). This "delayed risk" that the authors felt to have discovered has not been evident in much larger datasets, including evaluations in both the claudicant and critical limb ischemia patient populations (Dinh et al., 2020; Gutierrez et al., 2021; Katsanos et al., 2018).

To date, the US Food and Drug Administration (FDA) has fully removed their concern and no longer suggests limits to paclitaxel use (https://www.fda.gov/medical-devices/cardiovascular-devices/paclitaxel-coated-balloons-and-stents-peripheral-arterial-disease; Food and Drung Administration (FDA); Hess et al., 2021). The initial stance by the FDA led to a significant quandary for the PAD interventionalist since to date, since limus-based device for PAD have only recently been placed into clinical trials in the United States.

DES

The lack of benefit seen in the first polymeric limus-based DES studies may have been secondary to the nonoptimized, coronary-based polymer platforms utilized. These polymers were designed for stagnant, balloon-expandable stents and may not have been suitable for the self-expanding stent platforms used in the peripheral vasculature. The first drug-coated PAD stent device approved for use in the United States, interestingly, was a non-polymer-based, non-excipient paclitaxel-coated DES Zilver PTX (Cook Medical, Bloomington, IN). The Zilver PTX randomized investigational device exemption (IDE) trial that demonstrated the safety and effectiveness of the paclitaxel-coated Zilver PTX DES through 1–5 years had a mean lesion length of 5.5 cm and a stented length of 6.6 cm. There was significant, sustained clinical benefit evident at 1- and 5-year compared with PTA (90.5 vs. 72.3% and 79.8 vs. 59.3%, $P < .01$, respectively) with a widening difference compared with PTA (Dake, Ansel, et al., 2011; Dake et al., 2016). The concern for stent fracture was not born out in this trial with a core lab-adjudicated 2.1% rate of stent fracture. Interestingly, a posthoc analysis of restenotic lesions appears to demonstrate a less diffuse pattern of tissue growth compared with BMS. This pattern would potentially make the treatment of restenosis less complex (Ansel et al., 2017).

In a primarily European-based registry, Zilver PTX was evaluated early on in more real-world patients with more complex lesions and a mean lesion length of 10 cm. The results were very consistent with the Zilver PTX randomized trial (Dake, Scheinert, et al., 2011). This registry was followed by the Japan postmarket surveillance study 1-year results. This population was even more complex with mean lesion lengths of 14.7 cm (Yokoi et al., 2016).

The second approval of a drug-eluting stent was for a polymer-based paclitaxel stent. This Eluvia DES (Boston Scientific, Marlborough, MA) has been evaluated in the randomized ELUVIA trial and was compared with the non-polymer Zilver PTX stent. Designed as a noninferiority trial, the 1-year results demonstrated noninferiority for both efficacy and safety endpoints at 12 months; primary patency was 86.8% (231/266) in the Eluvia group and 81.5% (106/130) in the Zilver PTX group, ($P < .0001$). There was a trend toward improved freedom from clinically driven total lesion revascularization (CD-TLR) at 12 months but did not meet statistical significance (Gray et al., 2018). The rate of freedom of TLR for Eluvia was 95.5 versus 91.0, $P = .061$ for Zilver PTX (Nordmann et al., 2006). The data have now matured with follow-up results to 2 years demonstrating that Eluvia use was associated with a trend of improved patency that did not meet statistical significance. However, the clinically driven target lesion revascularization rate was significantly less for patients treated with Eluvia versus Zilver PTX (12.7% vs. 20.1%; $P = .0495$) (Müller-Hülsbeck et al., 2021). To add further light on the benefit seen with the polymer-based device studies, late lumen loss after implantation does appear to favor the polymer-based platform (Soga et al., 2020).

One-year data on longer lesions in a 62-patient group have been published using Eluvia. Lesions were de novo in 84% of patients with a mean lesion length of 20 cm. The Kaplan–Meier estimate of primary patency and freedom from target lesion revascularization was 87%. The investigators did note the formation of peristent lucency in five of the treated segments (8%), which were thought by the authors to be attributable to paclitaxel (Bisdas et al., 2018). The clinical relevance is unknown, however, and previous animal research demonstrated a similar finding attributed to a variable amount of inflammation affected by the amount of external force experienced by stents in the femoral versus popliteal arterial segments (Sakaoka et al., 2019). There have been, however, other animal data demonstrating this to be more common with this polymer-based platform (Sakamoto et al., 2021). Clinically what this all means has not been established with no evidence of associated complications in the first few years. Longer-term follow-up will potentially shed more light on the matter.

Full drug jacket?

There appears to be discrepancy in evaluating the optimal length of DES for longer lesions. Park et al. evaluated lesions over 150 cm in a multicenter randomized trial in 105 patients, followed for 1-year in Japan, comparing spot stenting versus long full lesion coverage. The trial was terminated before full enrollment due to a significant outcome advantage in the full coverage group. The average lesion lengths were approximately 24 cm for both groups. The freedom from CD-TLR was 91.7% versus 72.0%, $P = .044$, between the full coverage and spot stenting, respectively (Park et al., 2022). Our own group reported early, single center experience in the most complex patient population to date and followed for 2 years. We specifically evaluated our results in diffuse fempop disease of long (>20 cm) versus shorter lesions (<20 cm). In our center, the longer lesion population is common and treatment of these lesions with DES warranted formal clinical evaluation in an effort to better understand their durability and clinical effectiveness in this real-world setting. This is important since more complex lesion populations are typically excluded from device approval Investigational Device Exemption (IDE) study groups. In this registry (n = 89), CD-TLR rates in patients with more simple disease (mean lesion length 13.3 cm) were compared with the full drug jacket group with more diffuse disease (mean lesion length of 33 cm) for both denovo and in-stent restenosis lesions. A strong trend of higher restenosis was seen in the more diffuse disease group treated with a "full drug jacket" versus the simpler disease group at 1-year 40.5% versus 18.8% ($P = .050$) and 2-year 53.6% versus 38.9% ($P = .331$), respectively. The shorter lesion group was also associated with significantly lower rates of reintervention, both at 1 year (2.4% vs. 20.8% in full drug jacket group; $P = .009$), and at 2 years (12.2% vs. 33.3%; $P = .019$), respectively (Phillips et al., 2018). Hopefully, future datasets will allow us to figure out when too much stent may change the compliance of the vessel in such a way as to decrease their utility.

Restenosis and the use of DES

The efficacy of relining in-stent restenosis, i.e., putting in a second stent, has limited data on usefulness. The first data of the use of Zilver PTX for in = stent restenosis were from the early single arm study completed primarily in Europe. In this study, 108 pts with a mean in-stent restenosis lesion length of 13.3 cm and 31% with total occlusions were treated. The 2-year freedom from CD-TLR was 60.8% (Thomas et al., 2013).

Most recently, this was evaluated in the Zilver PTX Japan Post-Market Surveillance Study, a prospective, multicenter registry. The relining of instent restenosis with Zilver PTX was evaluated in 177 patients with a mean lesion length of 17.8 cm, and ⅓ being total occlusions. This study demonstrated a 5-year rate of freedom from CD-TLR of 73.4% with a 5% stent fracture rate (Sugimoto et al., 2021).

Tibial DES

Though there has been much excitement of transferring the success of coronary DES to the tibial vascular bed, there have been no randomized data, although there are have been some reports of success (Huntress et al., 2020).

The recent DES BTK Vascular Stent System versus PTA in Subjects With Critical Limb Ischemia (SAVAL) trial, which randomized a self-expanding polymer-based paclitaxel-eluting nitinol stent versus PTA, showed no patency benefit of the DES (Hans van Overhagen, 2022). The most recent developement is with the success in a drug coated bioabsorbable stent. The randomized LIFE BTK study demonstrated superiority against PTA with a freedom from multifactorial primary endpoint of 74% in the treatment group versus 44% in the control group, $P < .001$ (Ansel, 2024; Varcoe & LIFE BTK Investigators, 2023).

DCB

Numerous randomized controlled trials (RCTs) have demonstrated that DCBs are more effective for the treatment of patients with femoropopliteal lesions than uncoated balloon angioplasty (Kondapalli et al., 2017). Unlike the DES space, no DCB not utilizing an excipient has demonstrated benefit. In fact, all excipient utilizing DCBs to date evaluated in the fempop region have demonstrated favorable 1-year patency. Longer-term datasets beyond 2 years, especially 5-year data, are derived from the IN.PACT device. As evident in the DES IDE randomized trials, these trials were mostly for simple lesions to support device approval. Lutonix (Becton Dickson, Franklin Lakes, NJ) was the first DCB to gain approval by demonstrating a 1-year improvement in patency in patients undergoing angioplasty with the DCB versus conventional angioplasty (65.2% vs. 52.6%, $P = .02$). However, CD-TLR was not significantly different 12.3% versus 6.8%, respectively (Rosenfield et al., 2015). The approval of the IN.PACT DCB followed; the IN.PACT DCB appears to have more effect than the Levant DCB compared with PTA. In the IN.PACT SFA trial, DCB resulted in significantly higher primary patency versus PTA (82.2% vs. 52.4%; $P < .001$), as well as an improved rate of CD-TLR, 2.4% in the DCB arm compared with 20.6% in the PTA arm ($P < .001$) (Tepe, Laird, et al., 2015). The randomized dataset has been reported at 2−3 years. These datasets have demonstrated a lessening restenosis effect, but still both clinically and statistically significant benefit at these time periods (Schneider et al., 2018; Zeller et al., 2022). A third DCB, Stellarex (Philips Healthcare, Andover, MA), has also demonstrated significant benefit at 1-year in a single-arm trial as well. Primary patency was 81.4% and the freedom from CD-TLR was 94.8% (Stellarex, 2018). More recently, DCB comparative randomized IDE trials have started to be published or presented. The first randomized DCB evaluation was the Surmodics Surveil DCB (Surmodics, Eden Prairie, MN) Safety and Efficacy of the SurVeil Drug-Coated Balloon (TRANSCEND) Trial that demonstrated noninferiority with a 75% lower PTX dose and unique polymer compared with IN.PACT. At 24 months, the primary patency was 70.8% for SurVeil DCB versus 70.4% for IN.PACT Admiral DCB ($P = .991$). CD-TLR was also comparable (14.7% vs. 11.8%; $P = .453$) (Rosenfield, 2022). The second randomized evaluation was the evaluated in the Chocolate Touch Trial and compared with the Lutonix device. Chocolate Touch (TriReme Medical, Pleasanton, CA) demonstrated noninferiority with a CD-TLR 93.7% versus 88.6% for the Lutonix device (Shishehbor et al., 2022).

Similar patency and freedom from CD-TLR seen in IDE trials have also been evident in real-world registries for more complex disease, including longer lesions, chronic total occlusions, etc. This success has been demonstrated for most DCBs at 2 years and the IN.PACT device to 5 years (Schroeder et al., 2015; Steiner et al., 2022; Zeller, Brodmann, et al., 2022). The need for adjunctive stenting to optimize acute results in complex disease is significant, however, up to 40%. Thankfully, stented results appear to be similar to optimal DCB (Brodmann et al., 2022). However, whether adding BMS to optimize a suboptimal DCB result is equivalent to primarily using a DES for a suboptimal predilation is still in question and in need of clinical data.

Comparative DCB versus DES data

Recently published data may help to add some clarity on differentiating DES and DCB results and potential optimizing treatment pathways.

Utilizing propensity-matched score stratification, Zeller et al. performed a retrospective analysis of DCB and DES outcomes in 228 patients in long lesions >10 cm, with a mean of 19.3 cm. Stents were utilized in 18.3%. The clinical outcomes were not significantly different. Binary restenosis rates were 23.9% (26/109) and 30.4% (24/79, $P = .319$) in the DCB and DES cohorts, respectively. CD-TLR rates did not demonstrate a significant difference at 15.6% versus 19.0%, $P = .543$, respectively (Zeller et al., 2014). Bausback et al. randomized 150 patients with symptomatic femoropopliteal disease to primary Zilver PTX implantation or DCB angioplasty (IN.PACT Admiral) with bailout stenting after stratification for lesion length (<10 cm, >10 cm to <20 cm, and >20 cm to < 30 cm). The primary effectiveness endpoint was primary patency at 12 months assessed by Kaplan–Meier. Secondary endpoints comprised major adverse events including death, major amputations, and CD-TLR. More than one-half of lesions were total occlusions, and the stenting rate was 25.3% in the DCB group. Kaplan–Meier estimates of primary patency were 79% and 80% for DES and DCB at 12 months ($P = .96$), but decreased to 54% and 38% through 36 months ($P = .17$), respectively. Freedom from CD-TLR was >90% at 12 months but decreased to approximately 70% for both groups at 36 months. Though the 12-month findings for clinical outcomes appeared similar at 1 year, a more detailed look at the longer term outcome trend, especially in stenotic and medium-to-long length lesions, appeared to have improved outcomes with DES. For stenotic disease, the 3-year event-free survival for DES was 74.8% versus 49.3% for DCB, $P = .04$. While the difference was not significant for total occlusions, at 34.9% and 27.8%, $P = .93$, for mid-to-long lesions, there was a nonsignificant trend of 3year event-free survival with DES 45.2% and DCB 25.8%, $P = .19$. As noted, the bailout stenting rate was 25% of the DCB group overall and increased to over 35% in the long lesion group (Bausback et al., 2019).

Treatment of in-stent restenosis with DCB/DES

Though registry data have demonstrated acceptable CD-TLR rates in patients with in-stent restenosis treated with DCB, it will only be in randomized trials that we can truly evaluate their effect. The use of DCB's for in-stent restenosis has demonstrated reasonable results at 1 year. However, after that time point there is typically a significant drop off in patency. The somewhat small study, Copa Cabana trial evaluated DCB use in patients with in-stent restenosis and recurrent in-stent restenosis. A double dose DCB was utilized for patients with more than a single episode of in-stent restenosis. Those with a single-episode were randomized between uncoated PTA and DCB (Tepe et al., 2020). Following treatment the 12-month follow-up, CD_TLR was performed in 49% patients in the uncoated group, 14% in the single-dose DCB group $P = .001$. No patients from the recurrent ISR group. At 2 years, significant number 52% of TLRs were recorded in the single-dose DCB group. The use of laser atherectomy has been evaluated but not difference was evident at 1 and 2 years (Böhme et al., 2021).

Vessel prep and DCB

As previously noted, the presence of calcification and thrombus may decrease results of drug-based devices. Devices directed at preparing the lesion are currently most focused on atherectomy, which may lead to removal and or fractures of calcification and potentially some removal of underlying chronic thrombus. A small pilot study evaluating the use of orbital atherectomy before DCB certainly demonstrated the feasibility of this technique but no significant difference at 1-year in freedom from major adverse events, CD-TLR, major amputation, and all-cause mortality rates were similar between both groups (Zeller, Giannopoulos, et al., 2022).

Directional atherectomy, which may be associated with more tissue removal, has been evaluated in the multicenter REALITY trial. This registry study in a very complex group of patient s (mean lesion length 22.6 ± 8.6 cm); 86.2% of lesions exhibited moderate-to-severe bilateral calcification demonstrated a low rate of provisional stenting 8.8%. Twelve-month primary patency rate was 76.7% (66/86), and freedom from CD-TLR rate was 92.6%. No device- or procedure-related deaths and one index-limb major amputation were reported (Rocha-Singh et al., 2021). An underpowered, randomized definitive AR trial data did not demonstrate a difference at 1 year (Zeller et al., 2017).

The use of lithoplasty before DCB has been studied in a randomized trial. The use of lithoplasty/DCB demonstrated benefit. The requirement for provisional stenting was significantly lower in the IVL group (4.6% vs. 18.3%, $P < .0001$). Freedom from clinically driven target lesion revascularization (IVL: 95.7% vs. PTA: 98.3%, $P = .94$) and restenosis rates (IVL: 90.0% vs. PTA: 88.8%, $P = .48$) were similar between the two groups at 1 year. At 2 years, primary patency remained significantly greater in the IVL arm (70.3% vs. 51.3%, $P = .003$) (Tepe et al., 2022).

Tibial DCB

The success of DCB in the fempop region was eagerly anticipated to be transferred to the critical limb ischemia patient population with tibial arterial disease. Subsequently, two key trial results have dampened the enthusiasm. The INPACT DEEP (Randomized IN.PACT Amphirion Drug-Coated Balloon) trial has results to 5 years of follow-up. Initially, there was concern at 1 year of an increased amputation risk with DCB use. However, to 5 years, there was no patency benefit or significantly increased risk of amputation found by the investigators (Zeller et al., 2020). The first FDA-approved DCB in the United States, Lutonix, did not demonstrate significant enough clinical improvements to warrant approval by the FDA or subsequent FDA panel (Case et al., 2021).

This lack of perceived benefit in the tibial arterial vascular bed may have many reasons. First, in a recent pathologic dissection series in amputated patients with CLI demonstrated that over half of the tibial blockage was thrombotic in nature and thus may limit drug uptake. Second, medial arterial calcification is very common, especially in diabetes, and may be decreasing the uptake of paclitaxel into the arterial tissue (Fanelli et al., 2014; Hwang et al., 2005).

Economic impact of drug-based technologies

The economic benefits of all drug based technologies depend on where you stand in the healthcare spectrum (Pietzsch et al., 2014). Currently, healthcare delivery institutions are at greatest risk for the cost of adopting these technologies, which carry a cost premium but to date do not enjoy any increased reimbursement. Patients benefit from a decreased number of procedures and potential copay or out-of-pocket expenditures. Public payors or insurers have the most to gain as there is currently no increase in cost and significantly decreased downstream costs associated with their use. Physicians pay no procedural cost in hospital settings though in "off hospital campus" delivery of this care where reimbursements are even tighter use may be more difficult. However, to sum the dilemma up, widespread adoption of drug-eluting endovascular therapies for femoropopliteal disease would add meaningful clinical benefit at reasonable additional costs; hopefully, this will be reinforced by the payors.

Summary

The addition of drug-based technology has significantly reduced the restenosis and subsequently repeat CD-TLR of endovascular fempop lesions. Though a leave nothing behind strategy may seem to be desirable, it is the patency and reduced risk of repeat procedures that should be the ultimate goal. As lesions become more complex, there is typically a significantly increased need for adjunctive stenting. Randomized data on patency appear to favor DES in medium/long length stenotic disease. Whether DCB followed by bailout BMS are equal to a primary DES stent is still unknown. Confirmatory randomized datasets are still needed to allow for more insight. Until then, a reasonable practice is to see how the vessel responds to predilation with a plan for drug-based stent usage when predilation is unsatisfactory and possibly optimal for stenotic and longer lesion lengths. Whether vessel preparation before device use and in which lesions is still in question. However, with proper case selection, DES and DCB are both useful clinically and economically. Lesion characteristics should help the operator choose the theoretically most optimal device.

References

Ansel, G. M., et al. (2024). Five-year safety and effectiveness of paclitaxel drug-coated balloons alone or with provisional bare metal stenting for real-world femoropopliteal lesions: IN. PACT global study subgroup analysis. *Circulation: Cardiovascular Interventions, 17*(2), e013084.

Ansel, G. M., Jaff, M. R., Popma, J. J., et al. (2017). A quantitative angiographic comparison of restenotic tissue following placement of drug-eluting stents and bare metal stents in symptomatic patients with femoropopliteal disease. *Endovascular Theraphy, 24*, 499–503.

Bausback, Y., Wittig, T., Schmidt, A., et al. (2019). Drug-eluting stent versus drug-coated balloon revascularization in patients with femoropopliteal arterial disease. *Journal of the American College of Cardiology, 73*, 667–679.

Bisdas, T., Beropoulis, E., & Argyriou. (2018). 1-Year all-comers analysis of the eluvia drug-eluting stent for long femoropopliteal lesions after suboptimal angioplasty. *A2JACC Cardiovascular Intervention, 11*, 957–966.

Böhme, T., Noory, E., Beschorner, U., et al. (2021). Photoablative atherectomy followed by a paclitaxel-coated balloon to inhibit restenosis in instent femoro-popliteal obstructions (PHOTOPAC). *Vasa, 50*, 387–393.

Brodmann, M., Lansink, W., Guetl, K., et al. (2022). Long-term outcomes of the 150 mm drug-coated balloon cohort from the IN.PACT global study. *CardioVascular and Interventional Radiology, 45*(9), 1276–1287.

Case, B., Torguson, R., Zhang, C., & Waksman, R. (2021). Overview of the virtual 2021 FDA's circulatory System devices advisory panel on Lutonix 014 drug-coated percutaneous transluminal angioplasty catheter for below-the-knee lesions in critical limb ischemia. *Cardiovascular Revascularization Medicine, 33*, 55–61.

Dake, M. D., Ansel, G. M., Jaff, M. R., et al. (2011). Paclitaxel-eluting stents show superiority to balloon angioplasty and bare metal stents in femoropopliteal disease: Twelve-month zilver PTX randomized study results. on behalf of the Zilver PTX Investigators *Circulative Cardiovascular Intervention, 4*, 495–504.

Dake, M. D., Scheinert, D., Tepe, G., et al., Zilver PTX Single- Arm Study Investigators. (2011). Nitinol stents with polymer-freepaclitaxel coating for lesions in the superficial femoral and popliteal arteries above the knee: Twelve-month safety and effectiveness results from the zilver PTX single-arm clinical study. *Journal of Endovascular Therapy, 18*, 613–623.

Dake, M. D., Ansel, G. M., Jaff, M. R., et al., Zilver PTX Investigators. (2016). Durable clinical effectiveness with paclitaxel-eluting stents in the femoropopliteal artery: 5-year results of the zilver PTX randomized trial. *Circulation, 133*, 1472–1483.

Dinh, K., Gomes, M. L., Thomas, S. D., et al. (2020, April). Mortality after paclitaxel-coated device use in patients with chronic limb-threatening ischemia: A systematic review and meta-analysis of randomized controlled trials. *Journal of Endovascular Therapy, 27*(2), 175–185.

Duda, S. H., Bosiers, M., Lammer, J., et al. (2005). Sirolimus-eluting versus bare nitinol stent for obstructive superficial femoral artery disease: The SIROCCO II trial. *Journal of Vascular and Interventional Radiology, 16*, 331–338.

Fanelli, F., Cannavale, A., & Gazzetti, M. (2014). Calcium burden assessment and impact on drug-eluting balloons in peripheral arterial disease. *Cardiovascular and Interventional Radiology, 37*, 898–907.

Food and Drug Administration (FDA). UPDATE: Paclitaxel-coated devices to treat peripheral arterial disease unlikely to increase risk of mortality – Letter to health care providers. https://www.fda.gov/medical-devices/letters-health-care-providers/update-paclitaxel-coated-devices-treat-peripheral-arterial-disease-unlikely-increase-risk-mortality#:~:text=Based%20on%20the%20FDA's%20review,is%20now%20providing%20updated%20information

Garcia, L. A., Rosenfield, K. R., Metzger, C. D., et al. (2017). SUPERB final 3-year outcomes using interwoven nitinol biomimetic supera stent. *Catheterization and Cardiovascular Interventions, 89*, 1259–1267.

Gray, W. A., Keirse, K., Soga, Y., et al. (2018). A polymer-coated, paclitaxel-eluting stent (eluvia) versus a polymer-free, paclitaxel-coated stent (zilver PTX) for endovascular femoropopliteal intervention (IMPERIAL): A randomised, non-inferiority trial. *Lancet, 392*, 1541–1551.

Gutierrez, J. A., Rao, S. V., Jones, W. S., et al. (2021). Survival and causes of death among veterans with lower extremity revascularization with paclitaxel-coated devices: Insights from the veterans health administration. *Journal of American Heart Association, 10*, e018149. https://doi.org/10.1161/JAHA.120.018149

Hans van Overhagen. (2022). *Hans van Overhagen cardiovascular and interventional radiological society of Europe (CIRSE)*. Barcelona, Spain.

Hess, C. N., Patel, M. R., Bauersachs, R. M., et al. (2021). Safety and effectiveness of paclitaxel drug-coated devices in peripheral artery revascularization: Insights from VOYAGER PAD. *Journal of the American College of Cardiology, 78*(18), 1768–1778.

Ho, K. J., & Owens, C. D. (2017). Diagnosis, classification, and treatment of femoropopliteal artery in-stent restenosis. *Journal of Vascular Surgery, 65*, 545–557.

Huntress, L., Fereydooni, A., Dardik, A., et al. (2020). Endovascular revascularization incorporating infrapopliteal coronary drug-eluting stents improves clinical outcomes in patients with critical limb ischemia and tissue loss. *Annals of Vascular Surgery, 63*, 234–240.

Hwang, C. W., Levin, A., Jonas, M., et al. (2005). Thrombosis modulates arterial drug distribution for drug-eluting stents. *Circulation, 11*, 1619–1626.

Katsanos, K., Spiliopoulos, S., Kitrou, P., et al. (2018). Risk of death following application of paclitaxel-coated balloons and stents in the femoropopliteal artery of the leg: A systematic review and meta-analysis of randomized controlled trials. *This Journal of American Heart Association, 7*(24), e011245. https://doi.org/10.1161/JAHA.118.011245

Kondapalli, A., Danek, B. A., & Khalili, H. (2017). Drug-coated balloons: Current outcomes and future directions. *Interventional Cardiology Clinic, 6*, 217–225.

Krankenberg, H., Schlüter, M., Steinkamp, H. J., et al. (2007). Nitinol stent implantation versus percutaneous transluminal angioplasty in superficial femoral artery lesions up to 10 cm in length: The femoral artery stenting trial. *Circulation, 116*, 285–292.

Laird, J. R., Schneider, P. A., Tepe, G., et al. (2015). Sustained durability of treatment effect using a drug-coated balloon for femoropopliteal lesions: 24-month results. *Journal of the American College of Cardiology, 66*, 2329–2338.

Lammer, J., Bosiers, M., Zeller, T., et al. (2011). First clinical trial of nitinol self-expanding everolimus-eluting stent implantation for peripheral arterial occlusive disease. *Journal of Vascular Surgery, 54*, 394–401.

Lammer, J., Zeller, T., Hausegger, K. A., Schaefer, P. J., et al. (2013). Heparin-bonded covered stents versus bare-metal stents for complex femoropopliteal artery lesions: The randomized VIASTAR trial (viabahn endoprothesis with PROPATEN bioactive surface [VIA] versus bare nitinol stent in the treatment of long lesions in superficial femoral artery occlusive disease). *Journal of the American College of Cardiology, 62*, 1320–1327.

Müller-Hülsbeck, S., Benko, A., Yoshimitsu, S., et al. (2021). Two-year efficacy and safety results from the IMPERIAL randomized study of the eluvia polymer-coated drug-eluting stent and the zilver PTX polymer-free drug-coated stent. *CardioVascular and Interventional Radiology, 44*, 368–375.

Narula, N., Dannenberg, A., Olin, J., et al. (2018). Pathology of peripheral artery disease in patients with critical limb ischemia. *Journal of the American College of Cardiology, 72*, 2152–2163.

Nordmann, A. J., Briel, M., & Bucher, H. C. (2006). Mortality in randomized controlled trials comparing drug-eluting vs. bare metal stents in coronary artery disease: A meta-analysis. *European Heart Journal, 27*, 2784–2814.

Park, j, Ko, Y. G., Lee, Y. J., et al. (2022). Long coverage with drug-eluting stents is superior to spot coverage for long femoropopliteal artery disease: APARADEII study. *Frontiers in Cardiovascular Medicine, 19*(9), 1—8.

Phillips, J. A., Falls, A., & Kolluri, R. (2018). Full drug-eluting stent jacket: Two year results of a single-center experience with Zilver PTX stenting for long lesions in the femoropopliteal arteries. *Journal of Endovascular Therapy, 25,* 295—301.

Pietzsch, J. B., Geisler, B. P., Garner, A. M., Zeller, T., & Jaff, M. R. (2014). Economic analysis of endovascular interventions for femoropopliteal arterial disease: A systematic review and budget impact model for the United States and Germany. *Catheterization and Cardiovascular Interventions, 84,* 546—554.

Rocha-Singh, K. J., Jaff, M. R., Crabtree, T. R., et al. (2007). Performance goals and endpoint assessments for clinical trials of femoropopliteal bare nitinol stents in patients with symptomatic peripheral arterial disease. *Catheterization and Cardiovascular Interventions, 69,* 910—919.

Rocha-Singh, K. J., Sachar, R., DeRubertis, B. G., et al. (2021). Directional atherectomy before paclitaxel coated balloon angioplasty in complex femoropopliteal disease: The VIVA REALITY study. *Catheterization and Cardiovascular Interventions, 98,* 549—558.

Rosenfield, K., Schainfeld, R., Pieczek, A., et al. (1997). Restenosis of endovascular stents from stent compression. *Journal of the American College of Cardiology, 29,* 328—338.

Rosenfield, K. (2022, November). Intermediate-term (24-Month) results of the TRANSCEND study comparing a next-generation paclitaxel drug-coated balloon (SurVeil DCB) to IN.PACT DCB in the treatment of femoropopliteal artery disease. *Vascular Interventions Advances (VIVA).*

Rosenfield, K., Jaff, M., White, C., et al. (2015). Trial of a paclitaxel-coated balloon for femoropopliteal artery disease. *New England Journal of Medicine, 373,* 145—153.

Sakamoto, A., Torii, S., Jinnouchi, H., et al. (2021). Vascular response of a polymer-free paclitaxel-coated stent (zilver ptx) versus a polymer-coated paclitaxel-eluting stent (eluvia) in healthy swine femoropopliteal arteries. *Laboratory Investigation, 32,* 792—801.

Sakaoka, A., Souba, J., Rousselle, S. D., et al. (2019). Different vascular responses to a bare nitinol stent in porcine femoral and femoropopliteal arteries. *Toxicologic Pathology, 47,* 408—417.

Schillinger, M., Sabeti, S., Loewe, C., et al. (2006). Balloon angioplasty versus implantation of nitinol stents in the superficial femoral artery. *New England Journal of Medicine, 354,* 1879—1888.

Schneider, P. A., Laird, J. R., Tepe, G., et al. (2018). Treatment effect of drug-coated balloons is durable to 3 Years in the femoropopliteal arteries: Long-term results of the IN.PACT SFA randomized trial. IN.PACT SFA trial investigators. *Circulation of Cardiovascular Interventions, 11,* e005891.

Schroeder, H., Meyer, D. R., Lux, B., et al. (2015). Two-year results of a low-dose drug-coated balloon for revascularization of the femoropopliteal artery: Outcomes from the ILLUMENATE first-in-human study. *Catheterization and Cardiovascular Interventions, 86,* 278—286.

Shishehbor, M. H., Zeller, T., Werner, M., et al. (2022). Randomized trial of chocolate Touch compared with Lutonix drug-coated balloon in femoropopliteal lesions (chocolate Touch study). *Circulation, 145,* 1645—1654.

Soga, Y., Fujihara, M., Tomoi, Y., et al. (2020). One-year late lumen loss between a polymer-coated paclitaxel eluting stent (eluvia) and a polymer-free paclitaxel coated stent (zilver ptx) for femoropopliteal disease. *Journal of Atherosclerosis Thrombosis, 27,* 164–171.

Steiner, S., Schmidt, A., & Zeller, T. (2022). Low-dose vs high-dose paclitaxel-coated balloons for femoropopliteal lesions: 2-Year results from the COMPARE trial. *JACC: Cardiovascular Interventions, 15,* 2093–2102.

Stellarex drug-coated balloon for treatment of femoropopliteal arterial disease-the ILLUMENATE global study: 12-Month results from a prospective, multicenter, single-arm study. *Catheterization and Cardiovascular Interventions, 91,* (2018), 497–504.

Stone, G. W., Moses, J. W., Ellis, S. G., Schofer, J., et al. (2007). Safety and efficacy of sirolimus- and paclitaxel-eluting coronary stents. *New England Journal of Medicine, 356,* 998–1008.

Sugimoto, M., Komori, K., Yokoi, H., et al. (2021). Long-term effectiveness of a drug-eluting stent for femoropopliteal in-stent restenosis: Subanalysis of the zilver PTX Japan post-market surveillance study. *Journal of Endovascular Therapy, 28,* 229–235.

Tepe, G., Laird, J., Schneider, P., Brodmann, M., Krishnan, P., Micari, A., Metzger, C., Scheinert, D., Zeller, T., Cohen, D. J., Snead, D. B., Alexander, B., Landini, M., Jaff, M. R., & IN.PACT SFA Trial Investigators. (2015). Drug-coated balloon versus standard percutaneous transluminal angioplasty for the treatment of superficial femoral and popliteal peripheral artery disease: 12-month results from the IN.PACT SFA randomized trial. *Circulation, 131,* 495–502.

Tepe, G., Schnorr, B., Albrecht, T., et al. (2015). Angioplasty of femoropopliteal arteries with drug-coated balloons; 5-year follow-up of the thunder trial. *JACC: Cardiovascular Interventions, 8,* 102–106.

Tepe, G., Schroeder, H., Albrecht, T., et al. (2020). Paclitaxel-coated balloon vs uncoated balloon angioplasty for treatment of in-stent restenosis in the superficial femoral and popliteal arteries: The COPA CABANA trial. *Journal of Endovascular Therapy, 27,* 276–286.

Tepe, G., Brodmann, M., Bachinsky, W., et al. (2022). Intravascular lithotripsy for peripheral artery calcification: Mid-term outcomes from the randomized disrupt PAD III trial. *JASCAI, 1,* 10031.

Thomas, Z., Dake, M., Tepe, G., et al. (2013). Treatment of femoropopliteal in-stent restenosis with paclitaxel-eluting stents. *JACC: Cardiovascular Interventions, 6,* 274–281.

Varcoe, R., LIFE BTK Investigators, et al. (2023). Drug-eluting resorbable scaffold versus angioplasty for infrapopliteal artery disease. *New England Journal of Medicine, 390*(1), 9 19.

Yokoi, H., Ohki, T., Kichikawa, K., et al. (2016). Zilver PTX post-market surveillance study of paclitaxel-eluting stents for treating femoropopliteal artery disease in Japan. *JACC: Cardiovascular Interventions, 9,* 271–277.

Zeller, T., Rastan, A., Macharzina, R., et al. (2014). Drug-coated balloons vs. drug-eluting stents for treatment of long femoropopliteal lesions. *Journal of Endovascular Therapy, 21,* 359–368.

Zeller, T., Gaines, P. A., Ansel, G. M., & Caro, C. G. (2016). Helical centerline stent improves patency: Two-year results from the randomized mimics trial. *Circulation of Cardiovascular Interventions, 9,* 1–8.

Zeller, T., Langhoff, R., Rocha-Singh, K. J., et al. (2017). Directional atherectomy followed by a paclitaxel-coated balloon to inhibit restenosis and maintain vessel patency: Twelve-month results of the DEFINITIVE AR study. *Circulation of Cardiovascular Interventions, 10*, e004848.

Zeller, T., Micari, A., Scheinert, D., et al. (2020). The IN.PACT DEEP clinical drug-coated balloon trial: 5-Year outcomes. *JACC: Cardiovascular Interventions, 13*, 431−443.

Zeller, T., Brodmann, M., Ansel, G. M., et al. (2022). Paclitaxel-coated balloons for femoropopliteal peripheral arterial disease: Final five-year results of the IN. *PACT Global Study. Euro Intervention, 18*, e940−e948.

Zeller, T., Giannopoulos, S., Brodmann, M., et al. (2022). Orbital atherectomy prior to drug-coated balloon angioplasty in calcified infrapopliteal lesions: A randomized, multicenter pilot study. *Journal of Endovascular Therapy, 29*, 874−884.

Zollikofer, C. L., Antonucci, F., Pfyffer, et al. (1991). Arterial stent placement with use of the wallstent: Midterm results of clinical experience. *Radiology, 179*, 449−456.

12

Surgical treatment of PAD: Open and endovascular repair

Nabil Chakfe[2] and Arielle Bellissard[1,2]

[1]CVPath Institute, Gaithersburg, MD, United States; [2]Department of Vascular Surgery and Kidney Transplantation, Strasbourg University Hospitals, Strasbourg, France

Introduction

Revascularization of peripheral arterial disease (PAD) is considered in case of intermittent claudication with functional life-limiting impairment, after failure of optimal medical management and exercise therapy (Aboyans et al., 2018). On the other hand, patients with chronic limb-threatening ischemia (CLTI) need aggressive management and optimal revascularization,

Pathophysiology and Treatment of Atherosclerotic Disease in Peripheral Arteries. https://doi.org/10.1016/B978-0-443-13593-4.00012-3

with a focus on pain management and limb salvage (Conte et al., 2019). Historically, open repair has been the gold-standard for peripheral vascularization, with good patency at the price of high perioperative risk and mortality. However, the last decades have witnessed the great development of minimally invasive approaches to peripheral arterial reconstruction.

Strategies for revascularization differ according to the anatomical level and the morphology of the lesions. Surgical management of PAD often reveals to be challenging due to multilevel occlusive disease and fragile patients with severe disease stage and severe comorbidity. This chapter aims to summarize the techniques we presently hold for peripheral revascularization both in supra- and infrainguinal levels, and the current state of knowledge on their safety and efficacy.

Aortoiliac lesions

Severe aortoiliac occlusive lesions can be responsible of a variety of clinical presentation including intermittent claudication, impotence in male patients, and CLTI. In case of CLTI, aortoiliac disease is most often associated with infrainguinal lesions and can require multilevel hybrid revascularization procedures (Aboyans et al., 2018).

Revascularization options are impacted by the morphology of the lesions. The Transatlantic Intersociety Consensus (TASC) II guidelines provides anatomic artery lesions classifications for guiding optimal treatment decision (Jaff et al., 2015; Norgren et al., 2007). Currently, primary endovascular therapy (EVT) is recommended in case of short iliac stenosis or occlusions (TASC A and B lesions). For longer lesions and lesions involving multiple segments, open surgical reconstruction is preferred for TASC C lesions in good-risk patients and the treatment of choice in TASC D lesions.

With the rapid development of EVT and devices and increased surgeons' experience, more severe and complex lesions are being treated with endovascular methods. Several meta-analyses comparing open surgical reconstruction to EVT have shown that EVT is a viable alternative to open repair in patients with TASC C and D lesions (Indes et al., 2013; Premaratne et al., 2020; Salem et al., 2021). Mortality and morbidity are lower in endovascular-treated patients, with a shorter average hospital stay. Complications reported for open surgery are mostly cardiac, respiratory, and intestinal, whereas complications for EVT are pseudoaneurysms, arterial dissection, or perforation. Distal embolization was reported higher in endovascular-treated patients by Indes et al., in 2013, but a more recent meta-analysis by Premaratne et al., in 2020 described an absence of difference between both groups. The rate of renal failure is the same in both groups. Primary patency at 1, 3, and 5 years is significantly higher in open repair patients; however, secondary patency is reported equivalent in two recent meta-analyses (Premaratne et al., 2020; Salem et al., 2021).

Open repair

Aortobifemoral bypass grafting is the most commonly recommended open reconstruction for long aortoiliac occlusive lesions (Aboyans et al., 2018; Norgren et al., 2007). In case of proximal lesions sparing the common femoral arteries (CFAs), aortobiiliac bypass can be considered, hence allowing the preservation of hypogastric perfusion; the risk for wound infection is also reduced in the absence of groin incision. Transperitoneal or retroperitoneal approaches can be used for exposure of the infrarenal aorta. A retroperitoneal approach may be preferred in case of prior abdominal surgeries and allows for better control of the visceral aorta if needed; however, distal access of the right iliac artery and graft tunneling are made easier by a transperitoneal approach. In case of extension of the occlusion to the juxtarenal aorta, proximal endarterectomy can be performed. Femoral bifurcations are exposed via bilateral groin incisions. The dissection should allow control of the proximal superficial femoral artery (SFA) and profunda femoris artery (PFA), with additional exposure if extended endarterectomy is needed (Clair & Beach, 2015; Marrocco-Trischitta et al., 2012; Velazquez-Ramirez & Rosenberg, 2021, pp. 185—202). Use of a bifurcated synthetic graft of either expanded polytetrafluorethylene or polyethylene terephthalate is dependent on the surgeon's preference (Norgren et al., 2007; Roll et al., 2008).

In case of unilateral lesion without involvement of the infrarenal aorta, unilateral bypass such as iliofemoral bypass can be considered, as an alternative for high-risk patients. Surgical approach can be done with a retroperitoneal incision, and total aortic cross-clamping can be avoided, limiting the mortality compared to abdominal aortic surgeries. However, a systematic review by Chiu et al. reported a tendency to lower primary patency for iliofemoral bypasses (Chiu et al., 2010).

Aortic thromboendarterectomy (TEA) is not as widely practiced but may be considered in case of focal aortic or proximal iliac lesions, or in association with visceral arteries lesions

(Connolly & Price, 2006). The technique avoids graft insertion and lowers mortality and complication rates compared to aortobifemoral bypass, although it performs poorly in case of lesions extended to the external iliac arteries (Chiu et al., 2010; Clair & Beach, 2015).

Overall mortality rate after open aortic repair is reported between 2.6% and 4.1%; morbidity rate is reported between 12% and 19%. Main complications include cardiac and pulmonary morbidity, renal failure, intestinal or lower limb ischemia, bleeding, injury to ureters during dissection or during tunneling, sexual dysfunction, graft thrombosis or infection, wound dehiscence or infection especially in the groin incisions. Primary patency and secondary patency rates are estimated over 94% and 95% at 1 year, and over 83% and 91% at 5 years, respectively (Bredahl et al., 2015; Chiu et al., 2010; Indes et al., 2013; Salem et al., 2021).

Descending thoracic aortobifemoral bypass can be considered for direct aortic inflow but presents high mortality and morbidity rates, with a primary patency rate significantly inferior to other procedures (79.6% at 5 years). As such, it should be reserved for patients with no other alternative (Bismuth & Duran, 2013; Chiu et al., 2010).

Laparoscopic repair

Minimally invasive approaches to aortobifemoral bypass surgery are laparoscopic or robotic-assisted aortic surgery. With aortobifemoral bypass remains the gold standard for severe aortoiliac occlusive disease, laparoscopic repair allows for reduced morbidity (Bismuth & Duran, 2013; Pascarella & Aboul Hosn, 2018). A systematic review of the literature concluded satisfactory results of laparoscopic aortobifemoral bypass compared to open repair, with shorter hospital stays and a suggested reduction in blood loss and peri- and postoperative complications, although operating and clamping times were longer. Survival was comparable between the two groups (Helgetveit & Krog, 2017). However, studies included in the analysis presented a high level of heterogeneity and lacked a higher grade level of evidence, as few centers perform this procedure (Rusch et al., 2022). Laparoscopic aortic repair is deemed an advanced technique that requires an experienced surgeon. Robotic-assisted surgery seems to offer an advantage as it tends toward a quicker learning curve than total laparoscopic surgery, and perhaps allows for faster and more accurate skill acquiring (Lucereau et al., 2016).

Extraanatomic reconstruction

Extraanatomic bypasses, such as axillobifemoral or crossover femorofemoral bypasses, can be considered for high-risk patients, in the absence of alternative for revascularization. Patients with advanced disease and severe comorbidities or contraindications to abdominal surgeries can qualify for such procedures, but with poor patency rates (Aboyans et al., 2018; Bismuth & Duran, 2013; Clair & Beach, 2015; Norgren et al., 2007).

Endovascular repair

EVT has developed greatly in the last decades, with an increasing role in the management of complex aortoiliac occlusive lesions. The minimally invasive aspect of EVT makes it a seducing alternative for patients with severe comorbidities and advanced stage disease who are not eligible for open repair (Aboyans et al., 2018).

EVT requires careful preprocedure planning, including the choice of access. Most often, unilateral or bilateral femoral artery is the first option; the left brachial artery can also be used for antegrade access, depending on the lesion location and extension (Clair & Beach, 2015; Pascarella & Aboul Hosn, 2018). Ultrasound guidance for arterial puncture is recommended to reduce access site complications (Appelt et al., 2021; Sobolev et al., 2015). Arterial closure can be achieved through closure device or manual compression with comparable safety, efficacy, and outcomes (Das et al., 2011; Noori & Eldrup-Jørgensen, 2018). Depending on the operation plan and patient, EVT can be performed under local anesthesia with sedation, avoiding the morbidity–mortality of general anesthesia in populations of elderly and comorbid patients.

Crossing the lesion must be done with care, particularly for recanalization of long occlusions. One possibility is to create a subintimal plane, with or without the use of reentry devices, but caution is required. Major risks are arterial perforation or dissection with retrograde extension through the aorta (Pescatori et al., 2020).

Either percutaneous transluminal angioplasty (PTA) alone, PTA with stenting, or primary stenting can be performed. Primary stenting for TASC C and D aortoiliac lesions seems to offer better success and patency rates over PTA with selective stent placement (Bekken et al., 2014; Ye et al., 2011). However, data extracted from randomized controlled trials showed no significant difference in technical success, resolution of symptoms, primary patency at 2 years, and rate of reintervention between the two techniques. One trial reported on significantly higher rate of distal embolization in the selective stenting group (20% vs. 5%; $P = .01$), leading to a premature stop of the study (Jongsma et al., 2020; Koeckerling et al., 2023). Studies are lacking on the comparative use of self-expending stent (SES) versus balloon-expending stent (BES); the ICE randomized trial suggests lower 1-year restenosis and target lesion revascularization rates with SES in common and external iliac arteries (Krankenberg et al., 2017). Similarly, the comparison between covered stents (CS) and bare-metal stents (BMS) needs more investigation; however, studies suggest that there is no significant difference in technical success, primary and secondary patency, major complications, limb salvage, and survival. The need for reintervention could be lower in CS versus BMS, with higher ankle-brachial index after treatment with CS (Ghariani et al., 2022; Hajibandeh et al., 2016). One randomized trial showed improved patency and lesser target lesion revascularization at 5 years for CS (Mwipatayi et al., 2016).

When lesions are located near the origin of the common iliac artery, they are best treated with bilateral kissing stent to avoid occlusion of the contralateral iliac axis (Fig. 12.1).

A systematic review of kissing stent reported a technical success rate of 98.7%, with a complication rate of 11% (mostly groin hematoma). Primary and secondary patency were 89% and 92% at 1 year, and 69% and 83% at 5 years, respectively. Mean percentage of reintervention was 21% (Groot Jebbink et al., 2017).

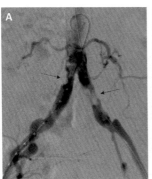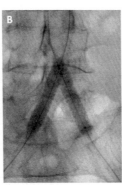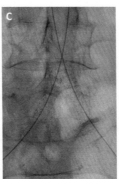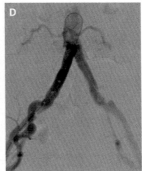

Figure 12.1 Angiography of iliac kissing stents. A 71-years-old man with a history of past smoking, dyslipidemia, chronic obstructive pulmonary disease, presenting with bilateral intermittent claudication occurring at 300 m and no improvement after exercise therapy. (A) Is the original angiography with visualization of two stenotic lesions (*red arrows*) on the common iliac arteries. (B) Is the simultaneous deployment of the two balloon-expandable iliac stents. (C) Is the radiographic image of the kissing stent after stent deployment. (D) Is the completion angiography.

In case of extension to the aorta, a Covered Endovascular Reconstruction of Aortic Bifurcation (CERAB) can be performed. The technique consists of a CS in the distal aorta, and two iliac CS inside the aortic stent (Fig. 12.2).

The geometry of CERAB has been studied in vitro in order to overcome the flow disturbances and restenosis risk of kissing stents, due to their protrusion in the aorta. Primary and secondary patency rates of CERAB are reported at 88% and 97% at 1 year and 82% and 97% at 3 years, respectively (Reijnen, 2020; Salem et al., 2021).

Overall, the last decades have shown that EVT in complex, extensive aortoiliac occlusive lesions can be performed safely and efficiently. Reported technical success rates range from 86% to 100%. Mortality rates are estimated at 0.7% and morbidity rates at 10%−14%. Main complications are access site hematoma, pseudoaneurysm, distal embolization, arterial dissection, and arterial rupture. Primary patency rates are over 86% at 1 year and 71% at 5 years, and secondary patency rates are over 90% at 1 year and 82% at 5 years (Indes et al., 2013; Jongkind et al., 2010; Premaratne et al., 2020; Salem et al., 2021).

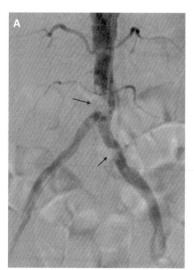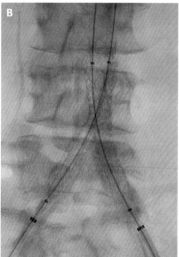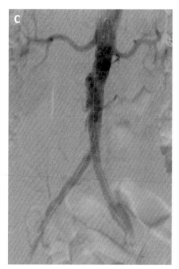

Figure 12.2 Angiography of a covered endovascular reconstruction of aortic bifurcation (CERAB). A 58-years-old woman with history of active smoking, hypertension, and dyslipidemia presenting with bilateral intermittent claudication occurring at 200 m. (A) Is the original aortography with visualization of two stenotic lesion in the distal aorta and the common left iliac artery (*red arrows*). (B) Is the covered endovascular reconstruction of aortic bifurcation radiographic image after balloon expansion of the aortic stent and the two iliac stents. (C) Is the completion aortography.

Hybrid procedures

The combination of EVT on the iliac segment with open surgery of the femoral bifurcation, mainly endarterectomy or bypass reconstruction, has been shown to improve primary patency in case of iliofemoral lesions compared to EVT alone, with comparable rates to open surgery (Premaratne et al., 2020). As such, primary hybrid procedures are recommended for iliofemoral lesions, including long occlusions (Aboyans et al., 2018). Hybrid procedures can also be performed to reestablish iliac inflow through EVT for crossover femorofemoral bypass, in patients considered unfit for total open reconstruction (Norgren et al., 2007) (Fig. 12.3).

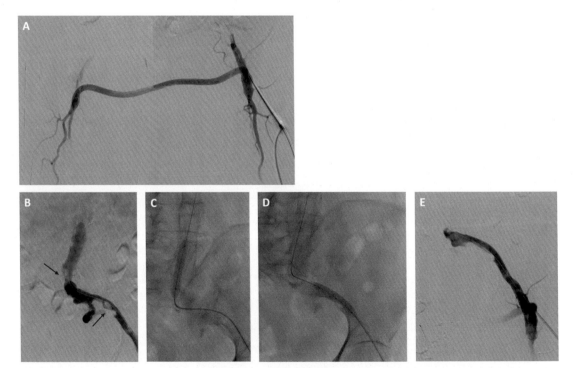

Figure 12.3 Angiography of a crossover left common femoral to right common femoral artery bypass and concomitant left iliac angioplasty and stenting. A 91-years-old woman with history of diabetes and hypertension, with preserved autonomy and ambulation, presenting for 1 month with a third toe necrosis on the right foot and bilateral rest pain. Doppler ultrasound and computed tomography angiography show total occlusion of the right iliac axis and severe stenosis of the left common iliac artery. Decision of revascularization considering her age and general state with a crossover femorofemoral bypass and endovascular therapy on the left iliac artery. (A) Is the angiographic result after prosthetic crossover femorofemoral bypass with bilateral implantation on the common femoral artery. (B) Shows the angiography of the left iliac axis before treatment. Two severe stenotic lesions are seen on the common and external iliac artery (*red arrows*). (C) Is the angioplasty of the common iliac artery. (D) Is the angioplasty of the external iliac artery, followed by stenting due to a residual stenosis. (E) Is the completion angiography, showing the persistence of a calcified plaque on the external iliac artery causing a residual stenosis, which was deemed acceptable.

Femoropopliteal lesions

Femoral bifurcation

The gold standard for repair of symptomatic CFA lesions is femoral TEA, offering high success rates (over 93%) and excellent outcomes. TEA is the surgical removal of the atherosclerotic plaque, generally performed with patch angioplasty. The procedure also allows for reestablishment of inflow in the PFA, which is crucial for long-term limb prognosis (Conte et al., 2019). Primary and secondary patency rates at 1 year are reported at 93% and 97% respectively, and target lesion revascularization rates are around 4% (Shammas et al., 2020; Wong et al., 2019).

Lately, EVT has been increasingly suggested for treatment of the femoral bifurcation. Recent reviews have reported a correct success and safety of EVT procedure for CFA, with a primary patency rate of 82% and a secondary patency rate of 93% at 1 year. Target lesion revascularization remains however in favor of TEA, with a rate of 8%−19% for EVT. Primary stenting seemed to yield better patency rates than selective stenting (Bath & Avgerinos, 2016). Mostly, EVT offers significantly lower morbidity rates, estimated at 5%−8% versus 16%−22% for TEA. Principal complications of open repair include lymphoceles, hematomas, wound dehiscence, and wound infection. On the other hand, mortality rates are similar for both procedures and estimated around 2% (Boufi et al., 2021; Changal et al., 2019; Hoffmann-Wieker et al., 2022).

Endovascular repair

The femoropopliteal segment is characterized by its mobility and is subjected to highly dynamic forces of flexion, extension, and torsion, especially in areas of hip and knee flexion. These mechanical forces uniquely impact how SFA reacts to revascularization and device implantation (Dieval et al., 2003; Jadidi et al., 2021).

In the femoropopliteal segment, EVT can be the primary choice of treatment for lesions under 25 cm (Aboyans et al., 2018). The TASC classification also recommends EVT as the treatment of choice for TASC Λ lesions and as the preferred treatment for TASC B lesions, which includes single or short lesions, or lesions with absence of correct tibial outflow (Norgren et al., 2007). The Global Vascular Guidelines recommends basing the choice of revascularization strategy on both the anatomic complexity of the lesion and the limb severity (Conte et al., 2019) (Fig. 12.4).

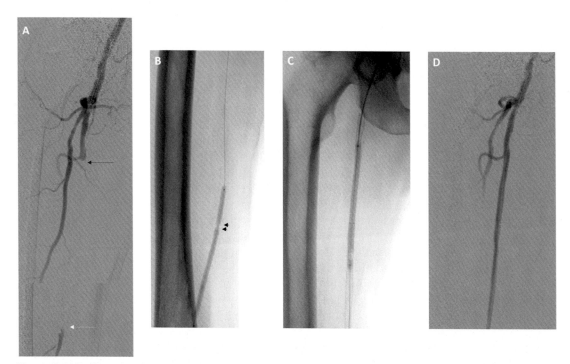

Figure 12.4 Angiography of an occluded right superficial femoral artery with recanalization, angioplasty, and stenting. A 81-years-old man with a history of type 2 diabetes, chronic kidney disease, and coronary artery disease, presenting with necrotic ulcers on the right leg. Doppler ultrasound shows an occlusion of the right SFA with popliteal reentry and a runoff of two below-the-knee arteries. (A) Shows the original angiography with occlusion of the SFA shortly after its origin (*red arrows*) and a mid-thigh reentry (*white arrow*). Access is made through the contralateral femoral artery with a crossover approach. Balloon angioplasty is performed (B) with constatation of a severe stenosis (*black arrows*), followed by stenting (C) with nitinol stent. (D) Is the completion angiography showing good permeability of the SFA.

Access is generally obtained from the contralateral femoral artery with a crossover approach. Ipsilateral access can be used when the targeted lesion is distal enough (Narins, 2009). Crossing a chronically occluded lesion can be challenging, in which case a retrograde ipsilateral can be used in a safe and efficient way (Martin et al., 2021).

PTA remains an acceptable first line of approach for EVT in infrainguinal disease. Strong data is still lacking in order to favor one type of endovascular approach. Primary stenting with BMS seems to yield slightly better patency and lower target lesion revascularization rates at short-term, which is not sustained at long-term. Drug-coated balloon (DCB) angioplasty shows lower target lesion revascularization, better primary patency rates, and less binary restenosis than simple angioplasty. Few studies have compared drug-eluting stents (DES) with BMS or PTA; data suggests a better patency at 1 year for DES which is not sustained at longer time-point. DES could show a significant reduction in target lesion revascularization rate in shorter length lesions (Antonopoulos et al., 2017; Caradu et al., 2019; Jens, Conijn, Koelemay, Bipat, & Reekers, 2014a, 2014b; Koeckerling et al., 2023; Varetto et al., 2019). It should be noted that recent concern has been raised about increased late mortality with the use of paclitaxel-coated devices in peripheral arteries (Katsanos et al., 2018; Rocha-Singh et al., 2020).

Infrainguinal bypasses

In patients with reasonable surgical risk and life expectancy >2 years, open bypass surgery is recommended for long, complex femoropopliteal lesions (*i.e.*, TASC C and D) (Aboyans et al., 2018; Norgren et al., 2007). Adequate inflow and runoff are required in order to provide correct patency and limb vascularization. In case of multilevel disease, blood flow in and out of the bypass graft might be improved with endovascular means to achieve complete revascularization.

Significantly better long-term patency is achieved with autologous vein substitute. A good quality great saphenous vein would be the first choice, with the use of the contralateral vein in case there is none on the ipsilateral side. Acceptable alternative may be small saphenous, arm, or spliced vein. In the absence of suitable autologous material and alternative revascularization choice, prosthetic graft can be used (Aboyans et al., 2018; Lejay et al., 2020).

There is no significant difference between mortality rates (1% −7%), amputation rates (up to 7%), and secondary patency rates in both EVT and bypass surgery (50%−96% at 1 and 5 year). However, primary patency remains better with bypass surgery (40% −80% vs. 38%−64% for EVT at 5 years). Studies also suggest better improvement of symptoms and less recurrence with bypass surgery (Abu Dabrh et al., 2016; Almasri et al., 2018; Antonopoulos et al., 2017; Lemos et al., 2022). On the other hand, local and systemic complications rates are significantly higher in bypass surgery than in EVT. Main local complications of bypass surgery are surgical site infection, graft failure, and amputation (Komshian et al., 2017). As such, choice of revascularization procedure in infrainguinal segments is regulated by many parameters: patient's general status and life expectancy, perioperative risk, severity of the disease, anatomical morphology and complexity of the lesion, and presence of an autologous material.

Infrapopliteal lesions

Revascularization of below-the-knee lesions is almost exclusively done in patients with CLTI and is often part of a multilevel arterial disease. Infrapopliteal lesions are often associated with age, diabetes, and chronic kidney disease. Hence, patients with infrapopliteal lesions and CLTI often represent a challenging cohort for revascularization, due to age, comorbidities, disease severity, anatomical complexity of the lesions, and the prevalence of chronic total occlusion and medial calcification (Chaudery et al., 2021; Conte et al., 2019; Jaff et al., 2015).

Endovascular repair

EVT tends to be preferred in those patients for its lower perioperative mortality and complication rates. Advance in technologies offers promising results for EVT in infrapopliteal arteries and improve in patency. EVT with DES, especially in focal lesions, shows better results in term of restenosis, target lesion revascularization, wound healing, and amputation-free survival. Use of DCB could also lead to better wound healing and symptom relief, and less binary restenosis and target lesion revascularization in long infrapopliteal lesions compared to simple PTA (Fusaro et al., 2013; Jaff et al., 2015; Jens et al., 2014a, 2014b; Katsanos et al., 2016). Despite these progress, restenosis, and patency failure rates remains high in infrapopliteal revascularization, with frequent need for reintervention. Performance of repeat infrapopliteal revascularization lacks specific recommendations. However, adequate runoff and particularly pedal arch quality has been identified as a predictor of outcome; hence, revascularization of distal inframalleolar arteries could be an important therapy (Spiliopoulos et al., 2021; Steiner & Schmidt, 2021).

Bypass

Similar to above-the-knee bypass, open surgery for infrapopliteal disease is recommended with the use of an autologous vein (Fig. 12.5).

Prosthetic substitutes have shown decreased durability and higher complication rates (Chakfe et al., 1997; Jaff et al., 2015; Lejay et al., 2020). There seems to be no difference in wound healing, limb salvage, or amputation-free survival when favoring a single-tibial vessel revascularization versus a multiple vessel revascularization. However, single vessel offers lower fluoroscopy time and contrast agent use, lower complication and lower

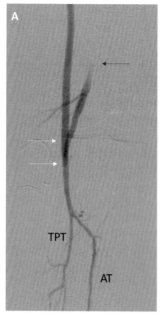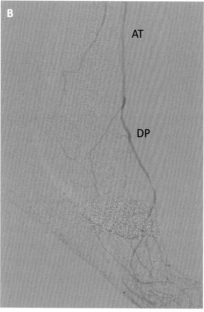

Figure 12.5 Angiography of a left femoro-popliteal bypass using the great saphenous vein with infrapopliteal distal anastomosis. An 57-year-old man with history of active smoking, hemodialysis for end-stage renal disease, coronary artery disease, and left above-the-knee femoro-popliteal bypass, presenting with a chronic right foot ulcer. Doppler ultrasound shows a complete occlusion of the bypass. Considering his young age and good general state despite his comorbidity, a below-the-knee femoro-popliteal bypass is performed by using the great saphenous vein. (A) Is the angiographic result of the distal anastomosis (*white arrows*), with retrograde vascularization in the native popliteal artery showing the proximal occlusion (*red arrow*). (B) Is the angiography of the foot showing a correct vascularization of the dorsal and plantar pedal arch. Resolution of the symptoms is observed at 2 weeks follow-up. *AT*, Anterior tibial artery; *DP*, dorsal pedis artery; *TPT*, Tibio-peroneal trunk.

perioperative mortality rates (Anand et al., 2020). Revascularization following the angiosome concept, meaning achieving the bypass on the target artery corresponding to the territory of the wound, suggests better results in wound healing and limb salvage (Dilaver et al., 2018; Lejay et al., 2014).

Amputation

Limb salvage and preservation of mobility is a major aspect of medical and surgical treatment in CLTI. Both endovascular and open repair have proven effective in preserving limb integrity. However, amputation will still be needed in some patients as part of CLTI management. In case of revascularization failure and in the absence of further option, amputation should be offered with the goal of infection control, pain relief, and autonomy rehabilitation. In patients with poor general state and life expectancy, and inability to achieve rehabilitation to ambulation, primary amputation can be offered. Decision of amputation should always involve multidisciplinary team discussion and anticipate a postoperative care route for optimal rehabilitation (Conte et al., 2019).

Conclusion

Aortobifemoral bypass remains the more durable option but with higher mortality and morbidity for extensive aortoiliac lesions. Late technical developments made EVT a safe and efficient option even for TASC C and D aortoiliac lesions; as such, EVT could be considered an appropriate first line of treatment in certain patients. In infrainguinal lesions, EVT is generally the first choice of treatment with good results and safety; however, bypass surgery offers better patency and is considered in case of long lesions, in patients fit for open surgery and with reasonable life expectancy. Autologous vein substitute allows for significantly better patency than prosthetic material and should be favored when available, especially for infrapopliteal bypasses.

The recent and continuous development of EVT and devices allows now for treatment of high-risk patients, with reasonable patency and decreased morbidity—mortality. The choice of procedure should be made after careful consideration of all treatment options and should be individually tailored to the patient, lesion, and risks. Hybrid procedures may offer advantage in the management of multilevel disease and enable complete revascularization with less operative risk.

References

Aboyans, V., Ricco, J. B., Bartelink, M. L. E. L., Björck, M., Brodmann, M., Cohnert, T., Collet, J. P., Czerny, M., De Carlo, M., Debus, S., Espinola-Klein, C., Kahan, T., Kownator, S., Mazzolai, L., Naylor, A. R., Roffi, M., Röther, J., Sprynger, M., Tendera, M., … Obiekezie, A. (2018). 2017 ESC guidelines on the Diagnosis and treatment of peripheral arterial diseases, in collaboration with the European Society for Vascular Surgery (ESVS). *European Heart Journal, 39*(9), 763—816. https://doi.org/10.1093/eurheartj/ehx095

Abu Dabrh, A. M., Steffen, M. W., Asi, N., Undavalli, C., Wang, Z., Elamin, M. B., Conte, M. S., & Murad, M. H. (2016). Bypass surgery versus endovascular interventions in severe or critical limb ischemia. *Journal of Vascular Surgery, 63*(1), 244—253.e11. https://doi.org/10.1016/j.jvs.2015.07.068

Almasri, J., Adusumalli, J., Asi, N., Lakis, S., Alsawas, M., Prokop, L. J., Bradbury, A., Kolh, P., Conte, M. S., & Murad, M. H. (2018). A systematic review and meta-analysis of revascularization outcomes of infrainguinal chronic limb-threatening ischemia. *Journal of Vascular Surgery, 68*(2), 624−633. https://doi.org/10.1016/j.jvs.2018.01.066

Anand, G. M., Conway, A. M., & Giangola, G. (2020). Single versus multiple vessel endovascular tibial artery revascularization for critical limb ischemia: A review of the literature. *International Journal of Angiology, 29*(3), 175−179. https://doi.org/10.1055/s-0040-1714662

Antonopoulos, C. N., Mylonas, S. N., Moulakakis, K. G., Sergentanis, T. N., Sfyroeras, G. S., Lazaris, A. M., Kakisis, J. D., & Vasdekis, S. N. (2017). A network meta-analysis of randomized controlled trials comparing treatment modalities for de novo superficial femoral artery occlusive lesions. *Journal of Vascular Surgery, 65*(1), 234−245.e11. https://doi.org/10.1016/j.jvs.2016.08.095

Appelt, K., Takes, M., Zech, C. J., Blackham, K., & Schubert, T. (2021). Complication rates of percutaneous brachial artery puncture: Effect of live ultrasound guidance. *CVIR Endovascular, 4*(1). https://doi.org/10.1186/s42155-021-00262-2

Bath, J., & Avgerinos, E. (2016). A pooled analysis of common femoral and profunda femoris endovascular interventions. *Vascular, 24*(4), 404−413. https://doi.org/10.1177/1708538115604929

Bekken, J. A., Jongsma, H., de vries, J. P. P. M., & Fioole, B. (2014). Self-expanding stents and aortoiliac occlusive disease: A review of the literature. *Medical Devices: Evidence and Research, 7*(1), 99−105. https://doi.org/10.2147/MDER.S60594

Bismuth, J., & Duran, C. (2013). Bypass surgery in limb salvage: Inflow procedures. *Methodist DeBakey cardiovascular journal, 9*(2), 66−68. https://doi.org/10.14797/mdcj-9-2-66

Boufi, M., Ejargue, M., Gaye, M., Boyer, L., Alimi, Y., & Loundou, A. D. (2021). Systematic review and meta-analysis of endovascular versus open repair for common femoral artery atherosclerosis treatment. *Journal of Vascular Surgery, 73*(4), 1445−1455. https://doi.org/10.1016/j.jvs.2020.10.026

Bredahl, K., Jensen, L. P., Schroeder, T. V., Sillesen, H., Nielsen, H., & Eiberg, J. P. (2015). Mortality and complications after aortic bifurcated bypass procedures for chronic aortoiliac occlusive disease. *Journal of Vascular Surgery, 62*(1), 75−82. https://doi.org/10.1016/j.jvs.2015.02.025

Caradu, C., Lakhlifi, E., Colacchio, E. C., Midy, D., Bérard, X., Poirier, M., & Ducasse, E. (2019). Systematic review and updated meta-analysis of the use of drug-coated balloon angioplasty versus plain old balloon angioplasty for femoropopliteal arterial disease. *Journal of Vascular Surgery, 70*(3), 981−995.e10. https://doi.org/10.1016/j.jvs.2019.01.080

Chakfe, N., Jahn, C., Nicolini, P., Kretz, J. G., Edah-Tally, S., Beaufigeau, M., Lebras, Y., Beaujeux, R., Durand, B., & Eisenmann, B. (1997). The impact of knee joint flexion on infrainguinal vascular grafts: An angiographic study. *European Journal of Vascular and Endovascular Surgery, 13*(1), 23−30. https://doi.org/10.1016/S1078-5884(97)80046-9

Changal, K. H., Syed, M. A., Dar, T., Mangi, M. A., & Sheikh, M. A. (2019). Systematic review and proportional meta-analysis of endarterectomy and endovascular therapy with routine or selective stenting for common femoral artery atherosclerotic disease. *Journal of Interventional Cardiology, 2019*. https://doi.org/10.1155/2019/1593401

Chaudery, M. A., Patel, S. D., & Zayed, H. (2021). Outcomes of open and hybrid treatments in below the knee pathology for critical limb threatening ischemia. *The Journal of Cardiovascular Surgery, 62*(2), 111–117. https://doi.org/10.23736/S0021-9509.21.11654-4

Chiu, K. W. H., Davies, R. S. M., Nightingale, P. G., Bradbury, A. W., & Adam, D. J. (2010). Review of direct anatomical open surgical management of atherosclerotic aorto-iliac occlusive disease. *European Journal of Vascular and Endovascular Surgery, 39*(4), 460–471. https://doi.org/10.1016/j.ejvs.2009.12.014

Clair, D. G., & Beach, J. M. (2015). Strategies for managing aortoiliac occlusions: Access, treatment and outcomes. *Expert Review of Cardiovascular Therapy, 13*(5), 551–563. https://doi.org/10.1586/14779072.2015.1036741

Connolly, J. E., & Price, T. (2006). Aortoiliac endarterectomy: A lost art? *Annals of Vascular Surgery, 20*(1), 56–62. https://doi.org/10.1007/s10016-005-9101-9

Conte, M. S., Bradbury, A. W., Kolh, P., White, J. V., Dick, F., Fitridge, R., Mills, J. L., Ricco, J. B., Suresh, K. R., Murad, M. H., Forbes, T. L., AbuRahma, A., Anankwah, K., Barshes, N., Bush, R., Dalman, R. L., Davies, M., Farber, A., Hingorani, A., … Diamant, M. (2019). Global vascular guidelines on the management of chronic limb-threatening ischemia. *Journal of Vascular Surgery, 69*(6), 3–125S.e40. https://doi.org/10.1016/j.jvs.2019.02.016

Das, R., Ahmed, K., Athanasiou, T., Morgan, R. A., & Belli, A. M. (2011). Arterial closure devices versus manual compression for femoral haemostasis in interventional radiological procedures: A systematic review and meta-analysis. *CardioVascular and Interventional Radiology, 34*(4), 723–738. https://doi.org/10.1007/s00270-010-9981-0

Dieval, F., Chakfé, N., Wang, L., Riepe, G., Thaveau, F., Heintz, C., Mathieu, D., Le Magnen, J. F., Kretz, J. G., & Durand, B. (2003). Mechanisms of rupture of knitted polyester vascular prostheses: An in vitro analysis of virgin prostheses. *European Journal of Vascular and Endovascular Surgery, 26*(4), 429–436. https://doi.org/10.1016/S1078-5884(03)00257-0

Dilaver, N., Twine, C. P., & Bosanquet, D. C. (2018). Editor's choice — direct vs. indirect angiosomal revascularisation of infrapopliteal arteries, an updated systematic review and meta-analysis. *European Journal of Vascular and Endovascular Surgery, 56*(6), 834–848. https://doi.org/10.1016/j.ejvs.2018.07.017

Fusaro, M., Cassese, S., Ndrepepa, G., Tepe, G., King, L., Ott, I., Nerad, M., Schunkert, H., & Kastrati, A. (2013). Drug-eluting stents for revascularization of infrapopliteal arteries: Updated meta-analysis of randomized trials. *JACC: Cardiovascular Interventions, 6*(12), 1284–1293. https://doi.org/10.1016/j.jcin.2013.08.007

Ghariani, M. Z., Vento, V., Kuntz, S., Schwein, A., Sonetto, A., D'Ospina, R., Lejay, A., Freyrie, A., Gargiulo, M., & Chakfe, N. (2022). Covered stents versus bare metal stents in kissing reconstructions of the aortic bifurcation. *EJVES Vascular Forum, 54*, e17–e18. https://doi.org/10.1016/j.ejvsvf.2021.12.023

Groot Jebbink, E., Holewijn, S., Slump, C. H., Lardenoije, J. W., & Reijnen, M. M. P. J. (2017). Systematic review of results of kissing stents in the treatment of aortoiliac occlusive disease. *Annals of Vascular Surgery, 42*, 328–336. https://doi.org/10.1016/j.avsg.2017.01.009

Hajibandeh, S., Hajibandeh, S., Antoniou, S. A., Torella, F., & Antoniou, G. A. (2016). Covered vs uncovered stents for aortoiliac and femoropopliteal arterial disease: A systematic review and meta-analysis. *Journal of Endovascular Therapy, 23*(3), 442–452. https://doi.org/10.1177/1526602816643834

Helgetveit, I., & Krog, A. H. (2017). Totally laparoscopic aortobifemoral bypass surgery in the treatment of aortoiliac occlusive disease or abdominal aortic aneurysms — A systematic review and critical appraisal of literature. *Vascular Health and Risk Management, 13*, 187–199. https://doi.org/10.2147/VHRM.S130707

Hoffmann-Wieker, C. M., Ronellenfitsch, U., Rebelo, A., Görg, N., Schwarzer, G., Ballotta, E., Gouëffic, Y., & Böckler, D. (2022). Open surgical thrombendarterectomy versus endovascular treatment in occlusive processes of the femoral artery bifurcation. *Deutsches Arzteblatt international, 119*(47), 803–809. https://doi.org/10.3238/arztebl.m2022.0331

Indes, J. E., Pfaff, M. J., Farrokhyar, F., Brown, H., Hashim, P., Cheung, K., & Sosa, J. A. (2013). Clinical outcomes of 5358 patients undergoing direct open bypass or endovascular treatment for aortoiliac occlusive disease: A systematic review and meta-analysis. *Journal of Endovascular Therapy, 20*(4), 443–455. https://doi.org/10.1583/13-4242.1

Jadidi, M., Razian, S. A., Anttila, E., Doan, T., Adamson, J., Pipinos, M., & Kamenskiy, A. (2021). Comparison of morphometric, structural, mechanical, and physiologic characteristics of human superficial femoral and popliteal arteries. *Acta Biomaterialia, 121*, 431–443. https://doi.org/10.1016/j.actbio.2020.11.025

Jaff, M. R., White, C. J., Hiatt, W. R., Fowkes, G. R., Dormandy, J., Razavi, M., Reekers, J., & Norgren, L. (2015). An Update on methods for revascularization and expansion of the TASC lesion classification to include below-the-knee arteries: A supplement to the inter-society consensus for the management of peripheral arterial disease (TASC II). *Vascular Medicine, 20*(5), 465–478. https://doi.org/10.1177/1358863X15597877

Jens, S., Conijn, A. P., Koelemay, M. J. W., Bipat, S., & Reekers, J. A. (2014a). Randomized trials for endovascular treatment of infrainguinal arterial disease: Systematic review and meta-analysis (part 1: Above the knee). *European Journal of Vascular and Endovascular Surgery, 47*(5), 524–535. https://doi.org/10.1016/j.ejvs.2014.02.011

Jens, S., Conijn, A. P., Koelemay, M. J. W., Bipat, S., & Reekers, J. A. (2014b). Randomized trials for endovascular treatment of infrainguinal arterial disease: Systematic review and meta-analysis (part 2: Below the knee). *European Journal of Vascular and Endovascular Surgery, 47*(5), 536–544. https://doi.org/10.1016/j.ejvs.2014.02.012

Jongkind, V., Akkersdijk, G. J. M., Yeung, K. K., & Wisselink, W. (2010). A systematic review of endovascular treatment of extensive aortoiliac occlusive disease. *Journal of Vascular Surgery, 52*(5), 1376–1383. https://doi.org/10.1016/j.jvs.2010.04.080

Jongsma, H., Bekken, J., Ayez, N., Hoogewerf, C. J., Van Weel, V., & Fioole, B. (2020). Angioplasty versus stenting for iliac artery lesions. *Cochrane Database of Systematic Reviews, 2020*(12). https://doi.org/10.1002/14651858.CD007561.pub3

Katsanos, K., Kitrou, P., Spiliopoulos, S., Diamantopoulos, A., & Karnabatidis, D. (2016). Comparative effectiveness of plain balloon angioplasty, bare metal stents, drug-coated balloons, and drug-eluting stents for the treatment of infrapopliteal artery disease: Systematic review and Bayesian network meta-analysis of randomized controlled trials. *Journal of Endovascular Therapy, 23*(6), 851–863. https://doi.org/10.1177/1526602816671740

Katsanos, K., Spiliopoulos, S., Kitrou, P., Krokidis, M., & Karnabatidis, D. (2018). Risk of death following application of paclitaxel-coated balloons and stents in the femoropopliteal artery of the leg: A systematic review and meta-analysis of randomized controlled trials. *Journal of the American Heart Association, 7*(24). https://doi.org/10.1161/JAHA.118.011245

Koeckerling, D., Raguindin, P. F., Kastrati, L., Bernhard, S., Barker, J., Quiroga Centeno, A. C., Raeisi-Dehkordi, H., Khatami, F., Niehot, C., Lejay, A., Szeberin, Z., Behrendt, C.-A., Nordanstig, J., Muka, T., & Baumgartner, I. (2023). Endovascular revascularization strategies for aortoiliac and femoropopliteal artery disease: A meta-analysis. *European Heart Journal, 44*(11), 935–950. https://doi.org/10.1093/eurheartj/ehac722

Komshian, S. R., Lu, K., Pike, S. L., & Siracuse, J. J. (2017). Infrainguinal open reconstruction: A review of surgical considerations and expected outcomes. *Vascular Health and Risk Management, 13,* 161–168. https://doi.org/10.2147/VHRM.S106898

Krankenberg, H., Zeller, T., Ingwersen, M., Schmalstieg, J., Gissler, H. M., Nikol, S., Baumgartner, I., Diehm, N., Nickling, E., Müller-Hülsbeck, S., Schmiedel, R., Torsello, G., Hochholzer, W., Stelzner, C., Brechtel, K., Ito, W., Kickuth, R., Blessing, E., Thieme, M., ... Sixt, S. (2017). Self-expanding versus balloon-expandable stents for iliac artery occlusive disease: The randomized ICE trial. *JACC: Cardiovascular Interventions, 10*(16), 1694–1704. https://doi.org/10.1016/j.jcin.2017.05.015

Lejay, A., Georg, Y., Tartaglia, E., Gaertner, S., Geny, B., Thaveau, F., & Chakfe, N. (2014). Long-term outcomes of direct and indirect below-the-knee open revascularization based on the angiosome concept in diabetic patients with critical limb ischemia. *Annals of Vascular Surgery, 28*(4), 983–989. https://doi.org/10.1016/j.avsg.2013.08.026

Lejay, A., Vento, V., Kuntz, S., Steinmetz, L., Georg, Y., Thaveau, F., Heim, F., & Chakfé, N. (2020). Current status on vascular substitutes. *The Journal of Cardiovascular Surgery, 61*(5), 538–543. https://doi.org/10.23736/S0021-9509.20.11592-1

Lemos, T. M., Coelho, A., & Mansilha, A. (2022). Critical appraisal of evidence on bypass surgery versus endovascular treatment for intermittent claudication: A systematic review and meta-analysis. *International Angiology, 41*(3), 212–222. https://doi.org/10.23736/S0392-9590.21.04791-X

Lucereau, B., Thaveau, F., Lejay, A., Roussin, M., Georg, Y., Heim, F., Lee, J. T., & Chakfe, N. (2016). Learning curve of robotic-assisted anastomosis: Shorter than the laparoscopic technique? An educational study. *Annals of Vascular Surgery, 33,* 39–44. https://doi.org/10.1016/j.avsg.2015.12.001

Marrocco-Trischitta, M. M., Bertoglio, L., Tshomba, Y., Kahlberg, A., Marone, E. M., & Chiesa, R. (2012). The best treatment of juxtarenal aortic occlusion is and will be open surgery. *The Journal of Cardiovascular Surgery, 53*(3), 307–312.

Martin, G., Covani, M., Saab, F., Mustapha, J., Malina, M., & Patrone, L. (2021). A systematic review of the ipsilateral retrograde approach to the treatment of femoropopliteal arterial lesions. *Journal of Vascular Surgery, 74*(4), 1394–1405.e4. https://doi.org/10.1016/j.jvs.2021.04.050

Mwipatayi, B. P., Sharma, S., Daneshmand, A., Thomas, S. D., Vijayan, V., Altaf, N., Garbowski, M., Jackson, M., Benveniste, G., Denton, M., Anderson, J., Dubenec, S., Neale, M., Puttaswamy, V., & Fletcher, J. (2016). Durability of the balloon-expandable covered versus bare-metal stents in the Covered versus Balloon Expandable Stent Trial (COBEST) for the treatment of aortoiliac occlusive disease. *Journal of Vascular Surgery, 64*(1), 83–94.e1. https://doi.org/10.1016/j.jvs.2016.02.064

Narins, C. R. (2009). Access strategies for peripheral arterial intervention. *Cardiology Journal, 16*(1), 88–97.

Noori, V. J., & Eldrup-Jørgensen, J. (2018). A systematic review of vascular closure devices for femoral artery puncture sites. *Journal of Vascular Surgery, 68*(3), 887–899. https://doi.org/10.1016/j.jvs.2018.05.019

Norgren, L., Hiatt, W. R., Dormandy, J. A., Nehler, M. R., Harris, K. A., & Fowkes, F. G. R. (2007). Inter-society consensus for the management of peripheral arterial disease (TASC II). *European Journal of Vascular and Endovascular Surgery, 33*(1), S1–S75. https://doi.org/10.1016/j.ejvs.2006.09.024

Pascarella, L., & Aboul Hosn, M. (2018). Minimally invasive management of severe aortoiliac occlusive disease. *Journal of Laparoendoscopic & Advanced Surgical Techniques, 28*(5), 562–568. https://doi.org/10.1089/lap.2017.0675

Pescatori, L. C., Tacher, V., & Kobeiter, H. (2020). The use of re-entry devices in aortoiliac occlusive disease. *Frontiers in Cardiovascular Medicine, 7.* https://doi.org/10.3389/fcvm.2020.00144

Premaratne, S., Newman, J., Hobbs, S., Garnham, A., & Wall, M. (2020). Meta-analysis of direct surgical versus endovascular revascularization for aortoiliac occlusive disease. *Journal of Vascular Surgery, 72*(2), 726–737. https://doi.org/10.1016/j.jvs.2019.12.035

Reijnen, M. M. P. J. (2020). Update on covered endovascular reconstruction of the aortic bifurcation. *Vascular, 28*(3), 225–232. https://doi.org/10.1177/1708538119896197

Rocha-Singh, K. J., Duval, S., Jaff, M. R., Schneider, P. A., Ansel, G. M., Lyden, S. P., Mullin, C. M., Ioannidis, J. P. A., Misra, S., Tzafriri, A. R., Edelman, E. R., Granada, J. F., White, C. J., & Beckman, J. A. (2020). Mortality and paclitaxel-coated devices: An individual patient data meta-analysis. *Circulation, 141*(23), 1859–1869. https://doi.org/10.1161/CIRCULATIONAHA.119.044697

Roll, S., Müller-Nordhorn, J., Scholz, K. T., Eidt, H., Greiner, D., & et al.. (2008). Dacron vs. PTFE as bypass materials in peripheral vascular surgery–systematic review and meta-analysis. *BMC Surgery, 8.*

Rusch, R., Hoffmann, G., Rusch, M., Cremer, J., & Berndt, R. (2022). Robotic-assisted abdominal aortic surgery: Evidence and techniques. *Journal of Robotic Surgery, 16*(6), 1265–1271. https://doi.org/10.1007/s11701-022-01390-0

Salem, M., Hosny, M. S., Francia, F., Sallam, M., Saratzis, A., Saha, P., Patel, S., Abisi, S., & Zayed, H. (2021). Management of extensive aorto-iliac disease: A systematic review and meta-analysis of 9319 patients. *CardioVascular and Interventional Radiology, 44*(10), 1518–1535. https://doi.org/10.1007/s00270-021-02785-6

Shammas, N. W., Doumet, A. A., Karia, R., & Khalafallah, R. (2020). An overview of the treatment of symptomatic common femoral artery lesions with a focus on endovascular therapy. *Vascular Health and Risk Management, 16*, 67–73. https://doi.org/10.2147/VHRM.S242291

Sobolev, M., Slovut, D. P., Chang, A. L., Shiloh, A. L., & Eisen, L. A. (2015). Ultrasound-guided catheterization of the femoral artery: A systematic review and meta-analysis of randomized controlled trials. *Journal of Invasive Cardiology, 27*(7), 318–323.

Spiliopoulos, S., Del Giudice, C., Manzi, M., Reppas, L., Rodt, T., & Uberoi, R. (2021). CIRSE standards of practice on below-the-knee revascularisation. *CardioVascular and Interventional Radiology, 44*(9), 1309–1322. https://doi.org/10.1007/s00270-021-02891-5

Steiner, S., & Schmidt, A. (2021). Repeat BTK revascularization: When, how and what are the results? *The Journal of Cardiovascular Surgery, 62*(2), 118–123. https://doi.org/10.23736/S0021-9509.21.11679-9

Varetto, G., Gibello, L., Boero, M., Frola, E., Peretti, T., Spalla, F., Verzini, F., & Rispoli, P. (2019). Angioplasty or bare metal stent versus drug-eluting endovascular treatment in femoropopliteal artery disease: A systematic review and meta-analysis. *The Journal of Cardiovascular Surgery, 60*(5), 546–556. https://doi.org/10.23736/S0021-9509.19.11115-9

Velazquez-Ramirez, G., & Rosenberg, M. L. (2021). *Suprainguinal peripheral artery disease: Open management.* Elsevier BV. https://doi.org/10.1016/b978-0-12-822959-0.00041-9

Wong, G., Lahsaei, S., Aoun, J., & Garcia, L. A. (2019). Management of common femoral artery occlusive disease: A review of endovascular treatment strategies and outcomes. *Catheterization and Cardiovascular Interventions, 93*(3), 514–521. https://doi.org/10.1002/ccd.27983

Ye, W., Liu, C. W., Ricco, J. B., Mani, K., Zeng, R., & Jiang, J. (2011). Early and late outcomes of percutaneous treatment of TransAtlantic Inter-Society Consensus class C and D aorto-iliac lesions. *Journal of Vascular Surgery, 53*(6), 1728–1737. https://doi.org/10.1016/j.jvs.2011.02.005

13

PAD: Future directions

Ji-Eun Park[1] and Aloke V. Finn[2]

[1]*Division of Cardiovascular Medicine, Department of Medicine, University of Maryland Medical Center, Baltimore, MD, United States;* [2]*CVPath Institute, Gaithersburg, MD, United States*

The rapidly changing field of vascular disease has changed treatment options for millions of people worldwide. As the population ages and the awareness of peripheral arterial disease (PAD) grows, PAD will be diagnosed earlier and become more commonplace, indicating the great need for evidence-based therapies to reduce major cardiovascular, and specifically limb, events and improve quality of life. Already, incorporating artificial intelligence and machine learning to improve the diagnosis and detection of PAD is being studied. Much of what we currently use as medical therapies for primary and secondary prevention of PAD is a result of data generated from coronary atherosclerosis. As our understanding of the pathophysiology of the disease advances, directed targeted therapeutics, for example, using molecular therapies and genomics, can be further honed to treat specific disease pathways and processes. Pharmacologic and exercise therapy remains at the cornerstone of treatment of PAD. We foresee the wider adoption of anticoagulants for the treatment and prevention of PAD, in tune with increasing evidence that more of lower extremity disease results from embolic initiators than previously thought.

Intervention therapeutic options, especially for those with symptomatic PAD, which limits quality of life or in the extreme causes critical limb ischemia, may require invasive therapies. With the approval of drug-coated balloons, primarily coated with paclitaxel, outcomes have been improved with lower risks of reintervention. Although recent controversies about safety of paclitaxel for treatment of peripheral arteries were raised, subsequent data have reassured the community about the safety of these devices. Perhaps one of the most anticipated invasive therapies on the horizon is the advent of sirolimus-coated balloons, which have recently been granted investigational device exemption for the treatment of superficial femoral arteries. Many further innovations are also being explored and should help to improve outcomes. Below the knee, PAD remains a difficult-to-treat area with not as many options, but new data from bio-absorable scaffolds (Abbott Vascular) as well as use of venous conduits to feed blocked arteries (LimboFlo) provided new options for these patients. As the population ages, calcium modification for invasive therapies may also become more widely utilized. As our understanding of the complexity of peripheral arterial disease expands, it is our hope that that knowledge is used to treat the millions of patients worldwide affected by PAD.

Index

Note: 'Page numbers followed by *f* indicate figures, *t* indicates tables'